The Dean in the University

For Tatiana Fumasoli:
Thank you for your contribution
on our future,

Chris &
Notes

Christian Scholz
Volker Stein
editors

The Dean in the University of the Future

Rainer Hampp Verlag   München, Mering   2014

Bibliographic information published by the Deutsche Nationalbibliothek

Deutsche Nationalbibliothek lists this publication in the Deutsche Nationalbibliografie; detailed bibliographic data are available in the Internet at http://dnb.d-nb.de.

ISBN 978-3-86618-888-4 (print)
ISBN 978-3-86618-988-1 (e-book)
DOI 10.1688/978386618988-1

First published 2014

© 2014   Rainer Hampp Verlag   München, Mering
           Marktplatz 5   86415 Mering, Germany

           www.Hampp-Verlag.de

CONTENTS

PART I: CONFERENCE THEME

PART II: CONFERENCE CONTRIBUTIONS

Session 1: Strategy of Deans and Faculties in Higher Education

Session 2: Management of Faculties and Dean's Competence Profile in Higher Education

Session 3: Faculty's Autonomy in Higher Education

Session 4: External Relations of Faculties in Higher Education

Session 5: Performance Controlling of Faculties in Higher Education

PART III: CONFERENCE OUTCOME

PART I

CONFERENCE THEME

WELCOME ADDRESS FOR THE CONFERENCE

Michael Olbrich

Chair for Accounting, Universität des Saarlandes, Campus B4, 66123 Saarbrücken, Germany
olbrich@iwp.uni-saarland.de

Dear colleagues!

The conference organisers asked me to open this conference with a few words. It is a pleasure for me to do so, although the subject "The Dean in the University of the Future" is very broad and therefore difficult to contain.

When I prepared my short speech, I was looking for quotes and found two which I considered as useful to get an idea of the subject. The first quote is by Mahatma Gandhi. He said:

"The future depends on what you do today."

This is true, I guess, but requires a specification, because what we do today depends on what we want today. From my point of view, we can observe two different models of the University of the Future that people aim for today.

One is the model of serfdom: Proponents of this model strive for a university that treats students as pupils and professors as employees. Control can be found everywhere in this model. Students are controlled by compulsory attendance and continuous examinations. Professors are controlled, for example, by teaching evaluations, and the setting of targets, like the amount of raised funds or the number of published papers. And the university itself is interpreted as a corporation and therefore controlled by a supervisory board.

The second model is the model of liberty: Supporters of this model advocate a university which goes for research carried out regardless of its exploitability. Teaching is strongly influenced by the outcomes of such research and students are considered to be self dependent individuals at eye level.

We must decide on the model which we want as the University of the Future, because it will determine the role of the dean in this university. In the model of liberty, he is a faculty's temporary primus inter pares, whereas in the model of serfdom he is superior to the faculty and subordinate to the president.

Well, which model of the University of the Future should we aim for now? I guess a second quote which was made by Confucius is suitable to answer this question: He said:

"Study the past if you would define the future."

Indeed, the study of the past is quite revealing. The history of the model of liberty goes back 200 years, with regard to the work of Humboldt, or even longer, when we consider its roots in the era of Humanism. It is an awesome series of achievements that led to an immense outcome of knowledge and education for broad levels of the population.

The history of the model of serfdom goes back 15 years, at least in Germany and with regard to the work of Edelgard Bulmahn, who was secretary of education then. It produced an immense growth of bureaucracy, killed creativity in research and teaching, degraded the universities and transformed them into vocational schools and achieved all this at large costs.

In my opinion, the University of the Future will therefore either be a university in accordance with the model of liberty, or it will not be a university at all.

Hence, I am looking forward to the findings of this conference. Not only with regard to the "Dean in the University of the Future" but also to the dean's part on the road to achieve this university and to overcome the dead-lock we are facing today.

Have a successful conference and a warm welcome to Saarland University!

Michael Olbrich is acting Vice Dean of the Faculty of Law and Management at Universität des Saarlandes. He is Director of the "Institut für Wirtschaftsprüfung" (Chair for Auditing) at the Universität des Saarlandes and has been Visiting Professor at the Ecole des Hautes Etudes Commerciales (HEC) in Paris and in Joensuu University/Finland. His research interests cover, among others, due diligence, separate and consolidated financial statements, convergence of external and internal accounting, analysis and critics of accounting law and company law, and accounting challenges related to the corporate life cycle. Michael Olbrich is author of a wide range of books, journal articles and conference contributions and member of the editorial board of the German scientific journal "Betriebswirtschaftliche Forschung und Praxis (BFuP)".

CONFERENCE KEYNOTE
THE NEED FOR ACADEMIC MANAGEMENT OF UNIVERSITIES – A CENTRAL ROLE FOR THE DEAN

Martin Paul

Executive Board of Maastricht University, Minderbroedersberg 4-6, Maastricht, Netherlands
m.paul@maastrichtuniversity.nl

1. ACADEMIA – QUO VADIS?

Universities are among the oldest institutions in Europe which over centuries have survived the plague, wars, cultural and industrial revolutions and many other threats. The current political and financial environment has put them under intense pressure. The call for a "return of investment" by national and regional governments, dwindling financial resources at a time of on-going economic crisis, as well as the emergence of apparently disruptive technologies such as massive open online course (MOOCs) are just a few trends that appear to be threatening universities as we know it. These factors have recently been summarised in the publication "An avalanche is coming" (Barber/Donnelly/Rizvi 2013) that compares universities to snow covered mountains that appear to be stable at the surface but where under this snow layer, multiple changes occur that will lead to catastrophe. Century old academic traditions are under risk to become obsolete and the value of a university degree appears to be dwindling. These are indeed scary scenarios – and they lead to sometimes fearful responses by those who are responsible for universities, supervisory and executive boards as well as state ministries and lawmakers alike.

Their response is very often to adapt organisational and administrative changes in the university organisation to implement a more top down approach in running the universities and try to improve the chances of their institution on the market, leading in fact to a policy that is not in line with the bottom-up spirit of universities. This has created indeed concern about the "marketisation" of universities plays in many countries. On the other hand universities need to be aware of their surroundings, particularly in countries where they are financed from taxpayers money. Concepts of indefinite academic freedom and university autonomy, therefore, come under pressure. But accountability and autonomy must not be counteracting each other and universities should not be afraid to be held accountable, but they unfortunately sit in a comfort zone and are not communicating their value, the value of knowledge, by educating not only the professionals of the future, but also by doing basic and applied research for the long term benefit of society. In the end, universities need a "license to operate" from their stakeholders, independently whether they are in the public or private sector.

Because of this complex situation, university leadership is crucial as it needs to be convincing at the same time to the internal stakeholders such as students and staff as well as to the external players, such as board of trustees, ministries and the public in general. The management of universities, therefore, has a very special flavour as it cannot be neither carried out by simply transferring management practices (or personnel) from the industrial sector to universities nor by leaving them without any strategic goals. Universities, therefore, need a very specific brand of leadership, leadership from the heart of the organisation.

2. MIDDLE MANAGEMENT OR MANAGEMENT FROM THE MIDDLE?

If one works in the economic sector in a managerial position, to be in middle management is not seen as a goal of life, it is natural in these surroundings to strive for the top. The darwinistic principle of survival of the fittest and vertical structures do, however, badly apply for universities. Here middle management is the key for an organisation functioning according to academic principles. And the dean plays a central role in such a structure.

These principles are brilliantly laid out in what in my view is still the best book on the subject, *The Essential Academic Dean – A Practical guide to College Leadership* by Jeffrey R. Buller (2007), a book that every dean or academic that wants to take a role in academic administration should read. In his book, Buller lays out clearly the specific needs of universities for academic leadership (i.e. leadership by academics) and gives many practical examples of the dos and don'ts within such structures. For him management is performed from the middle of the organisation by deans who come from the heart of academia with a background as researchers and educators are key. "…few aspects of the dean's tasks are as essential as the ability to see the institutions needs from the middle and address these needs adequately" is a key statement from Buller's book. He also states that the mode of operation of deans should be based on something that he calls *collegial candor*. Buller defines this as follows: „Your method of interacting with department chairs, division directors and faculty members should be a reflection of the role you want to play in the larger institutional structure: in fact, how you treat others should be based on how you want to

be treated yourself by upper management.". This is indeed a key feature of academic management: it must be based on collegiality and therefore, on natural authority from deans who understand very well the position of their colleagues because they have been in this situation themselves. And university presidents can give mandates to their deans to provide faculty leadership because they can be assured that they are "honest brokers" to implement university strategy in a balanced way.

Again, Buller gives us a good description what is the key for this specific academic environment by addressing two key characteristics:

(1) "Creating a working environment in which individuals feel free to provide their perspectives and understand that you will agree or disagree based on the argument's merits." and

(2) "Fostering an environment in which individuals feel safe to provide their perspectives where the overall mission of the institution, rather than the personal convenience of its individual members, is the guiding principle behind all deliberations. "

Unfortunately, these obvious principles providing true academic spirit in university management are not always implemented, and often deans are not selected based on academic track records or the qualities as managers from the middle. Election of dean's by faculty council, although a cherished academic tradition, can lead to inappropriate situations. Buller quotes Fogarty (2006) who gave some examples in his book for "bad deans" and provides a number of case studies. Table 1 gives a summary of such examples.

Paul

Table 1: Examples for Bad Deans
(Buller, based on Fogarty, 2006)

The indecisive dean	Has difficulty making any kind of decision
The clue-less dean	Doesn't really understand academic administration as a whole or the local culture
The hoarder	Cannot delegate authority
The shaker	Promotes change simply for the sake of change, not because it is needed

Clearly, all of us have seen such or similar examples. "Bad deans" are usually chosen for political, opportunistic and/or convenience and always out of the absence of a clear vision of academic leadership.

Also, the dean's profession has no formal training. Knowledge by individuals is acquired auto didactically or based on natural talent. There is, therefore, a clear need to provide a format to make sure that candidates to become "good deans" can gear up for the occasion to take over academic leadership. This requires a number of key features:

(1) Deans should have a strong academic track record, for example by having served as a professor or senior academician in the university.
(2) Deanships should be always organised as temporary roles, which mean that it is based on the fact that academics step out of their usual role as a professor after which they can return o after their deanship.
(3) The periods of deanship should be defined, they should be reasonably long enough to allow the dean to implement successful achievements but also not permanent to make sure the dean can rotate back after his term into the academic roster.
(4) In order to make these positions appealing for academics, a "reintegration package" should be negotiated combining for example a sabbatical and a new start-up package for the dean stepping down.
(5) Deans should get feedback from the organisation and be evaluated in regular

intervals both by the university leadership, but also by the organisation.
(6) Most importantly: there must be a reference or best practice database for successful candidates for deanship. In my view this can be best achieved by learning from peers, i.e. self-organised professional organisations focusing on academic management and run by academics.

If adapting to these principles, there is a good chance that adequate candidates for deanship should not be in shortage but a reality. I can support this by having worked for years in such a professional organisation at the European level, DEAN (Dean's and academic managers European Academic Network). In this network, deans and junior academic managers from all over Europe and all disciplines came together to share their experiences and develop together best practices on all pertinent issues and challenges of academic university management. Similar activities are needed for the future as – and I would like to reiterate this important point here, academic management in universities belongs in the hand of academics.

3. ACADEMIC MANAGEMENT AT MAASTRICHT UNIVERSITY – AN EXAMPLE

Maastricht University is a young university in the Netherlands and as of this writing 38 years of age. It has been founded in an area of the country that had been hit by economic crisis, as the major source of employment, coal mining, had been abandoned due to insufficient natural resources. The Dutch government at the time made the bold decision to replace coal mines with knowledge by founding a research university in this region. This decision proved to be right. Today the economic situation is improved and the university as well as the associated academic hospital are major employers in the region, there are a large number of additional and secondary jobs created, for example by spin-off companies, support businesses and new industrial developments. Studies

15

on the economic impact of our university have shown that one new knowledge worker creates 5 to 6 new additional jobs directly and indirectly. And the almost 16,000 students of Maastricht University also have a positive impact on the economic development of the region.

Even more importantly, as a new university, the institution was founded on modern principles, being an innovator in education by becoming the first European university to implement problem based learning across the board in all faculties, by choosing its research hotspots carefully and by implementing flat hierarchies.

On the first view the Dutch governance model of universities looks rather undemocratic and top-down. Members of the executive board and deans are, for example, not elected but appointed. The Dutch minister of Higher Education appoints a supervisory board which must consist explicitly of members outside the political sector and should come, for example from industry, academia and public institutions. This structure already generates a certain distance from the ministry which takes its supervisory role mostly in budgeting universities and controlling the implementation and quality of research and education.

The supervisory board, among other things, appoints the members of the executive board, a president (equivalent to vice chancellor), a rector magnificus (equivalent to provost) and a vice president (with different portefeuilles, mostly responsible for administration). Executive board members are appointed for four years with the option of one (and only one) extension for another four years. The executive board functions as collegiate body, i.e. decisions are based on consensus and not on a majority of votes.

The executive board is responsible for appointing the deans of faculties. This occurs in parallel for a maximum of two consecutive terms of four years. In order to become dean, candidates must hold a professorship at Maastricht University and must be ranking academics. This is very important since in order to run a faculty, deans must be accepted by their peers, i.e. the professors within their faculties and the other person-

nel. In order to stimulate outstanding academics to take on this role of a dean for a certain period (four or eight years), a number of actions are taking such as the guarantee of a "reintegration" project at the end of the deanship consisting in a paid one year sabbatical and start-up funds for new research projects.

But what is even more important is that the deans and their faculty boards get a strong mandate from the executive board to be indeed responsible and accountable for the primary process of research and education. As is shown in the strategic program of the University (2012) states this very clearly.

"Teaching, research and support services are located within the faculties, with support services shared as much as possible. The dean is ultimately responsible for all aspects of running a faculty. The primary role of the Executive Board is to facilitate the faculties so that they can carry out their tasks as optimally as possible" (Inspired by Quality: Strategic Programme Maastricht University 2012 – 2016).

But how is this top-down system actually controlled, what is the role of participation from the organisation, i.e. by consultative bodies representing the employees, both academic and non-academic? To guarantee organisational participation, an elected university council consisting of employee's en students (both making up 50% of the council respectively) is interacting with the executive committee, largely in an advisory function. The same is true for the faculty level, where faculty councils interact with the deans and faculty boards, in a largely advisory way. There are also subjects that require approval of these councils, largely those dealing with issues of education.

But what is very important to know is that despite the largely advisory role of these bodies, one should not underestimate their influence, because their advice is taken seriously. For example no dean or university president could "survive" a permanent situation where he or she are not listening and are operating against negative advice. And to support this, there are certainly examples in the Netherlands, where this has led to discharging deans and executive board members at universities. This system of informal checks and balances works just because management is academic i.e. is happening within a family of peers. The deans are an essential part of this governance system run by peers. At Maastricht University, they are, therefore, integrated in a group called "management team" that is a central decision making body in the university and characterised in figure 2.

Table 2: The Management Team

▪ 10 members, executive board, deans and head of administration
▪ The strategic board of the university
▪ Represents the matrix structure of the university
▪ Decisions based on consensus
▪ Resolves issues between central and decentral organisation

4. CONCLUSION

In summary, there is a strong need for academic leadership of universities but to achieve this, academics must be ready to take over management tasks, at least for a certain period of time. This generates the

need to work on management proficiency also in academic circles, not only to generate a database for best practices, but also to identify those who will be ready to take on academic management tasks in the future. This will generate a *high trust system* where rules and regulations will be less important than the common understanding of the task at hand, making and keeping the university viable as a central ingredient of the knowledge society.

REFERENCES

Barber, Michael/Donnelly, Katelyn/Rizvi, Saad, An avalanche is coming. Higher education and the revolution ahead. London (Institute of Public Policy Research) 2013.

Buller, Jeffrey R., The essential academic dean: a practical guide to college leadership. Jossey-Bass (San Francisco) 2007.

Fogarty, Timothy, J., The good, the bad and the ugly: Knowing your dean, in: The department chair, 17 (1/2006), 10-11.

Maastricht University, Strategic Programme of Maastricht University 2012 – 2016. http://www.maastrichtuniversity.nl/web/show/id=5740056/langid=42, accessed 28 January 2013.

Martin Paul is President of Maastricht University since May 2011. From 1997 to 2003 he was Dean of the Medical Faculty of the Freie Universität Berlin and from 2004 to 2008 Dean and Vice President of the Executive Board of the Medical Faculty of the Charité Medical Center in Berlin, the joint medical school of the Freie Universität and Humboldt University in Berlin. Martin Paul has authored more than 200 research papers in the fields of molecular medicine, clinical and experimental pharmacology and cardio-vascular disease. He has been active in several professional organisations, for example as president of German Society of Experimental and Clinical Pharmacology and Toxicology and as Chairman of the European Council for Cardiovascular Research. Apart from his career as a scientist and educationalist, Martin Paul has worked actively to improve academic management on the European level. In this context he has acted as chair of DEAN, a European Network of deans and academic managers from all academic disciplines. In addition he has been serving on the board of ESMU, the European Center for Strategic Management of Universities.

THE DEAN IN THE UNIVERSITY OF THE FUTURE – CHALLENGE FOR AN ACADEMIC CONFERENCE

Christian Scholz[1] and Volker Stein[2]

[1]*Chair for Organisational Behaviour, Human Resource Management and Information Systems, Universität des Saarlandes, Campus A5 4, 66123 Saarbrücken, Germany*
[2]*Chair for Human Resource Management and Organisational Behaviour, University of Siegen, Hoelderlinstrasse 3, 57076 Siegen, Germany*
[1]*scholz@orga.uni-sb.de,* [2]*volker.stein@uni-siegen.de*

Initial statement for the International Academic Conference "The Dean in the University of the Future. Learning From and Progressing With Each Other", organised by Univ.-Professor Dr. Christian Scholz (University of Saarland/Germany) and Univ.-Professor Dr. Volker Stein (University of Siegen/Germany), taking place June 26-28, 2013 in Saarbrücken/Germany. The conference is part of KORFU ("Korporatismus als ökonomisches Gestaltungsprinzip für Universitäten") – a research programme funded by the German Federal Ministry of Education and Research (BMBF) and administered by the German Aerospace Center (DLR); see www.kor-fu.de.

1. INTRODUCTION

Within the past decade and on a worldwide scope, higher education has been affected by major reforms. In the face of challenges such as financial deficits and international convergence pressure, higher education should be made more efficient and effective. Therefore, constantly recurring reforms mainly resulted in structural transformations. As a secondary effect, they provoked new problems and increased existing obstacles. Mapping the problem areas of contemporary universities, two prevalent topics can be identified:

External: Political, social, and cultural pressure

Starting within public administration in the early 1990s, reforms under the umbrella of "New Public Management" (Aucoin 1990; Hood 1991) were initiated in order to increase performance through the implementation of competition and management (Schimank 2005; Santiago/Carvalho 2008; Bogumil/Heinze 2009) and to deliver services to different social – and taxpaying – stakeholders such as adults and elderly, employees and employers. Spilling over to universities, new definitions of legitimate and illegitimate organisational goals (Hüther 2010) affected self-conception, mission, strategies and the overall image of universities.

This development forced universities to develop new objectives such as meeting third-party demands, but also new competencies in order to adequately cope with the claims of internal and external stakeholders. In particular, a dynamic sampling of university competencies is needed to keep up with national and international, with "real" and "internet-based" competitors in the field of higher education.

This leads to the need for organisational learning of dynamic capabilities (Teece et al. 1997; Eisenhart/Martin 2000) in order to establish efficiency and effective performance, particularly in higher education institutions (Fumasoli/Lepori 2011). In the end, the traditional model of universities, which follows Humboldt's ideas, is in danger of being completely replaced by a corporate model of universities which follows the rationale of corporations – with the open question being whether the underlying corporate framework is from the 1980s or from the 2010s. Consequently, the identity of universities is shifted as well, reflecting cultural changes in self-conception.

Internal: Strategic, structural, and organisational pressure

This problem area concerns the structural field, in particular the position of faculties as the core organisational units of universities. Within universities, two opposing principles can be found regarding the structural evolution of university governance (Scholz/Stein 2011).

One principle is the corporate model of universities with *strong control of the president*. While public financial resources are allocated to universities as global budgets, only the president is entitled to make decisions in a completely centralised structure. He counteracts individual optimisation strategies of individual professors by increasing his own decision-making power to the disadvantage of the autonomy of faculties and professors. The underlying normative principle is the hierarchical mode of governance, which is that of private business (corporatisation). Based on formal law as well as on the shift in the policy paradigm towards central planning, the president can decide on the whole range of university and faculty matters, including overall strategy, election of deans, appointment of professors, budget allocation and additional pay. At the same time, the role of the dean is characterised as recipient of orders, having to execute the decisions of the president within their faculty.

The other principle is the *collegial approach*, which revives subsidiarity, decentralisation and participative bottom-up management (collegialisation). It reflects that tasks and problems within a university are carried out by groups of professors in a cooperative way. This democratic structure tries to strengthen the academic freedom and competition of the professors as part of a faculty. Faculties are becoming the main organisational units within universities, providing services for professors, while the president is in charge of attracting funds and endowments for the university and concentrates on external representation, and the role of the dean is limited to implementing the decisions of the academic staff.

Putting this together, it becomes obvious that the first problem area can be located on the macro level of higher education, whereas the second problem area has to be located on the micro level of universities. Developments on the macro level shape developments on the micro level, while the micro level itself, additionally, follows a path with its own internal dynamics.

2. THE INTERNATIONAL CONTEXT

On a worldwide scale, systems of higher education differ very much, as international comparisons show (e.g. Paradeise et al. 2009). We perceive that national university systems can be located in different developmental stages of corporatisation. While, for example, the Australian, New Zealand and US universities are far ahead in the application of New Public Management reforms (e.g. Christensen 2011, 503) that are supposed to reflect "modern management principles", Japanese (e.g. Yamamoto 2004), Latin American, African (e.g. Waswa/Swaleh 2012) and Dutch universities are on the way and German universities are still close to the starting point.

The condition of faculties can serve as a useful indicator for the maturation level of a national university system. It is fascinating to compare faculties around the globe, which are run in different ways. It is an empirical task to relate the autonomy of the different systems to their performance, their effectiveness and their overall competitiveness.

Given the international competition in higher education, it seems reasonable to depart from the idea of international convergence and assimilation of university systems for two reasons: first, the situational factors differ from country to country, and second, competitive advantages can only be achieved if different systems compete. However, today's prevalent management rationale still pushes university systems internationally in the same direction of centralistic governance (e.g. Kamola/Meyerhoff 2009). Interestingly, the concept underlying that is the corporation of the 1980s – the centralised, departmental, regulated company with strong top-down management. The related problem is complexity: The more players and the more links between them, the more complex the system and the less appropriate a centralistic leadership (e.g. Birnbaum 1988, 198–199).

Taking different national systems of higher education together, they represent a system of benchmarks in which different intensities of university corporatisation can be assessed. Especially in international dialogues, faculties and deans will be able to learn from their different experiences.

3. THE FACULTY AS PLAYGROUND

It is not only that the system of higher education is facing turbulent times; moreover, it seems that it has entered a critical phase. The future of higher education, of the universities as we know them today, but also of the people who are responsible for innovative research and excellent teaching, is uncertain.

Interestingly, there are a lot of "players" involved in the macro system of higher education: ministries which set the budgets, donors who give endowments, companies who are willing to cooperate or to instrumentalise universities for their purposes, consultants who have discovered universities as a profitable business area, professional associations which fight for the interests of their members.

This situation must be characterised as outsiders' interventionism.

As if that were not enough, in the university micro system, there are even more "players": the president is interested in power, the administration has to find its position between service and cost efficiency, the staff are supposed to do the work and the students are customers of the system, even though

"students as customers" is already a paradigm to be disputed in detail.

In any case: the faculties are caught in the middle.

Consisting of academic staff (such as professors, associate professors, assistant professors, research assistants, lecturers) and administrative staff, faculties can be seen as university divisions being responsible for academic research and teaching. Usually, they are headed by a dean who is supported by a management team made of vice deans, some parliament-like structures such as the faculty council, and the faculty administration. Most faculties include more than one department.

Although they are often not the prevalent players themselves, faculties are the areas where opposing interests clash. Faculties have to pay for the decisions taken by others:

- They must adapt, in teaching and research, to every new reform imposed on them – even if acceptance of the system changes is missing.
- They must themselves provide external funds – even if resources such as money for new requirements and time for their complex workload are missing.
- They must create services for new stakeholders such as corporations or accreditation agencies – even if sense and directedness to faculty goals are missing.
- They must execute orders of faculty outsiders and abandon their own decision rights – even if this contradicts the purpose of faculty autonomy.
- They must motivate faculty members – even if all structural changes strongly contribute to the demotivation of the academic staff.

It can be observed that players outside of the faculty tend even to increase the problems for faculties. They, for example, install new service units with decision powers which are dependent on the president, they impose time-consuming bureaucracy and accreditation efforts on faculties (Amaral/Magalhães 2004), they implement new systems of control, or they shift financial resources to central administration.

Translated to organisation theory, university structures are to be seen as the result of a wide and complex sphere, designed by stakeholders such as educational politicians, professional associations or companies: "In fact, not only do the professionals control their own work, but they also seek collective control of the administrative decisions that affect them – decisions, for example, to hire colleagues, to promote them, and to distribute resources. Controlling these decisions requires control of the middle line of organisation, which professionals do by ensuring that it is staffed with 'their own'. Some of the administrative work the operating professionals do themselves. [...] Moreover, full-time administrators who wish to have any power at all in these structures must be certified members of the profession and preferably be elected by the professional operators or at least appointed with their blessing. What emerges therefore, is a rather democratic administrative structure" (Mintzberg 1983, 197).

This professional bureaucracy (Mintzberg 1983, 189) can be found in faculties as the "natural" structure of a university, characterised by democracy and decentralisation. Professors are the operating core of the university, the faculties are their democratically institutionalised organisational frame and the deans are their heads.

Given the directedness by outsiders on the one hand and the alternative option of a decentralised, autonomous faculty on the other, faculties have reached a crossroads, not knowing who will have enough commitment and engagement to do the core work of faculties in the future – serving the students and being innovative. Therefore, the question is raised: what will be necessary for faculty survival and sustainability and what will be necessary for improvement of the faculty's contribution to the overall system of higher education?

4. THE HISTORICAL EVOLUTION

Before answering these questions, it has to be stated that we are not dealing with "the faculty". Beside national differences, there is also a historical process going on: the evolutionary process of structural change leads to different stages of faculty development and therefore different types of faculties. The stages – but not the effectiveness of the different national systems of higher education – are widely country-independent, since they describe a sequential pattern derived from basic organisation theory on the dynamics of intrasystem change (e.g. Greiner 1972).

A stage model of faculty evolution describes six archetypical developmental stages of university governance (Scholz/Stein 2010; 2011):

Faculty Silos depicts the situation where faculties as the core organisational units of the traditional university are divided along professional boundaries. Independently providing research and teaching, they fulfil their tasks according to the standards developed by their respective scientific community. The president of a university – an academic – plays a rather weak role; his managerial tasks are more or less restricted to representation. Centralised service units provide services to the faculties. The relationship between faculties and university top management is based on partnership and not on formal top-down authority. Professors have relatively high academic autonomy, which is supposed to bring about creativity and open up an appropriate scope of action to succeed within the competition for scientific reputation (Reichwald 1997, 7; Kern 2000, 29).

Academic Kindergarten is the structural degeneration of "Faculty Silos", sketching the relationship of the university with individual professors who are opportunistic, with opportunism defined as self-interest-oriented individual behaviour without taking third-party implications into account (Williamson 1975). Some professors, left to themselves and not being compelled into

21

loyalty, begin to seek their own advantages, in particular financial resources, staff and prestige. Free access to a broad range of university services favours free-rider behaviour of individual university members (Wilkesmann 2011, 305-306), coming alongside a deficit of the individual professors' accountability.

Presidential Feudalism reflects the corporatisation model of universities. The university president is the key player, who decides on everything which affects the future of the university. His completely centralised structure helps him to interfere in the remotest corners of the university. He counteracts individual optimisation strategies of individual professors by increasing his own decision-making power, to the disadvantage of the autonomy of faculties and professors who have only a minor voice in the university.

Individual Negotiation Jungle is the structural degeneration of "Presidential Feudalism". Professors who got rid of a great amount of their individual autonomy, as well of faculty autonomy, start to adapt to their new role and increase their negotiation capacity focused on extrinsic motivation. Since the professors only have one negotiation partner left – the president – they will all go to him to deal with every single problem: they will ask for moral support, more research money, higher salaries, new target agreements, bonuses, incentives, etc. The logical consequence is that the president's negotiation capacity will sooner or later be exceeded. System complexity will lead to a system overload. The collapse of the whole university system has to be taken into account as a realistic possibility. The president's authority decreases because he faces hundreds of well-trained negotiation partners. Faculties become obsolete, since each professor negotiates his working conditions opportunistically, even at the expense of the faculty's interests and the interests of his colleagues. University effectiveness and efficiency become a zero-sum game among all university members.

University Collegialism reflects that tasks and problems within a university are carried out by groups of professors in a co-

operative way. This democratic structure resembles "Faculty Silos" but, in order to resolve its negative results, introduces new elements. Collegialism – understood as the translation of the German term "Korporatismus" – follows a normative principle shaped by academic freedom and competition. On the one hand, professors regain full autonomy. They make decisions according to the principle of collegiality regarding the services portfolio provided by their university. On the other, professors become accountable for their decisions. They are responsible for meeting the demands of stakeholders and, therefore, undertake the risk of failure. The accountability of professors is supposed to lead to their participation in working groups in order to deliver excellent research and teaching. Faculties are strengthened as service providers for the professors, with deans being responsible for the implementation of the academic staff's decisions. The influence of the president, however, is reduced to external representation and fundraising.

Dean Steering is the structural degeneration of "University Collegialism". Deans turn out to behave opportunistically, taking advantage of the withdrawn role of the president as well of the professors who were sidetracked by coordination efforts. They develop their own agenda, pleading the faculty's interests, and behave within the faculty in as feudalistic a manner as the president in the stage of "Presidential Feudalism".

These stages differ in regard to the distribution of power within the university and result in different extents of effectiveness and efficiency.

5. THE COMPLEX ROLE OF A DEAN

The changing role of deans in an arena of complex and conflicting political interests and in the structural evolution of higher education and universities is being increasingly discussed in international literature on university governance. There are a growing number of comprehensive overviews (e.g.

Wolverton et al. 2001; Bray 2008; de Boer/ Goedegebuure 2009; Gmelch et al. 2011; Scholz/Stein/Fraune 2012) on this topic.

Leading a faculty is an activity that mediates between the interests of the professors and the interests of the university management.

While intending to bridge this gap, the crucial question becomes on which side the dean sees himself: on the side of the professors who are the key unit for the production of academic output, or on the side of the powerful presidential university management? Both tend to have different and often conflicting views on the relevance of external university stakeholders such as companies and their influence on research and teaching contents. The dean's role strongly influences the degree of academic autonomy of the professors and the degree of decision power of the university president.

Two alternative models for the dean position can be observed:

- There are collegial deans who are elected by the faculty members for a limited period of time. They are academics and not specifically trained for the dean's job, but have prior experience in how universities work from internal faculty and university politics in committees, councils or the senate, and they know that they are in a "primus inter pares" role compared to their colleagues.
- Alternatively, there are professional, full-time executive deans, who are usually installed by the president and serve as the president's messenger. Being an executive dean means telling the faculty completely what to do in order to conform to the president's will.

Both are responsible for faculty performance and sustainable development. Therefore, they have to be professionalised. A collegial dean is not naturally qualified because he is already a professor in the university system. He has, for example, to train in managerial competences as well as negotiation skills, learn about the faculty and university system, and understand all numbers and indicators he will be dealing with. An executive dean has even more to learn. He is not automatically a better type of dean because he is from the outside and a non-academic. On the contrary, it might be highly dysfunctional for an over-the-hill company manager to try to become a university specialist without understanding the system and culture.

The determination process also shapes the role of the dean. Collegial deans are elected by their peers, while executive deans are selected by the president or elected by their peers but not instated against the will of the president who has the final veto power. Dependent on their determination, deans will later behave according to the psychological contract they have concluded.

6. THE DEAN'S SCOPE OF ACTION

Facing very complex configurations of inter-related interests, which are additionally moderated by academic discipline (Del Favero 2006), the dean's main managerial challenge is how to meet the different demands placed upon him. In their international comparison of the most important areas of a dean's work, Scott/Coates/Anderson (2008) identify for academic deans in Australian universities a task list ranked by perceived priority. It consists of "managing relationships with senior staff – strategic planning – identifying new opportunities – managing other staff – developing policy – chairing meetings – networking within the university – participating in meetings – liaising with external constituents – developing organisational processes". This task list not only shows the different domains involved, such as planning, policy development, networking, management and administration (Scott/Coates/Anderson 2008), but also reveals that between 2008 and today, the task list may even have been extended.

In order to strengthen his position in university policy, a dean has to reflect his activities on five fields:

(1) Strategy of deans and faculties: in which direction can deans influence the development of faculties within the university of the future? This domain includes, for

example:
- Overall identity of a faculty
- Formulation of a faculty strategy
- Dean's accountability for academic freedom in research and teaching

(2) Management of faculties and deans' competence profiles: which management tasks should a dean institutionalise and which competences should he acquire in order to build a faculty with competitive strengths? This domain includes, for example:
- Training requirements for deans
- Interface optimisation between dean and president
- Transparency between dean and faculty members

(3) Faculty autonomy: what significance will the autonomy of faculties have in the university of the future? This domain includes, for example:
- Decision-making principles within the faculty
- Power in budget negotiations
- Administrative independence of the faculty

(4) External relations of faculties: which external relations of a faculty can and should a dean shape in the university of the future? This domain includes, for example:
- Autonomy in respect to firm cooperation
- Independence of horizontal cooperation among faculties
- Faculty internationalisation strategy

(5) Performance control of faculties: how will a dean be able to direct and control the performance of a faculty member, as well as of the whole faculty, in future competition in higher education? This domain includes, for example:
- Significance of rankings, accreditations, and evaluations
- Weight of performance indicators
- Overall model of university governance

These five fields each include the most important and relevant instruments of higher education policies (Reale/Seeber 2013). Deans are responsible for the implementation of their ideas regarding faculty management. Although their influence on professors, presidents, administration and external stakeholders is restricted, they still have some room for manoeuvre to influence faculty management and performance. The dean can find activity fields, for example, in respect to faculty strategy development, faculty funding, faculty leadership, faculty administration and faculty information systems.

Without stressing all the above points in detail (see Scholz/Stein/Fraune 2012), a dean can follow the "executive" model with authority or the "collegial" model with loyalty towards the faculty members. The formal power of the dean is decisive for his effectiveness, i.e. whether he will be able to successfully formulate the comprehensive strategy for the faculty, create motivating working conditions including material resources as well as immaterial support, shape the faculty's internal relations among its members and negotiate the faculty's external relations with other faculties and all stakeholders. The cooperative fulfilment of all these tasks requires a dean's capabilities in negotiation, creativity and innovation, as well as in strategic planning in higher education (Zechlin 2010), but foremost an interest in working towards the faculty's objectives rather than towards individual goals.

7. CONCLUSION

It emerges that – especially in international competition in higher education – the way to shape faculties will be decisive for the sustainability of the university in the future. To sum up the focal questions:

How should a dean influence the faculty so that it can be internationally competitive in research and teaching? What type of dean should he be?

These questions will shape the most important discussion lines of the international academic conference "The Dean in the University of the Future: Learning From and Progressing With Each Other".

The scope of discussion will range between conventional strategies and alternative strategies. While conventional action focuses on centralisation, an alternative method could be decentralisation or (in the terminology of the university system) collegialism and academic autonomy. What does that mean for faculties?

Applying conventional strategies could – related to the five fields presented in paragraph 3 – exemplarily mean making the following moves:

(1) Strategy of deans and faculties: to serve the university's performance criteria, such as maximisation of external funds;

(2) Management of faculties and deans' competence profiles: to train deans to be effectively performing faculty heads in the eyes of the president;

(3) Faculty autonomy: to support centralised service units in order to generate synergies;

(4) External relations of faculties: to implement cooperation with companies which are politically relevant for the university;

(5) Performance controlling of faculties: to optimise the system of key performance indicators for faculty-directed control and president-directed reporting.

Modern organisation theory, however, has developed organisational alternatives structurally based on federal concepts such as lean management, delegation, flexibilisation or virtualisation. Increasing complexity is met by an increase in decentralised problem solution capacity. Again linking action to the five fields presented in paragraph 3, examples of alternative strategies could be found in:

(1) Strategy of deans and faculties: to restore the ideal of a university as a location of unbiased innovation instead of obedient performance;

(2) Management of faculties and deans' competence profiles: to involve the faculties in the economisation discussion and let them decide autonomously about their contributions to save financial resources;

(3) Faculty autonomy: to empower faculties

so they can directly negotiate their budgets with the public ministries;

(4) External relations of faculties: to create inter-faculty cooperation without involving the president as "process owner";

(5) Performance controlling of faculties: to release faculties from non-productive tasks such as permanent accreditation.

The necessary discussions about the future of universities will be difficult and partly controversial. But first of all, it will be decisive to be precise in what is meant. New insight cannot be derived when there is only common agreement on the surface, while below there is vagueness, with room for every possible interpretation.

Faculties might be less the "problem" than the "solution" to university sustainability and effectiveness.

REFERENCES

Amaral, Alberto/Magalhães, António, Epidemiology and the Bologna saga, in: Higher Education 48 (2004), 79-100.

Aucoin, Peter, Administrative reform in public management: Paradigms, principles, paradoxes and pendulums, in: Governance. An International Journal of Policy and Administration 3 (1990), 115-137.

Birnbaum, Robert, How colleges work. The cybernetics of academic organization and leadership, San Francicso – London (Jossey-Bass) 1988.

Bogumil, Jörg/Heinze, Rolf G. (eds.), Neue Steuerung von Hochschulen. Eine Zwischenbilanz, Berlin (edition sigma) 2009.

Bray, Nathaniel J., Prospective norms for academic deans: Comparing faculty expectations across institutional and disciplinary boundaries, in: Journal of Higher Education 79 (2008), 692-721.

Christensen, Tom, University governance reforms: Potential problems of more autonomy, in: Higher Education 62 (2011), 503-517.

de Boer, Harry/Goedegebuure, Leo, The changing nature of the academic deanship, in: Leadership 5 (2009), 347-364.

Del Favero, Marietta, An examination of the relationship between academic discipline and cognitive complexity in academic deans' administrative behavior, in: Research in Higher Education 47 (2006), 281-315.

Eisenhardt, Katheleen M./Martin, Jeffrey A., Dynamic capabilities: What are they?, in: Strategic Management Journal 21 (2000), 1105-1121.

Fumasoli, Tatiana/Lepori, Benedetto, Patterns of strategies in Swiss higher education institutions, in: Higher Education 61 (2011), 157-178.

Gmelch, Walt/Hopkins, Dee/Damico, Sandra, Seasons of a dean's life. Understanding the role and building leadership capacity, Sterling, VA (Stylus) 2011.

Greiner, Larry E., Evolution and revolution as organizations grow, in: Harvard Business Review 50 (4/1972), 37-46.

Hood, Christopher, A public management for all seasons?, in: Public Administration 69 (Spring 1991), 3-19.

Hüther, Otto, Von der Kollegialität zur Hierarchie. Eine Analyse des New Managerialism in den Landeshochschulgesetzen. Wiesbaden (Verlag für Sozialwissenschaften) 2010.

Kamola, Isaac/Meyerhoff, Eli, Creating commons: Divided governance, participatory management, and struggles against enclosure in the university, in: Polygraph 21 (2009), 5-27.

Kern, Horst, Rückgekoppelte Autonomie. Steuerungselemente in lose gekoppelten Systemen, in: Hanft, Anke (ed.): Hochschule managen? Zur Reformierbarkeit der Hochschulen nach Managementprinzipien, Neuwied (Luchterhand) 2000, 25-38.

Mintzberg, Henry, Structure in fives: Designing effective organizations, New Jersey (Prentice Hall) 1983.

Paradeise, Catherine/Reale, Emanuela/Goastellec, Gaële, A comparative approach to higher education reforms in Western European countries, in: Paradeise, Catherine/Reale, Emanuela/Bleiklie, Ivar/Ferlie, Ewan (eds.), University governance. Western European comparative perspectives, Doordrecht (Springer) 2009, 197-225.

Reale, Emanuela/Seeber, Marco, Instruments as empirical evidence for the analysis of higher education policies, in: Higher Education 65 (2013), 135-151.

Reichwald, Ralf, Universitätsstrukturen und Führungsmechanismen für die Universität der Zukunft. Arbeitsbericht Nr. 13 des Lehrstuhls für Allgemeine und Industrielle Betriebswirtschaftslehre der Technischen Universität München, Munich (February 1997), http://www.aib.wiso.tu-muenchen.de/neu/eng/content/publikationen/arbeitsberichte_pdf/TUM-AIB%20WP%20013%20Reichwald%20Universitaetsstrukturen.pdf, accessed 18 June 2013.

Santiago, Rui/Carvalho, Teresa, Academics in a new work environment: The impact of New Public Management on work conditions, in: Higher Education Quarterly 62 (2008), 204-223.

Schimank, Uwe, 'New Public Management" and the academic profession: Reflections on the German situation, in: Minerva 43 (4/2005), 361-376.

Scholz, Christian/Stein, Volker, Bilder von Universitäten – Ein transaktionsanalytisch-agenturtheoretischer Ansatz, in: Betriebswirtschaftliche Forschung und Praxis, 62 (2010), 129-149.

Scholz, Christian/Stein, Volker, Les universités allemandes en mutation et les leçons à tirer par les administrations publiques pour leur gestion axée sur les connaissances, in: Télescope 17 (3/2011), 31-53.

Scholz, Christian/Stein, Volker/Fraune, Cornelia, Evolving structures of higher education institutions: The dean's role, in: Bergan, Sjur/Egron-Polak, Eva/Kohler, Jürgen/Purser, Lewis/Vukasović, Martina (eds.), Leadership and governance in higher education. Handbook for decision-makers and administrators, vol. 2, Berlin (Raabe) 2012, 1-24.

Scott, Geoff/Coates, Hamish/Anderson, Michelle, Learning leaders in times of change: Academic leadership capabilities for Australian higher education, Sydney (University of Western Sydney/Australian Council for Educational Research) 2008.

Teece, David. J./Pisano, Gary/Shuen, Amy, Dynamic capabilities and strategic management, in: Strategic Management Journal 18 (1997), 509-533.

Waswa, Fuchaka/Swaleh, Sauda, Faculty opinions on emerging corporatization in public universities in Kenya, in: Education and General Studies 1 (2012), 9-15.

Wilkesmann, Uwe, Governance von Hochschulen. Wie lässt sich ein Politikfeld steuern?, in: *Bandelow, Nils C./Hegelich, Simon* (eds.): Pluralismus – Strategien – Entscheidungen, Wiesbaden (Verlag für Sozialwissenschaften) 2011, 305-323.

Williamson, Oliver E., Markets and hierarchies. Analysis and antitrust implications, New York (Free Press) 1975.

Wolverton, Mimi/Gmelch, Walter H./Montez, Joni/Nies, Charles T., The changing nature of the academic deanship. ASHE-ERIC higher education research report vol 28, San Francisco, CA (Jossey-Bass) 2001.

Yamamoto, Kiyoshi, Corporatization of national universities in Japan: Revolution for governance or rhetoric for downsizing?, in: Financial Accountability & Management 20 (2004), 153-181.

Zechlin, Lothar, Strategic planning in higher education, in: *Baker, Eva/Peterson, Penelope/McGaw, Barry* (eds.), International Encyclopedia of Education vol 4, Oxford (Elsevier) 3. ed., 2010, 256-263.

Christian Scholz holds the Chair of Business Administration, especially Organisational Behaviour, Human Resource Management and Information Management. He is founding Director of the MBA School as part of the Europa-Institute at the Universität des Saarlandes. From 2010 until 2012 he was the Dean of the Faculty of Law and Business at the Saarland University. His research interests include human capital management, high performance teams, international human resource management, changes in the work environment (Darwiportunism) and "Korporatismus als ökonomisches Gestaltungsprinzip für Universitäten" (KORFU). In the field of Human Resource Management he has been voted several times as one of the Top 40 experts in Germany.

Volker Stein is Professor at the University of Siegen, Germany, Chair of Business Administration, especially Human Resource Management and Organisational Behaviour. He is Founding Director of the "Südwestfälische Akademie für den Mittelstand – University Siegen Business School" and Visiting Professor at EM Strasbourg Business School. His current research focuses on HRM especially in mid-sized companies, human capital management, international empirical organisational research, market-based leadership in organisations, and university governance, in particular the research project "Korporatismus als ökonomisches Gestaltungsprinzip für Universitäten" (KORFU). Among others, Volker Stein is co-editor of "Bologna-Schwarzbuch" (Black Book Bologna, 2009) together with Christian Scholz.

PART II

CONFERENCE CONTRIBUTIONS

Session 1

Strategy of Deans and Faculties in Higher Education

TO THE ETHICAL DIMENSION OF A DARWIPORTUNISTIC FACULTY SYSTEM

Stefanie Müller

Chair for Organisational Behaviour, Human Resource Management and Information Systems,
Universität des Saarlandes, Campus A5 4, 66123 Saarbrücken, Germany,
sm@orga.uni-sb.de

Faculties can be seen as behavioural systems in that the self-interest seeking behaviour of academic and administrative staff ("individual opportunism") meets the overall rationale of the faculty, i.e. performance and competitive strength in its hard-fought market for research and teaching ("collective Darwinism"). This results in so-called psychological contracts that can be described by the theory-based "Darwiportunism" framework. This article deals with the ethical questions related with different sets of psychological contracts in faculties. How can they be arranged so that a functional "good" realisation of collaborative work and joint performance will be reached? How can the interests of the faculty be bridged with those of its staff in order to implement effective psychological contracts and minimise conflicts? Guiding principles related to the Darwiportunism-Ethics will be presented that contribute to establish an intra-faculty regime of "clean" Darwiportunism.

1. CHALLENGE: "DARWIPORTUNISM" AS A REAL PHENOMENON

Charles Darwin became famous for his theory of evolution, which looked basically at the logic of variation, selection, and retention. One cornerstone in his theory of evolution is the idea of selection, which gives only the fittest a chance to survive. Finally, not the strong ones will survive, but those species that adapt best to the always-changing environment. This Darwinism can also be used as a paradigm for organisational behaviour and has an increasing relevance in markets, corporate cultures, and the society as a whole.

Changes within the working life on the one side concern the increased competitive pressure for companies, where companies have to fight and to survive within this global competition. This external pressure, results in internal performance pressure, where the employees have to perform. This development is called "collective Darwinism" (Scholz 2003; 2013): The external global markets decide which products, services, or companies survive. On an internal level assessment procedures decide which employee fits and contributes to the achievement of the objects of the organisation.

From an ethical point of view, we can discuss about the high internal performance orientation and the pressure for the employees, where only the most and best-performing employees will survive – everybody who failed has to leave this system. This darwinistic system can be characterised with catchwords as "exploitation" or "rat race". However, from a business and economic point of view, companies are forced to integrate competition and performance aspects within management if they want to stay at the market in a long-term view.

On the other side, the changes result from the idea, that companies also do not have a "permanent place" as employer regarding to their employees. Employees are no longer loyal to their organisation. Individuals act in order to maximise their own benefits, using their individual strengths to get ahead in the business world. They give priority to their own advancement, even if their goals are not concurrent with the objectives of the organisation or even if they may harm other people's interests. In consequence, there is no longer the assumption that the organisation's objectives are the same as the objectives of the employees. This development is called "individual opportunism" (Scholz 2003; 2013). These individuals are characterised by self-motivation and ambition. If they can get another, better paid job, they will seize this opportunity at once, without regard for loyalty to their current employer.

From an ethical point of view, we can discuss about the idea whether opportunistic behaviour is an ethical acceptable behaviour. Catchwords such as "missing loyalty" or "missing fairness" are called in this context. However, the own self-realisation is an important part within the working life and companies and employees have to discuss about the question how they will deal with this development, so that both parties have a good conscience.

Accepting the fact that we have at least to some degree Darwinism on the side of the organisation and opportunism on the side of the employees, we can blend this two concepts and get "Darwiportunism" (Scholz 2003) with its four different psychological contracts (figure 1):

(1) The first combination (*"Good old time"*) describes the traditional work life. The employees show their loyalty towards the organisation, the organisation provides the employees with a feeling of job security.

(2) The second combination (*"Kindergarten"*) is characterised by highly opportunistic behaviour of the employees. They seek to maximise their benefits and chances with little concern for the survival of the organisation in which they work.

(3) In the third combination (*"Feudalism"*), the employees accept that the main objective of the organisation is to survive in competition and that it cannot consider the problems and needs of its employees. The employees know that they must behave in a way decided by the organisation.

(4) The fourth combination (*"Pure Darwiportunism"*) is characterised by an open communication between the two parties. Both know that the other part will only maximise its own utility, but they also know that they only can maximise their utility together. The companies give the employees uncertainty and the employees show disobedience towards the organisation. Both parties accept this, if, on the one hand, the employees will do a good job as long as they work in the enterprise and if, on the other hand, the employees will receive the desired outcomes.

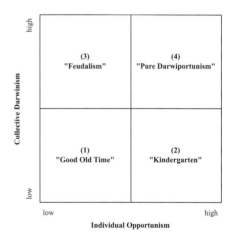

Figure 1: Darwiportunism-Matrix
(Scholz 2003, 89)

None of these four contracts is better than the other. Important is the transparency of the system and the "good" and "bad" realisation. Especially within the "bad" realisation we have more ethical conflicts, because one party (organisation or employee) has a disadvantage.

How companies and employees can solve this ethical conflicts is part of this article and it will be shown by an example of the faculty system.

2. SOLUTION: DARWIPORTUNISM-ETHICS

For solving the ethical conflicts as shown above, this article uses a framework, the four-step-model, for developing a Darwiportunism-Ethics (Müller 2011; 2012).

Step 1: Identify conflicts

The trigger for moral or ethical reflection is the location of a moral or ethical conflict. In working life, moral conflicts for instance are located by different interests within companies (employees, management other stakeholders).

Regarding to the Darwiportunism framework, the three contracts "Kindergarten", "Feudalism" and "Pure Darwiportunism" have conflict potential. Within the negative form of "Kindergarten", employees enforce their interests regardless of consequences. Often, these employees have a high qualification and the companies need them immediately. So, employees get what they want. In the contract "Feudalism" it is the other way around: In a bad way, companies demand high-performing people, which they exploit. The power lies on the side of the organisation. In the contract "Pure Darwinism" the two conflicts from "Kindergarten" and "Feudalism" come together: Each party searches for its own interests. If the benefit expectations do not fit, they leave.

Step 2: Appoint Philosophical Orientation

To solve these conflicts, ethical theories for the reason of right action go back to an isolated philosophical theory (as Kantianism) or

to various moral principles (as justice/fairness). The function of applied ethics is to transfer general, relevant maxims (e.g. mid-level principles), which are based on a higher moral principle, as well as to apply special topics, problems or situations (e.g., Bayertz 2007; Höffe 2010). The interesting questions are what the higher moral principle is and which general, relevant maxims are the right ones for applied ethics.

If we combine philosophical theories with Darwiportunism, we can find for each cell of the matrix a specific justification argument (figure 2):

(1) For the "Good Old Time" we can use ethics by *Prima-facie-duties*. The ethics of prima-facie-duties argues that maximising the good is only one of several prima-facie-duties (prima-facie-obligations) which plays a role in determining what a person ought to do in any given case (Ross 1930). Especially the contract "Good Old Time" is based on sense of duty, regarding companies and also employees. Examples are humanisation of the working world, employees' social engagement or the support from companies in case of family members in need of care.

(2) For the "Kindergarten" we can argue with ethics by *Kantianism*. Within Kants' ethics (Kant 1788) exists a single moral obligation, which he called the 'categorical imperative', that is derived from the concept of duty. Kant defines the demands for the moral law as 'categorical imperatives'. These imperatives are principles that are intrinsically valid and that are good in and of themselves. In this context, people have the obligation not to harm anybody and to do things, which promote oneself or other people. For the contract "Kindergarten" we can use these principles, with the claim not to harm the organisation in a sustainable context.

(3) For the "Feudalism" we can use ethics by *Utilitarism* (Bentham 1789). Regarding to utilitarianism, the moral value of an action is determined only by its resulting outcome. One can only weigh the morality of an action after knowing

all of its consequences. In the positive case the two criteria for right decisions, efficient fulfilment of an organisation's interest and the optimisation of the organisation's well-being, exist parallel. Especially in the case of the optimisation of the organisation's well-being or performance, employees could participate about incentive systems.

(4) For the "Pure Darwiportunism" we can argue with *ethics by discourse*. The basic idea is that the universal validity of a moral norm cannot be justified in an isolated individual reflection on an issue, but only in an ongoing dialogue between individuals. In that case opportunism and Darwinism are allowed, but only within boundaries. These boundaries result from a transparent reciprocal dialogue that is accepted by both parties.

Summing up, regarding to the psychological contract we need another justification argument. If we look at "Kindergarten" it makes no sense to use ethics by discourse, because it does not fit with the structure und the rules of the game within that contract.

Figure 2: Philosophical Orientation for Darwiportunism-Ethics

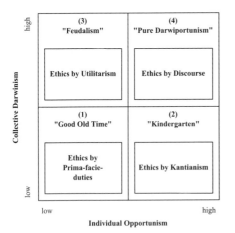

Step 3: Assure Pointers for Action

Based on the rationale of step two, strategies for action have to be derived. Applied ethics try to give orientation for action within a specific context. Norms and underlying values control human beings' behaviour in the context of culture. In management context, for instance, we talk about leadership norms which show how employees and leaders should work together. Regarding management ethics we have seen institutional regulations for the right moral behaviour, as codes of ethics, ethical audits, values and policies as well as whistle blowing systems.

Pointers for action means for the Darwiportunism-Ethics to show, how working life conflicts can be solved and what makes it easier in handling for companies as well as for employees.

(1) In the "Good Old Time" we have a balance between the interest groups. In that contract, people and organisation act as a "good businessman", based on virtues, which concentrate on a long-term economic success.

(2) In the "Kindergarten" companies should only fulfil claims of the employees, which not produce any damage for other people or for the organisation as a whole. On the other side, companies have to develop people if they want to keep them. In that case, organisations need a clear structure: The organisation plays on the one side the "parent part" and treats employees attentively. On the other side is the role of parents also to demonstrate the limits. Employees receive an incentive, if there is a success.

(3) In the "Feudalism" exist clear rules and performance indicators for the employees for achieving the organisational goals. The performance orientation leads on the one side to the maximisation of profits and on the other side to the adequate compensation of the high performer. A "good" Feudalism results in internal competition, which employees encourage to work better. In that case it is essential to have a clear and

well-structured performance agenda: How does the organisation measure performance on an individual level? How does the organisation pay additional work? How does the organisation define goals?

(4) In the "Pure Darwiportunism" the "good" case is based on mutual dialogue and negotiation of solutions. For instance, organisations negotiate for each employee his or her personal development. In that case personal development is more an investing, where employees also do one's bit in form of renunciation of vacation time, for example. So, employees have the possibility to develop themselves and organisations empower their position in competition.

The pointers for action can be achieved by playing the "good" form of the four cells.

Step 4: Formulate Recommendations

Actors need recommendations what they should do. The objective of applied ethics is to solve identified conflicts. In the context of management ethics, companies have to know which implications result from a specific theory and to which extent they solve the identified conflicts.

These recommendations in form of guiding principles are the following, which result from the identified conflicts in step 1 (table 1).

Table 1: Guiding Principles of the Darwiportunism-Ethics

Psychological Contract	Guiding Principle
In general	(0) Find out, which psychological contract is present – by organisation and by employee.
Good old Time	(1) Make sure, that the structures of the organisation, preferences and behaviour of the employees are not fixed.
Kindergarten	(2) Enable individual opportunism, but ensure clear limits.
Feudalism	(3) Create a working environment, which exploitation of employees not allow.
Pure Darwiportunism	(4a) Accept opportunistic behaviour of employees and renounce on contractual regulations, which try to limit opportunism. (4b) Accept darwinistic behaviour of organisations and renounce on mechanisms, which try to eliminate Darwinism.

The following example shows, how the Darwiportunism-Ethics can be disposed in a faculty system.

3. EXAMPLE: DARWIPORTUNISM-ETHICS IN A FACULTY SYSTEM

The psychological contracts also exist in the university context. Within the last years, the higher education system has changed dramatically, affected by national and international reforms as the Bologna process. Therefore, the following section shows how the Darwiportunism-Ethics can be applied to the faculty system.

Starting Situation

Within universities many interest groups are existing. Regarding to the psychological contracts in reality not only one contract exists, but a variety can be observed, as the following examples show:

(1) On the one side, there are members, which are very closely associated with the system "faculty", because of a long tradition of this department, for instance. They feel as a part of the system and have a high loyalty and emotional commitment to their faculty. On the other side, these members have less individual initiative regarding to change management and promoting new developments within the faculty. They are totally content with the existing system. These members follow the contract "Good old Time".

(2) Besides this, there are also members, which do what they want and focus on their own interests. A sense of belonging to the faculty only exits if they get an individual benefit. Transparency and fairness are for these members foreign words. In this situation they follow the contract "Kindergarten".

(3) Furthermore, there are members within a faculty which "execute commands" from higher instances. They adapt this hierarchical top down system within their own context. Keywords in this contract are "authority" and "obedience". The higher instances act feudalistically and say what is to do and what not. Therefore, this instance has the decision-making authority. Here, members are following the psychological contract "Feudalism".

(4) Finally, there are members, which act opportunistically on the one side, on the other side they also know, that the faculty is moving in a darwinistic environment where it competes with other faculties about financial or human resources. Therefore, the members anticipate that they have to adapt their behaviour. Also the faculty management knows about the darwinistic environment and expects from the members individual performance, which is directly connected to the faculty performance.

The conflicts result, for instance, from situations, where the faculty management board plays "Feudalism", and only a few members within the faculty follow the same psychological contract. This problem is reinforcing, if the faculty management board makes the contract not transparent: in a public environment they are signaling democracy and participation, behind the doors they play feudalism.

Conflict Solving

First of all, we have to find out, which psychological contract exists and if the assumptions and expectations between faculty management board and faculty members are the same.

(1) For the next guiding principle we look into the contract "Good Old Time". Here the faculty management has to ensure the "normal" operations: Employees (as professors and lectures) need a good infrastructure as good working rooms or good working administration procedures. Furthermore, this contract based on contingency, with a long planning horizon and without financial or economical ups and downs. All actors know their role.

(2) In the contract "Kindergarten" the faculty management may not allow that everybody has its will. Here the faculty management needs clear limits for the staff, which are bound for all faculty members. If there are faculties, which are promoted more than others (in case of excellent research for instance), a transparent communication and explanation for all university members is needed.

(3) In the contract "Feudalism" the faculty management has to play a transparent feudalism, where everybody knows that system. In case, that the working conditions and the working environment are organised in the interest of the members, they accept this feudalism system and also accept the decisions of the faculty management.

(4) In the contract "Pure Darwiportunism" it is important to look for a dialogue with all interest groups. In that contract, the faculty and the university management has to figure out that also universi-

ties and faculties have a huge external competitive pressure and everybody in the internal system has to make a contribution to performance. Furthermore, the faculty management has to satisfy requirements of the members, for instance in the case of contract negotiations with new professors.

However, first of all faculties and their members have to agree, which psychological contract is efficient. After that, changes in structure and behaviour are needed, that the preferred contract really gets true.

4. CONCLUSION: PLAY "CLEAN" DARWIPORTUNISM

An intervention within Darwiportunism is necessary, if "unclean" psychological contracts exist. Regarding to that, a "clean" playing of contracts is the better solution in a long-term-oriented and ethical perspective.

For universities, the environment becomes more and more complex and dynamic: Due to the Bologna reform in Europe, the competition between universities strongly increases. It is competition for students, high qualified staff, and financial resources. This external pressure leads to more internal pressure, where also faculties have to fight for their resources. In that game, universities and faculties needs a clear idea, how the rules of this game are. In that case Darwiportunism-Ethics can help to reach fair play.

REFERENCES

Bayertz, Kurt, Zur Selbstaufklärung der Angewandten Ethik, in: *Steenblock, Volker* (ed.), Praktische Philosophie/Ethik. Ein Studienbuch, Berlin (Lit) 3. ed., 2007, 153-171.

Bentham, Jeremy, An introduction to the principles of morals and legislation. (1798, Edition 2005) Whitefish MT (Kessinger Publishing).

Kant, Immanuel, Kritik der praktischen Vernunft, in: Kants Werke, Akademie Textausgabe (1877, Edition 1968), Berlin (de Gruyter), 1-162.

Höffe, Otfried, Philosophische Ethik. Fahne im Wind oder Fels in der Brandung?, in: http:www.zeit-fragen.ch/ausgabe/2010/nr-40-vom-11102010/philoso-phische-ethik-fahne-im-wind-oder-fels-in-der-brandung/, accessed 18 November 2010.

Müller, Stefanie, Humankapitalethik. Ein handlungsleitendes Modell zum verantwortungsvollen Umgang mit Humanvermögen, München – Mering (Hampp) 2011.

Müller, Stefanie, Human capital ethics: A framework for developing a more ethically human capital measurement, Paper presented at the 12th European Academy of Management Annual Conference, Rotterdam 6th – 8th June 2012.

Ross, William D., The right and the good, London (Oxford University Press) 1930.

Scholz, Christian, Spieler ohne Stammplatzgarantie. Darwiportunismus in der neuen Arbeitswelt, Weinheim (Wiley-VVCH) 2003.

Scholz, Christian, Darwiportunism: Fairness between darwinistic companies and opportunistic Employees?, Arbeitspapier Nr. 113 des Lehrstuhls für Organisation, Personal- und Informationsmanagement, Universität des Saarlandes, Saarbrücken 2013.

Scholz, Christian/Müller Stefanie, Darwiportunismusethik als Lösung für Arbeitsweltkonflikte, in: *Kaiser, Stephan/Kozica, Arjan* (eds.), Ethik im Personalmanagement, München – Mering (Hampp) 2012, 113-129.

To the Ethical Dimension of a Darwiportunistic Faculty System

Stefanie Müller is an assistant professor at the Chair for Organisational Behaviour, Human Resource Management and Information Systems at the Universität des Saarlandes. She received her doctoral degree for the research on ethics in human capital management. She is managing director of the Institute of Management Competence (imk) at the Universität des Saarlandes. Her research covers HRM in small and medium-sized enterprises, human capital measurement, employee surveys, and research on convergence versus divergence in HRM. Currently, she is member of the German research group for the ISO certification on Human Resource Management.

PROMOTING RESEARCH AND GRADUATE STUDIES IN THE UNIVERSITY OF THE FUTURE: THE ROLES OF DEANS AND VICE-PRESIDENTS

Graham Carr

Vice-President Research and Graduate Studies, Concordia University,
Montréal, Canada
gcarr@alcor.concordia.ca

One of the key challenges that will face academic administrators in the university of the future is how to align institutional practices with new trends in research and graduate education. Research and graduate training are the principle reputational drivers in the global world of higher education. Traditionally, faculties and departments have often been regarded as the principal units of research production and disciplinary formation. But the rise of large, project and programme-driven research networks and centres, as well as the growing emphasis on transdisciplinarity and inter-institutional partnerships highlight the need for new approaches to the organisation of research and graduate programme activities on campus. Drawing on North American and, more specifically Canadian examples, this paper focuses on three key pressure points—faculty hiring and mentorship, graduate programme development, and design of research space—where changing values and organisational practices are needed. It argues that successful research universities in the future will re-imagine the principles of faculty and departmental autonomy and foster new forms of collaborative, institution-wide leadership.

1. INTRODUCTION

Universities everywhere are at a critical juncture. The demand for access to higher education has never been greater. There are high expectations from government, industry, students, and the public at large that universities will be the primary generators of new knowledge and trained workforces capable of meeting and adapting to the rapidly changing realities of the global knowledge economy. Meanwhile, the proliferation of new teaching and learning technologies, growth of larger and larger research networks, unleashing of new mobility options for students and researchers, and transformation of the market context in which universities compete with each other, is fast putting pressure on university administrators to develop new models for success. Because research and graduate education are valorised as signature elements of leading universities and understood to be vital contributors to social value, many of the most urgent choices confronting stewards of higher education concern those key sectors of the university. While there are many dimensions to the 21st century transformations in research and graduate studies, one of the most basic challenges will be to achieve the best possible alignment between strategic decision-making at the institutional level and resource allocation both at the faculty and department levels, and in new cross-faculty research institutes and graduate programmes.

Focusing both on Canadian and international examples, this paper explores the transformative moment in which universities currently find themselves, particularly with regard to the delivery of high quality research and graduate education. Looking to the future, the paper argues that successful universities will be those that break free of traditional models of faculty and departmental autonomy, and instead achieve a coherent re-alignment of priorities, resources and actions that enables inter-sectoral opportunities and capitalises on transversal imperatives. This change will require faculty deans, as well as vice-presidents academic and research, to practice new steps in their administrative choreography and re-imagine how to define the scope and autonomy of their actions, both individually and collectively.

2. THE CANADIAN CONTEXT

In Canada, depending on who one's preferred source is, universities are either undergoing a massive crisis of funding, losing their bearings as bastions of free inquiry, and selling their souls to rampant corporatisation (Woodhouse 2009), or they are managing unprecedented growth in student numbers, expanding their community impact, and nurturing a flourishing of internationally-recognised research output (Davidson 2013). Some commentators would argue that those narratives are not mutually exclusive. Nor are they unique to Canada. The divergence illustrates a basic point, however, which is that there is no consensus about the state of higher education today, let alone, its directions for the future.

This is not just a matter of perception or ideology. The reality in Canada, and even more so on a global scale, is that there are many different types of universities facing vastly different challenges and opportunities. In Canada – where universities are publicly funded institutions operating under provincial jurisdiction – higher education systems in several parts of the country experienced significant multi-year compressions to their operating grants beginning in 2012-13. Similarly, since 2007, direct government investment in research has essentially flat-lined or shrunk against the pace of inflation (Davidson 2013, 114). These troubling recent trends follow a period of astonishing growth in the university sector, that included the

creation of many new regional universities, as well as the conversion to university status of a number of established polytechnic and arts institutes. Student numbers have swelled by 50 percent at the undergraduate level since 2000 and an astonishing 88 percent at the graduate level (Davidson 2013, 112). The recent, rampant growth in non-research, professional, graduate degrees is symptomatic of demands for new forms of credentialisation to meet training demands for 'the next economy' (Policy Horizons Canada 2012). But it also reflects the pressure on institutions to generate new revenue streams in order to sustain growth, particularly as other funding sources come under increasing strain.

3. INTERNATIONAL TRENDS

In other jurisdictions where universities also receive the bulk of their funding from the state, or have the status of para-public institutions answerable to government oversight, there is a marked intensification of government scrutiny and increased demands for academic and fiscal accountability. In the United Kingdom, severe government cutbacks and dramatic reorientations in national priorities for higher education are causing some administrators to talk about 'famine', 'convulsion' and 'the British disease' in the university sector (Thrift 2013, 26, 30, 42). The situation is also dire in many parts of the United States, where perilous public finances and some meddlesome legislatures, threaten the viability of many state university systems, while a number private universities are scrambling to maintain their pre-eminence given the vicissitudes of endowment funding.

By contrast, the higher education sector in China, Brazil and India is exploding by leaps and bounds due in large part to massive new levels of government investment. China now supports 'the world's largest higher education system,' surpassing the US in terms of overall enrolments and annual graduation at all levels. It is also second only to the US in terms of output of scientific papers (Zha 2013, 84). Rapidly emerging nations such as Malaysia, Singapore, and Vietnam are developing their university sectors at a prodigious rate, as are numerous countries in Central Europe, Africa and Latin America. Many of these universities are in a start-up phase. Lacking in tradition but eager to develop their reputations, their potential advantage is precisely that they are unencumbered by the weight of institutional history and bureaucratic stasis that often impedes change in more established institutions.

What the university of the future looks like, in other words, very much depends on how far into the future one casts a gaze, as well as the vantage point from which one poses the question. Some realities are universal, however. The world of higher education is far more competitive internationally than ever before. More and more students are seeking access to university and moving across borders, both real and virtual, to register. Large segments of today's student body have different learning expectations from previous generations, and increasingly students in the future will want higher education to be customised to their career, professional and entrepreneurial aspirations. Higher education is also reaching a technology crossroads with potentially revolutionary implications. The prevalent use of e- and blended-learning techniques, particularly in undergraduate education, and the emerging phenomenon of MOOCs (Massive Open Online Courses) are altering traditional modes of course delivery. They, or variations of them, also have the potential to transform the business model for many universities, not to mention the cost equation for students, as the example of Georgia Institute of Technology's online Masters degree in computer science strikingly demonstrates (Kahn 2013).

With so many factors potentially in flux, universities of the future are bound to confront an unprecedented mix of threats and opportunities, on a grand scale and at an accelerated pace. The problem is that universities tend not to be well equipped as 'quick responders' to change. Many institutions will strain to secure the infrastructure, financial and professional resources that will be necessary to accommodate the diverse web of demands that are being placed upon them, let alone to undertake or achieve the cultural change that will be required to meet and manage new realities.

4. FOSTERING RESEARCH AND GRADUATE EDUCATION

Yet in whichever direction one looks, it is also clear that a large component, perhaps the largest component, of institutional reputation and prestige is inextricably tied to quality in research and graduate training. Supporting successful research enterprises on campus is an expensive commitment, involving many different actors, and engaging a wide range of direct and indirect costs. Although modalities for calculating research revenue and expenditures as a percentage of overall institutional budgets vary from country to country, the basket of costs is pretty much the same everywhere. These include direct funding for specific research projects and programmes, but also recruitment and support of faculty and highly qualified personnel, the acquisition, construction, maintenance and support of infrastructure and equipment, and furnishing a range of quality professional research support, from technical expertise to financial administration and legal services.

Institutions that aspire to success in research must logically ask how best to organise themselves to support these key functions at a time when the landscape of university research and graduate training activities is rapidly shifting. Many features of that shift are plainly visible. There is a growing emphasis on transdisicplinarity, collaboration and partnerships, and there is a desire to promote greater mobility of graduate students and research personnel. Collaboration and internationalisation are becoming so ingrained in the world of research that it is almost possible to argue 'that there is no longer such a thing as an individual university', because 'the "university" has become a system of interaction which operates across the globe' (Thrift 2013, 36). There are also increased public and political expectations that research and training will serve society, that the outcomes of fundamental science and *recherche libre* will lead to the greater mobilisation, application and impact of knowledge. More and more the pattern of funding research is gravitating toward investments in large-scale projects and programmes, and with this comes a demand to house more research activity in centres, institutes, and core facilities. All of these trends are affecting the conventional organisation of research and graduate training activities on campus, inviting a re-alignment of resources that will surely transform the traditional role of faculties as units of research production.

Universities are administratively complex organisations in which a greater and greater degree of 'centralised management' (Thrift 2013, 28) is required to orchestrate a huge machinery of many moving parts and push them beyond established boundaries of performance. Therefore, it is logical to ask: what are the most productive roles for faculties and deans vis-à-vis other academic administrators in advancing strategic research graduate studies priorities? What new forms of administrative leadership and institutional governance will be required to intensify research activity? To address these questions it is useful to consider three issues – new faculty hiring, graduate recruitment and programme development, and space allocation – that are pivotal to illustrating how current administrative practices might best be adapted to support highly productive, novel research and graduate programmes in the future.

In Canada, faculty deans are sometimes referred to colloquially as 'baronial deans' because they are perceived to preside over fiefdoms, jealously guarding their resources and power against other faculties, and the central administration. Historically, the role and influence of the position of dean has been determined by the academic focus and reputation of the faculty they lead, and by its size, which is typically measured in student

numbers, the complement of full-time professors, and the amount of research revenue they generate. Even if god is on their side, deans of religion do not wield anywhere near the power in a research university that a dean of medicine or dean of arts and science does. Likewise, deans in professional schools, such as law, engineering or business, often march to different drummers because they are answerable to external accreditation criteria that deans of arts, humanities, environmental or social sciences, simply do not encounter.

At the risk of generalisation, these power relationships have tended to nurture a very conventional model of faculty autonomy that often privileges the local over the institution. The desire to construct a strong faculty identity can nurture a culture of difference that tips instinctively toward habits of segregation rather than collaboration across campus. While this traditional model of faculty identity and autonomy may have served some interests of universities well in the past, it increasingly seems misaligned with current and future directions in research and graduate studies.

5. ENABLING TRANSDISCIPLINARITY BEYOND FACULTY BOUNDARIES

Research and advanced training must always be grounded in fundamental know-ledge. Yet it is equally a truism that research in many leading-edge areas of inquiry can only go so far if it is contained within field or method-specific boxes, or a single stable of ideas. Many of the foremost research challenges of our time – from preventive health to energy sustainability, from human rights to omics or systems security – are of such a scale and complexity that they not only invite, but also require, the combined knowledge and problem-solving capacities of multiple types of scientific and intellectual discipline and training. It is an article of contemporary faith that science and scholarship must become more, not less, transdisciplinary. Smart universities are already borrowing lessons from the worlds of business, entrepreneurship and creative culture, where truly innovative thinking happens through collision, diversity and disruption (Page 2007; Chesbrough/West/Vanhaverbeke 2008; Christensen 2008). In the field of research, successful universities will be those that best and quickly develop formulas for bringing people together from different backgrounds, enabling them to collaborate on projects and re-imagine how technology and ideas can be deployed in novel ways.

Most universities profess to be incubators of diversity and transdisciplinarity and many offer advanced degrees under the rubric of interdisciplinary studies. Yet when one pulls back the rhetorical curtain, the problem is often that the institution, as an institution, presents more obstacles than pathways to boundary crossing. Ironically, for all their devotion to academic freedom and the spirit of unfettered inquiry, universities, as organisations, are not nimble institutions with a high degree of operational flexibility. On the contrary, they are process and procedure-rich establishments, held together by organisational structures and day-to-day modes of operating that tend to frustrate and impede permeability across departments and faculties. Where academic matters are concerned, the core operational activities – from the hiring of new faculty, to graduate curriculum design, student recruitment, or space allocation – are normally embedded, sometimes even fossilised, in the bedrock of faculties which are aggregates of monodisciplinary departments.

Universities also tend to be very conservative institutions that invest a lot of institutional pride in preserving tradition and maintaining the status quo. Full-time faculty hiring is the single most important function of a dean or department head. But the default tendency in many institutions is to engage primarily in 'replacement hiring' as a safe choice to replicate what already exists, or preserve what has worked in the past. This is especially the case if some proposed new initiatives or type of hiring cannot be funded independently but instead require a re-portioning of existing resources. These habits tend to reflect a version of faculty or

departmental autonomy that is protectionist and does little to incentivise or accommodate 'out of the box' thinking.

In the research realm, the limitation of these modes of thought and behaviour are thrown into stark relief by the current proliferation on campuses of parallel entities in the forms of large-scale research centres, institutes, *regroupements* and platforms. More and more, the terrain of cutting-edge research activity is being seeded by large scale, inter-institutional, projects and programmes. And more and more, the responsibility to cultivate this terrain is being assigned to targeted research units, rather than faculties. The Collaborative Research Centers funded by the German Research Foundation in the 1980s were an early example (Sagerer 2013, 99-100) of this trend, which has become increasingly common in other countries, not least in Canada and Québec.

In Canada, governments are the primary source of funding for university research activity. At the federal level, research is principally supported by five agencies: the Social Sciences and Humanities Research Council of Canada (SSHRC), the Natural Sciences and Engineering Research Council of Canada (NSERC), the Canadian Institutes for Health Research (CIHR), Genome Canada, and the Canada Foundation for Innovation (CFI). In Québec mirror agencies for research on *Société et culture*, *Nature et technologie* and *Santé* operate under the umbrella of the *Fonds de recherche Québec* (*FRQ*). Since its inception, the overarching philosophy of funding through *FRQ* has been to support new scholars, graduate students and trainees, but also to build up research capacity in Québec by supporting the formation of inter-institutional, and often cross-disciplinary, *Groupes* and *Regroupements stratégiques*. Each of these clusters is hosted by an individual university within the *réseau* of Québec higher education. Significantly, this emphasis on large-scale, cross-disciplinary research programmes is also more and more typical at the federal realm, as exemplified through programs such as the Network Centers of Excellence, Canada Excellence Research Chairs, and the SSHRC Partnership Grants programme. While some networks continue to be discipline or faculty-specific, many others reward or are designed to foster capacity building across disciplines.

Universities that compete successfully to host hubs funded under the auspices of these prestigious programmes benefit from the direct external funding that they receive from the granting agencies and affiliated partners. They also reap the rewards of institutional recognition attached to being known as a leader in a particular research domain. Of course, with success comes the obligation to provide institutional commitments for space, research administration expertise, faculty release time from teaching, support for graduate training and development of new programmes, and the recruitment of full-time faculty to boost research capacity. It is here where the internal governance dynamics of faculties and departments come into play for better or worse.

6. RE-IMAGINING ADMINISTRATIVE ROLES IN THE CHANGING RESEARCH LANDSCAPE

In most Canadian universities the responsibility to manage hiring, approve workloads, allocate space and authorise development of new programmes typically resides with faculty deans. Faculty deans, in turn, report to a provost or vice-president academic who wields considerable authority in terms of setting faculty budgets, assigning their hiring lines, and overseeing performance. In research-intensive universities, however, the core funding of centres or institutes, as well as oversight of their governance, is typically vested in offices of research, led by a vice-president for research whose mandate and responsibilities, like those of the provost, encompass the university as a whole. Offices of research provide ancillary professional support for the research community from aid with grant writing to management of intellectual property, and support for the acquisition of major infrastructure and instrumenta-

tion. The research office is also responsible for liaising with major funding agencies and industry, seeding and sustaining internal research activities, ensuring ethics compliance, and pro-actively pursuing inter-institutional collaborations and other funding opportunities, often in conjunction with an office of international relations.

Increasingly, too, the training component of research programmes is getting more emphasis on major grant applications. Many competitions place heightened expectations on universities to provide students with an enhanced training environment that frequently includes access to transdisciplinary formation and professional skills development. While programmes at the Masters and Ph.D. levels are typically delivered by departments within faculties, in most Canadian universities, the oversight of graduate studies and postdoctoral training is the responsibility of a dean of graduate studies. Unlike a faculty dean, deans of graduate studies may, depending on the institution, report either to a provost or a vice-president research. Schools of graduate studies play an important role in upholding standards, benchmarking national and international trends in graduate education, leading recruitment efforts, and fostering new programme development or programme reform. In terms of skills and budgetary resources, these activities require a breadth of professional expertise that is generally beyond the capacity of individual faculties to deliver on their own.

Because universities are 'loosely governed organisations,' the jurisdictional status of research centres, networks, institutes, schools of graduate studies or graduate programmes that live outside traditional departments and faculties, can be a source of ambiguity and tension if it is not clear 'who has the final say on matters that demand attention' (Cole 2009, 66). From both an operational and a strategic perspective, confusion – or worse, competition – over the place of faculty deans vis-à-vis deans of graduate studies or respective vice-presidents is especially damaging in the rapidly-changing, highly competitive national and global context of the 21st century, where speed and efficiency of decision-making matters greatly. It is vital that deans and vice-presidents have a shared commitment to the institution's long-term strategic priorities and pull together in a coordinated fashion. One way to encourage and facilitate this is to ensure that, in addition to reporting directly to a provost or vice-president academic, deans report at least functionally to vice-presidents of research.

This attention to common goals and emphasis on developing an overarching, strategic institutional perspective on research and graduate training does not mean undermining faculty autonomy. Instead, it involves reimagining autonomy and expressing it in different forms. Specifically, it means being open to the possibility that departmental needs and faculty interests may best be served if they are channelled in tandem with priorities in other faculties or research centres. In the university of the future, deans, like other senior academic and research administrators, must be impresarios of interdisciplinarity and innovation.

The imperative to re-imagine faculty autonomy is all the more urgent if one does a simple reality check on the constrained financial resources that deans in many institutions have at their disposal. It is not uncommon in Canadian universities for annual faculty budgets from institutional operating funds to be devoted almost entirely to salaries and other fixed costs. Deans in some faculties may control large budgets, but their margin for manoeuvre is often quite restricted, resembling more the profile of line-item managers who are pre-occupied with the day-to-day running of the faculty. Unless they are successful in raising non-operating funds through donations or endowments, it is very difficult for faculty deans to launch strategic initiatives let alone to ensure they are sustainable from one budget year to the next. This does not mean that deans' hands are tied, however.

7. STRATEGIC HIRING, PROGRAMME INNOVATION AND GRADUATE RECRUITMENT

The approach to faculty hiring is a key example. Managing the recruitment, mentoring and institutional socialisation of newly hired professors are the fundamental instruments by which deans can shape and advance the long-term vision of their faculty and university. At all universities across Canada, faculties, as well as the departments that comprise them, were created and designed to deliver academic programmes by providing core teaching. Although particular departments and faculties in many institutions have become recognised over time for the quality of research activity they support, the fact remains that the requirement to sustain viable teaching programmes is often pre-eminent in setting institutional priorities.

Today in Canada, more than half of the full-time professoriate has been hired since 2000 and the country is now ranked in the top four internationally in terms of quality of research output (Davidson 2013, 113-114). While many things will account for the future growth of universities' institutional reputations, their relative success in nurturing research productivity from this new cohort of tenured-faculty, and those who follow, will outweigh most, if not all other factors. This is not to say that all new hires will revolutionise their disciplines. While most professors do research, train graduate students and endeavour to publish regularly, 'relatively few scientists and scholars in fact influence their peers and the growth of knowledge' (Cole 2009, 178). Nevertheless, the challenge for research universities in the next phase of the 21st century will be to recruit and mentor faculty to build new research and scholarly directions, rather than automatically cloning what has been successful in the past.

The universities that best manage this critical turn will boast larger cohorts of productive faculty with transversal skills, who develop or engage in research programmes that are collaborative, rather than individual.

Yet many of these newly hired faculty will undoubtedly bump up against internal policies – performance reviews, teaching load assignments – that are localised in departments and disciplines and which may frustrate, rather than enable productive cross-fertilisation. Faculty deans have a key role to play in accompanying new hires through these procedures by making sure that there is a good alignment between institutional expectations for success, norms of assessment and mechanisms of support. Recent examples from the University of Connecticut–Storrs, and University of Southern California, illustrate how faculties and colleges were able first to salvage, then to grow and strengthen fledgling philosophy departments at a time when most humanities disciplines are reeling from declining enrolments and lack of institutional investment. At each institution, the pathway to success came by making crosscutting hires that linked to existing strengths in cognate fields in other colleges or faculties, such as health ethics and environmental science. The connections helped to nurture new transdisciplinary programme development. They also opened doors for humanities scholars to participate in novel STEM-based research opportunities and gain access to previously restricted funding streams (Straumsheim 2013).

In tandem with the recruitment and mentoring of new faculty, successful research institutions will also need to rethink their approach to graduate education and postdoctoral training. As a matter of public policy, many countries in the Middle East, as well as China, through the China Scholarship Council, and more recently Brazil, with its ambitious *Sciences without Borders* programme (Guimarães 2013), have sponsored large cohorts of students to gain advanced learning opportunities elsewhere. Universities in North America and Europe have long competed with each other to recruit highly qualified talent from afar because recruitment of the best and brightest trainees is deemed essential for sustaining high quality research productivity.

In North America the dependence on international students also reflects the reality that there are many disciplines where there is a dearth of domestic applicants. This helps to explain why a tremor went through the higher education community in the US in the spring, 2013, when the number of international applications to US graduate schools was discovered to have increased by a mere 1 percent in contrast to 9 percent in 2012 and 11 percent in 2011 (Council of Graduate Schools 2013). At a time when prospective students are more mobile and have far more options from which to choose than at any previous point in history, the statistics raised grave concerns about a tectonic shift occurring in recruitment patterns, and what that may imply for US enrolment models and research competiveness. Countries, such as China, that were net exporters of talent in the past are now positioning themselves to reverse this trend, with ambitions to host half a million international students by 2020 (Goldberger 2013, 69).

To compete effectively in the market for high performing students, universities will need to develop centralised recruitment strategies that are tied to strategic research priorities within their institutions. But they will also need to reform existing programmes or develop new ones, include online degrees, that are attractive to prospective domestic and international graduate students, because they are both affordable and closely aligned with the changing nature of research. This means developing next-generation programmes that capture cutting-edge developments in research, many of which will be transdisciplinary. But it also means fostering opportunities for inter-institutional mobility, or 'brain circulation,' in order to exploit the flow of networks associated with the internationalisation of research activity (Council of Graduate Schools 2012). Furthermore, universities that place a premium on high quality graduate education will also need to offer additional services, such as professional skills training and mentorship, that complement the academic formation students and postdoctoral fellows receive. Increasingly, this additional level of preparation is necessary for entry into a highly competitive, and rapidly changing global work environment

(Rose 2012; Fonds de recherche du Québec 2013).

The challenge is that many institutions are not equipped, administratively, to enable students or postdoctoral fellows to pursue these options. Once again, part of the reason has to do with the traditional focus on departmental and disciplinary identity and autonomy. Even highly attractive options such as developing robust *Co-tutelle*, double degree and *Erasmus Mundus* programmes often prove notoriously difficult to operationalise in existing institutional contexts. Intentionally or otherwise, many graduate programmes seem designed, at the department level, to frustrate transdisciplinarity, inter-institution-al mobility, or skills development opportunities by compelling students to meet tightly prescribed course requirements and observe minimum residency periods. In some disciplines, moreover, there is a significant disconnect between the type of training that students receive – which, at the Ph.D. level is often targeted to creating the next generation professoriate – and the employment opportunities that await doctoral degree-holders upon graduation. Furthermore, the capacity required to deliver supplementary options and services targeted specifically to the needs of graduate students and postdoctoral fellows, such as skills development training in areas such communications, second language acquisition, leadership and me management, often exceed what departments or faculties can reasonably supply.

There is a huge opportunity to innovate graduate education for the 21st century. While graduate training will always have its roots in disciplinary foundations, successful universities will capitalise on the innovation opportunity to develop truly interdisciplinary training opportunities for their students. The example of Stanford University's Design School (http://dschool.stanford.edu), which offers no degrees but welcomes students from all other graduate degree programmes at the university, is a marvellous case in point. The d.school aims to create an added layer of value for prospective students by engaging with them around particular research problems, thus creating a new experiential cohort is not defined or proscribed by a single programme.

To be successful, these types of pedagogic innovation require levels of elaboration and coordination beyond what most programmes and faculties currently deliver. Faculty deans, dean of graduate and postdoctoral studies, and vice-presidents responsible for academic affairs and research will need to play pivotal roles in encouraging programme renovation and innovation that will provide next generation students with truly inter-institutional and institution-wide access to transversal knowledge, skills and collaborative training environments.

8. MANAGING RESEARCH SPACE AND INFRASTRUCTURE

Finally, in anticipating the role that faculty deans and central administrators must play in the research and graduate studies intensive university of the future, it is worth reflecting on the physical space and infrastructure that will be required to support newly evolving forms of research and training activity. From parking to recreation to classroom allocations, physical space is one of the most contested issues on many campuses, and it has always been a defining element of departments and faculties. In the past, many faculty deans strove to acquire or construct dedicated facilities, including entire buildings and complexes precisely because they signified to the external world, the name, identity and autonomy of their particular faculty or school. This often made perfect sense from an institutional perspective because it created attractive naming opportunities for potential donors and allowed all departments in a faculty to be housed in proximity to each other and to the decanal administration. Of course the trade-off is that self-contained space can also promote a garrison mentality that reinforces tendencies to be inward looking and territorial.

Where research is concerned, the organisation of space in universities has traditionally been based on an old model of scholarship that assigned to each professor an individual office, lab or studio. The problem is that this space formula is anachronistic given the changing nature and scale of research-intensity in the 21st century. Indeed, the transformation of research physical space and infrastructure is already happening in many universities where common bench wet labs, black boxes, open innovation hubs, and core facilities are literally breaking down the walls between departments and faculties. Although graduate students in research programmes often select one institution over another because they are drawn by the opportunity to work with a particular supervisor or mentor, another attractive factor for many is the opportunity to study and train in a mixed environment, such as a research centre, a spatial environment that nurtures scientific and intellectual cross-fertilisation. While these developments undoubtedly signal a change in the classical alignment of space within faculties and departments, they do not have to lead to a diminishment in the power of those units.

To be sure, the old fiefdom model of research space may continue to work in some cases where institutions have already built up massive competitive advantages through infrastructure investments, and where it would be too costly or counter-productive to transform the space to a different model. But in general, the reality is that universities must become collaborative zones in order to meet the research and training requirements of the 21st century. This will require new attitudes by administrative leaders at all levels – department, research centre, faculty, and university – based on the common understanding that the re-organisation of space is not about protecting turf, but allowing science and scholarship on campus to flourish for the reputational benefit of all.

9. CONCLUSION

Successful universities of the future can no longer be what they once were. And for no area of their activity is this truer than re-search and graduate studies. Traditionally, departments and faculties were seen as the pivotal units of university research production and advanced training. By and large, the activities they sponsored were designed to promote disciplinary integrity and ensure the autonomy of scholarship. But the nature, scale and expectations for research and graduate studies are undergoing a seismic shift that runs counter to those models. Partnerships, collaboration, mobility, diversity, innovation and transdisciplinary are the scholarly and scientific values for the 21st century. Successful universities will need to learn not just how to articulate, but how to deliver on these values. This will require some reinvention of the traditional role that faculties and their deans have played in research and graduate studies administration to imagine and embrace new forms of collaboration and leadership.

REFERENCES

Chesbrough, Henry/West, Joel/Vanhaverbeke, Kim (eds.), Open Innovation: Researching a new paradigm, New York (Oxford University Press) 2008.

Christenson, Clayton, Disrupting class: How disruptive innovation will change the way the world learns, New York (McGraw-Hill) 2008.

Cole, Jonathan R., The great American university: Its rise to preeminence; its indispensable national role; Why it must be protected, New York (Public Affairs) 2009.

Council of Graduate Schools, From brain drain to brain circulation: Graduate education for global career pathways, in: http://www.cgsnet.org/global-summit-2012, 2012, accessed 26 November 2013.

Council of Graduate Schools, CGS International survey report: Applications, in: http://www.cgsnet.org/cgs-international-survey-report-applications, 8 April 2013, accessed 26 November 2013.

Davidson, Paul, The global university: How do we ensure Canada's universities continue to be at the forefront amidst growing competition, in: *Amrhein, Carl G./Baron, Britta* (eds.), Building success in a global university: Government and academia – redefine worldwide in the relationship, Bonn-Berlin (Lemmens) 2013, 111-120.

Fonds de recherche du Québec, Journée de réflexion sur la formation à la recherché, in: www.frq.gouv.qc.ca/presentations/journee-de-reflexion-sur-la-formation-a-la-recherche, 30 April 2013, accessed 26 November 2013.

Goldberger, Josef, Quantitative success will not bring long term stability: Variables and constants – the higher education system in the People's Republic of China has been and continues to be everything but uniform, in: *Amrhein, Carl G./Baron, Britta* (eds.), Building success in a global university: Government and academia – redefine worldwide in the relationship, Bonn-Berlin (Lemmens) 2013, 64-73.

Guimarães, Jorge A., Quality assurance of postgraduate education: The case of CAPES, the Brazlian agency for support and evaluation of graduate education, in: *Amrhein, Carl G./Baron, Britta* (eds.), Building success in a global university: Government and academia – redefine worldwide in the relationship, Bonn-Berlin (Lemmens) 2013, 54-63.

Kahn, Gabriel, The MOOC that roared: How Georgia Tech's new, super-cheap online Master's degree could radically change higher education, in: http://www.slate.com/articles/technology/technology/2013/07/georgia_tech_s_computer_science_mooc_the_super_cheap_master_s_degree_that.html, 23 July 2013, accessed 26 November 2013.

Page, Scott E., The difference: How the power of diversity creates better groups, firms, schools and societies, Princeton (Princeton University Press) 2007.

Policy Horizons Canada, The next economy: Transformation and resilience in times of rapid change, Ottawa (Government of Canada) 2012.

Rose, Marilyn, Graduate student professional development: A survey with recommendations, Ottawa (SSHRC) 2012.

Sagerer, Gerhard, Between regional embeddedness and international standard: How a young German university tries to position itself within the overarching conditions of the contemporary global scientific society, in: *Amrhein, Carl G./Baron, Britta* (eds.), Building success in a global university: Government and academia – redefine worldwide in the relationship, Bonn-Berlin (Lemmens) 2013, 97-110.

Straumshein, Carl, Defying the humanities crisis, in: http://www.insidehighered.com/news/2013/04/03/uconn-usc-philosophy-departments-defy-downwar-trend-humanities, 3 April 2013, accessed 26 November 2013.

Thrift, Nigel, Producers of systematic new knowledge and interpretation: Universities in British higher education – chief building blocks to answer the question: Where next?, in: *Amrhein, Carl G./Baron, Britta* (eds.), Building success in a global university: Government and academia – redefine worldwide in the relationship, Bonn-Berlin (Lemmens) 2013, 26-44.

Woodhouse, Howard, Selling out: Academic freedom and the corporate market, Montreal (McGill-Queen's University Press) 2009.

Zha, Qiang, Socialist cause and modernization drive: Anticipate the future – Chinese universities show a mixed story of success, crisis, promise, and rich educational traditions to be revitalized, in: *Amrhein, Carl G./Baron, Britta* (eds.), Building success in a global university: Government and academia – redefine worldwide in the relationship, Bonn-Berlin (Lemmens) 2013, 79-96.

Graham Carr is Vice-President, Research and Graduate Studies at Concordia University in Montréal. Previously, he served as the Dean of the School of Graduate Studies, Associate Dean, Research and Graduate Studies in the Faculty of Arts and Science, and Chair of the Department of History. He is past president of the Canadian Federation for the Humanities and Social Sciences. The Federation advocates on behalf of 80 universities and more than 80 scholarly associations, and hosts North America's largest, annual multidisciplinary congress. Dr. Carr has a Ph.D. in History from the University of Maine and holds an M.A. from Queen's University, where he also received his B.A.. His research interest is the cultural history of the Cold War.

HIGHER EDUCATION CHARTERS: IMPLICATIONS FOR FACULTIES

Dennis J. Farrington

President of the University Board, South East European University,
Ilindenska 335, 1200 Tetovo, Republic of Macedonia
d.farrington@seeu.edu.mk

The nature of Faculties and Deans within universities is reviewed in the context of legislation and practice in a number of member states of the European Higher Education Area, the emergence of New Public Management and managerialism generally. There are two conflicting approaches: (i) centralisation promoting interdisciplinarity and better control of resources in an increasingly competitive environment which is coupled with reductions in public funding, and (ii) decentralisation protecting coherent academic programmes, promoting subject-specific links with the outside world, enhancing individual responsibility and accountability. Overall the view is taken that maximising flexibility in the work of universities, addressing the risks attached to specific, relatively inexpensive subjects and aligning structures to potential major upheavals is best achieved by a new approach.

1. INTRODUCTION

Higher Education Charters

The term 'higher education charters' in the title of this paper set by the conference organisers is a generic term taken to mean the range of instruments which set out the way higher education institutions are governed and managed (such as the Royal Charter granted to most pre-1992 UK universities (Farrington et al. 2012); and to the colonial predecessors of some of the oldest universities in the US (Thelin 2011), and its equivalent in other countries.) There are other meanings of 'charter' in rights-based legal terminology, as for example the nature of the unwritten agreement between universities and society (Kezar 2004), student charters, the EU ERASMUS Charter and the Magna Charta Universitatum, but this paper concentrates on the traditional meaning. Governance in particular is a technically complex area with wide variations in practice, having developed since the beginning of mankind's notion of what is meant by 'higher' education, and with major changes taking place in the last half century.

The Nature of Faculties

The Faculty, or School or equivalent is in most countries of the European Higher Education Area (EHEA) an academic unit of a university or other higher education institution which comprises, usually, more than one academic discipline (e.g. Faculty of Humanities) or branch of a discipline (e.g. Faculty of Law). In most cases it has no legal personality of its own, although it may have functions which have legal consequences, e.g. determining the academic progress of students, conducting particular kinds of experiments subject to legal regulation, etc.

In some universities with a large number of Faculties, recent moves towards increasing the efficiency of operation have resulted in regroupings under Schools as a compromise between two main approaches, centralisation and decentralisation. A good example of this is the Technical University of Dresden (TUD), which is in the process of grouping 14 Faculties into five Schools. (TU Dresden 2013). TUD's objective is to achieve more autonomy, synergies, interdisciplinarity, strategic and operative scope. 'Governed by the principle of subsidiarity, academic plurality will be ensured and, simultaneously, synergetic advantages in research, education, administration and infrastructure will be supported.'

The Nature of a Dean of Faculty

The historical definition of 'dean' is a leader of a group of ten (1300-50; Middle English deen < Anglo-French deen, dean, Old French deien < Late Latin decānus chief of ten, equivalent to Latin dec(em) ten + -ānus -an), and the term came into use in the ecclesiastical, guild and other settings which were the models for the medieval constitutions of universities in Western Europe. In those early constitutions, Deans were mainly church officers attached to the colleges, but as the centuries progressed the office of Dean (or its equivalent) became associated with leadership of academic disciplines grouped in Faculties, subordinate to the overall authority of a Rector or Vice-Chancellor. The Dean is, in effect, a middle manager, whose authority in some cases, e.g. Dean of a Business or Medical School, is greater than in others, due to the emergence of international networks, and the significant resources managed in this type of School. It is the extent of the autonomy of Faculties generally, and thus of the Deans, which interests the present conference.

It has been recognised in recent years that there are issues common to Deans however they are defined, and whatever their relative status. The network DEAN run by the former European Centre for Strategic Management of Universities (ESMU) offered specialised workshops for academic leaders (deans of faculties/heads of schools) on 'cutting edge issues for the strategic management of their institutions'. From 2013,

ESMU is now incorporated into the European Foundation for Management Development (EFMD), which runs an invitation-only annual Deans and Directors General Conference confined to Deans and Directors of Business Schools. It seems that there is now no European-level programme for Deans in general, although other programmes formerly under the auspices of ESMU continue (e.g. HUMANE, the Heads of University Management and Administration Network in Europe, by which is meant the EU).

The Structure of Higher Education Legislation

The structure of legal regulation of universities is defined in terms of the framework proposed in the Council of Europe's (CoE) 1998 template adopted in the Final Report of the Council's Legislative Reform Programme for Higher Education and Research, 1991-2000 (Farrington 1998) which has been used as the basis for drafting a number of new laws. These should now be interpreted in the light of the CoE Committee of Ministers Recommendation R (2007)6 on the public responsibility for higher education and research, and the trend at both EU and national levels towards meta-governance, that is the process of steering devolved governance processes (Peters 2010). The aim of the template is to set out clearly what are the duties, responsibilities and rights of the three tiers of governance: Tier 1 (Parliament and Government), Tier 2 (Minister/Ministry) and Tier 3 (Institutions), with the aim of devolving as much authority as possible to the lowest relevant Tier. In which Tier the role and functions, and way of selecting or electing Deans, is located is one of the aspects of autonomy in governance of an institution, and important in determining the autonomy of the position.

2. THE PLACE OF THE FACULTY AND DEAN IN UNIVERSITY GOVERNANCE

The Origins of Faculties: Lower and Higher

Historically, universities' teaching and research was based on 'lower' Faculties and the 'higher' Faculties of Law (or Philosophy) Theology and Medicine. Student-run institutions like the University of Bologna admitted students from any nation: study was undertaken in the 'lower Faculty' of Arts and at least one of the 'higher Faculties' with the emphasis on Law. The hierarchical description of the Faculties, which excludes science and social sciences, management, and a whole range of subjects now studied at university, has been of legal significance almost to the present day, at least in the common law world. To qualify for the title 'university' in England, according to Vaisey J in St David's College Lampeter v Ministry of Education [1951] 1 All ER 559, based on the concept of the stadium generale, there had, among other old criteria, to be teaching in at least one of the 'higher' Faculties and this was missing from the College. Little notice was taken of this decision because of its specific facts, but for the avoidance of doubt, the ruling was effectively reversed by section 77(4) Further and Higher Education Act 1992, as amended by section 40 Teaching and Higher Education Act 1998, since a number of existing and new universities did not include any of these Faculties (Farrington et al. 2012, paras 3.05-3.08).

The Place of the Dean in Legislation

University governance is today a complex area with considerable differences between member states of the EHEA, as identified in the Trends and Autonomy Reports of the European Universities Association (EUA) over the past few years (e.g. EUA 2009a, 2010, 2011) by the European Commission (De Boer et al. 2010) and in the MODERN project (ESMU 2009). In some countries the responsible state administrations may be devolved in a federal (e.g. Germany) or quasi-federal (e.g. the UK) structure. Some have adopted higher education laws or codes (Tier 1) which specify precisely the role of the Dean of Faculty in a university, in others there are either only basic rules or none at all. Three examples of these differences are (i) the University of Saarland in Art 22 of Law Nr. 1556 of June 2004, as amended in 2006 which has quite detailed provisions; (ii) Chapter 11 of the Norwegian law of 2005 as to how heads of faculties are appointed, if the university board so decides, but the board has full responsibility – this provision can be assigned to Tier 3; (iii) in the UK, there is no provision at Tier 1 generally for university governance except in universities conducted by statutory corporations, but the appointment of Deans is not detailed in any modern law. (There are some exceptions to the general rule in the oldest universities operating under a specific, and of course old, legal framework, but their internal structure is anomalous. In most cases the internal organisation is specified at Tier 3.)

Page 11 of the first EUA Report on Autonomy (EUA 2009a) discusses this aspect of university governance. In two-thirds of the surveyed countries, universities are essentially free to determine their internal academic structures. In the remaining third, universities are subject to various restrictions in terms of their academic structure. The Report found that in 2008/9, in Turkey, Luxembourg and Cyprus, faculties are listed by name in the law. In Turkey, the law defines the number, name and disciplinary scope of each faculty. Departments can be established by the universities but need to be approved by the Turkish Council of Higher Education. In ten countries, universities must follow legal guidelines for their academic structure. However, in those cases the law does not contain provisions on the number and name of academic units. In the particular case of the Western Balkans, the previous status of Faculties as legal entities is gradually being changed with the introduction of integrated universities (EUA 2009a). Kosovo under its UN administration (UNMIK) was the first to achieve this, in 2003, as a result of a law and statutes devised by a Council of Europe team of which the present author was a member.

These differences are mainly historical, and to some extent reflect the degree of autonomy, which universities enjoy in their internal governance. The EUA Autonomy Scorecard (EUA 2011) does not include the appointment of Deans among its indicators, nor does it include Saarland (not included in the 2009 report either) or Norway (which was included); the UK score for organisational autonomy is 100%. The capacity to decide on academic structures (i.e. Faculties, etc.) has a weighting of 15% in considering academic autonomy.

3. DECENTRALISATION VS. CENTRALISATION

Corporate Structures

The introductory material for the conference raises the question of the role of the Dean, between two extremes 'agent of the president/rector' and 'CEO of the Faculty.' As generally speaking the Faculty has no legal status of its own, but functions as part of the university with authority delegated from the centre in a variety of ways described above, the corporatist term 'CEO' is strictly not applicable. Rather the Dean is the academic leader of the Faculty and responsible to central authorities, normally assisted by pro-deans and/or administrators depending on size and resources, for whatever the university's resource allocation model provides. The Dean may also have some responsibilities for curriculum development, quality assurance and in some cases human resource management within the Faculty. As one example, at the University of Bristol (UK), Deans have the following very wide functions and responsibilities (Bristol 2013):

- To oversee and guide the planning process within the Faculty and its integration within the overall University Plan

- To determine priorities for expenditure within the Faculty and to assist the Vice-Chancellor in the creation of departmental budgets
- To maintain and enhance academic standards within the Faculty
- To take a leading role in the formulation of University academic strategy
- To manage, encourage and guide heads of department within the Faculty
- To be the budget-holder for the Faculty

At University College London, Deans have a similar role but with less well-defined executive responsibilities (University College London 2013):

The Deans' principal duties include (inter alia): to advise the Provost and Vice-Provosts concerned on academic strategy, staffing matters and resources for academic departments within their faculty (which includes monitoring and ensuring achievement of budgetary targets); to oversee quality assurance and enhancement in curricula and programme management at faculty level; to liaise with Faculty Tutors on undergraduate admissions and on student academic matters; to oversee examination matters at faculty level; and to co-ordinate faculty views on library, IT and other matters relating to education and information support.

The concept was carried over to the US universities during colonial times (Columbia 2012):

'It shall be the duty of the dean of each Faculty, subject to the reserve powers of the President and the Provost or Provosts, to enforce the rules and regulations of such Faculty; to administer discipline in the school or college of which he or she is dean; and to report to the President the condition and needs of the Faculty to which he or she may have been appointed, as occasion may require.' Here the Dean is clearly subordinated to the central administration with delegated powers to enforce rules, etc.

Again generally speaking, it is the advice of the EUA Institutional Evaluation Programme to promote Faculty autonomy in well-defined academic – and to a limited extent, financial – areas to strengthen creativity and initiative in academic and research matters, and ensure that it is coupled with responsibility and accountability, while at the same time, to keep in mind that a strong university can exist only if it sustains unity and cohesion (e.g. EUA 2009b). Of course this presupposes that universities will continue either as they are now, or in reduced numbers through mergers and takeovers and that there is some logic in preserving the status quo of the fundamental structure which is more than one thousand years old. This paper goes on to suggest that this view may be out-dated, as we look at the title of the conference: The Dean in the University of the Future.

The Example of Portugal

A recent paper (Magalhães et al. 2013) discusses reforms in Portuguese higher education driven by managerial perspectives and New Public Management (NPM) approaches (Santiago et al. 2005) with the following arguments in favour of decentralisation to Faculties, etc.: a higher degree of subject-problem-related awareness and (presumably) higher degree of subject-related expertise; enhancement of staff motivation; safeguarding plurality. The arguments in favour of centralisation are: enhancement of interdisciplinarity; safeguarding professionalism outside subject-related competence (i.e., expertise in financial and legal constraints and requirements; market observation; time management); reduction of merely personalised considerations. In Portugal universities can opt to define structures at the middle management level when Faculties, etc. have self-governing bodies electing the head of the Faculty, or can maintain a centralised approach. In the former case, based on the traditional model of 'federation' of Faculties, there is fragmentation of decision-making processes by embedding the principle of subsidiarity (Moreira 2008) and Deans etc. have increasing authority which reinforces a need for institutional coordination.

A Contemporary Approach

The title of this paper 'Higher Education Charters: Implications for Faculties,' which was given by the organisers of the conference, suggests a new model of governance based on a highly autonomous university with a defined structure. In fact, one can go much further than that, and consider what is the future of universities as such, if decentralisation is taken to its logical conclusion, and if university diplomas become less significant than professional certification in most subjects, with the increasing use of online delivery and massive online open courses (MOOCs) supplanting traditional modes of delivery. This is not confined to expensive technical subjects. While relatively inexpensive 'traditional' subjects in the humanities may continue under 'Universities of the Arts' created by mergers of relevant Faculties, others such as law, accountancy, business, etc. are already offered by fully-accredited private sector bodies without any 'university umbrella', e.g. the BPP University College, a subsidiary of the Apollo Group (BPP 2011) or a single-subject university e.g. the newly-formed University of Law, (University of Law 2013) both examples from England.

Inspiration for this can be found in a report produced in Australia in 2012 (Ernst and Young 2012). Completely new models of higher education delivery are envisaged within a period of 10-20 years and the recommendations are as relevant for Europe as they are for Australia. The report recommends that universities should critically assess the viability of their institution's current business model, develop a vision of what a future model might look like, and develop a broad transition plan. Deliberations on future models need to include which customer segments to focus on, what 'products' or services they need, optimal channels to market, and the ideal role of the university within the education and research value chains. Support functions will need to be streamlined and in some cases fundamentally reconfigured. Regardless of the path chosen, universities will need to align new directions to their institution's core purpose and values.

What, then, of the role of the Faculty and its Dean in this process of change? Most, if not all, academic disciplines will go on with some in a continuous process of flux, and the need for most of them (albeit in changed form) will continue. But any new business model that is to compete with the private sector will almost certainly need to eliminate tiers of management and bureaucracy. One possibility is for Faculties in relevant disciplines to break away from a university structure and establish themselves as part of new business enterprises linked to the private sector as an integral part of a new knowledge-creation triangle education-research-industry. If this is to happen, or indeed is on the medium-term planning horizon, a new approach is needed to governance and to the selection and training of Deans as leaders of the new enterprises.

Re-Skilling of the Post of Dean

It is suggested that there is no future in the selection of Deans by a process of election. New Faculty enterprises will need to recruit inspirational and competent leaders to manage entirely reformed structures and modes of delivery. The onus now is on existing universities and Faculties to prepare students to take on such responsibilities at a relatively early stage in their careers, and think 'out of the box' in relation to traditional ways of academic progression. That is, abandon the slow-moving apprenticeship assistant/collaborator – docent/assistant professor – associate professor – full professor, with Deans only being found from those holding the last two titles. The new cadre of Deans need a range of skills outside normal academic pathways, in fact multi-skilling in languages, IT competence, managerial competence, fund-raising and friend-raising, international experience, business experience, public relations competence, and so on.

Implications for University Governance, Charters etc.

As discussed above, there is a wide variation among member states of the EHEA in how they regulate the place and role of Faculties and Deans. There is little prospect of creating any uniformity in such diverse systems, other than the voluntary complementarity created under the Bologna Process. All that can be done is to suggest to member states that they prepare for change by:

- Identifying by means of a risk analysis what is likely to be the locus of their universities in the international structure of higher education in future;
- Through a process of consultation with government and non-government stakeholders, identify which academic disciplines are likely to be viable;
- Ensuring that their higher education laws provide maximum flexibility to universities to adapt quickly to changing circumstances and in particular delegate to universities themselves how they are organised internally, both in respect of Faculties and their leadership;
- Ensuring that universities are supported nationally and/or internationally in developing the human resources needed to lead universities and Faculties in changing times;
- Promote joint degree programmes in educational management and leadership.

As a result, it should be possible clearly to define the role of the Dean, draw up a job description and person specification and the methodology of securing the most qualified and experienced personnel to fill these crucially important positions.

4. CONCLUSION

There are several different models adopted across the EHEA to adjust to trends towards NPM and managerialism in universities, with a variety of centralised and decentralised structures. In some cases the role and process of selecting the Dean is defined in the law, in some cases it is left to the university to determine the functions of the Dean and in many cases this has moved away from the concept of an elected short term office to a more managerial approach. In all cases it is fair to say however that no Dean can operate effectively if s/he does not have the support of a majority of staff affected by her/his decisions. However, everything of significance discussed in the academic literature so far is predicated on the continuance of universities as such, and naturally this is supported by the EUA. Now we need to look forward, in a rapidly escalating pace of change in higher education, to envisage the demise of old structures and the emergence of new models. There is a definite and potentially exciting role for academic disciplines and their leaders. Universities need to start now on identifying their future strategy and developing future leaders. Tomorrow may already be too late.

REFERENCES

BPP, http://www.apollo.edu/sites/default/files/files/Apollo-Group-BPP-Fact-Sheet.pdf , 2011, accessed 25 April 2013.

Bristol, http://www.bris.ac.uk/faculties/deans.html, 2013, accessed 30 April 2013.

Columbia (2012), Charters and Statutes of Columbia University, Statute 58(b) (2012), http://secretary.columbia.edu/files/secretary/university_charters_and_statutes/Charters_Statutes_October%202012.pdf , 2012, accessed 1 May 2013.

De Boer, Harry/Jongbloed, Ben/Enders, Jürgen/File, Jon, Progress in higher education reform across Europe: Governance reform. Brussels (European Commission) 2010.

Ernst and Young, University of the future: A thousand year old industry on the cusp of profound change, in: http://www.ey.com/Publication/vwLUAssets/University_of_the_future/$FILE/University_of_the_future_2012.pdf , 2012, accessed 24 April 2013.

ESMU, Higher Education Governance Reforms across Europe (MODERN project), in: http://www.highereducationmanagement.eu/images/stories/MODERN_Report_Governance.pdf, 2009, accessed 30 April 2013.

EUA, University Autonomy in Europe I: Exploratory Study. 2009a.

EUA, South East European University, Report of the Institutional Evaluation Programme, in: http://www.eua.be, 2009b.

EUA, Trends 2010: A decade of change in European higher education. 2010.

EUA, University Autonomy in Europe II: The Scorecard, 2011.

Farrington, Dennis, Governance in higher education: Issues arising from the work of the legislative reform programme for higher education and research of the Council of Europe (DECS/LRP (98) 28, reproduced as Appendix 1 to the Final Report of the LRP (CC-HER (2000) 40), 1998.

Farrington, Dennis/Palfreyman, David, The law of higher education, Oxford (Oxford University Press) 2. ed., 2012.

Kezar, Adrianna, Obtaining integrity? Reviewing and examining the charter between higher education and society, in: The Review of Higher Education 27 (4/2004), 429-459, 2004.

Magalhães, António/Veiga, Amélia/Ribeiro, Filipa/Amaral, Alberto, Governance and institutional autonomy: Governing and governance in Portuguese higher education, in: Higher Education Policy, 29.01.2013.

Moreira, Vital, O Estatuto Legal das Instituições de Ensino Superior, in: *Amaral, Alberto* (ed.) Políticas de Ensino Superior – quarto temas em debate, Lisbon: Conselho Nacional de Educação, 123-139, 2008.

Peters, Guy, Meta-Governance and Public Management in: *Osborne, Stephen* (ed.) The New Public Governance? Emerging Perspectives on the Theory and Practice of Public Governance, London:Routledge, 87-104, 2010.

Santiago, Rui/Magalhães, António/Carvalho, Teresa, O surgimento do Managerialismo no sistema de ensino superior Português, Masosinhos (CIPES) 2005.

Thelin, John, A history of American higher education, chapter 1, Baltimore (Johns Hopkins University Press) 2011.

Technical University of Dresden, in: http://tu-dreden.de/die_tu_dresden/fakultaeten?set_language=en&cl=en', 2013, accessed 23 April 2013.

University College London, http://www.ucl.ac.uk/provost/people/deans, 2013, accessed 30 May 2013.

University of Law, http://www.law.ac.uk/home/, 2013, accessed 25 April 2013.

Dennis Farrington is President of the Board and Professor of Law at South East European University (SEEU), Republic of Macedonia, being a founder in 2000. Since 1994 he has worked on h.e.legislation and governance in Europe. He is Visiting Fellow of OxCHEPS, University of Oxford, co-authoring *The Law of Higher Education* (2012, 2. ed., OUP).

LEARNING FROM AND PROGRESSING WITH EACH OTHER – INTERNATIONALISATION OF UNIVERSITY FACULTIES

Daniela Jänicke

Internationales Wissenschaftsmanagement,
Hamburg, Germany
janicke@science-management.eu

Internationalisation of higher education institutions around the globe is on the rise and means and methods to achieve this goal have been discussed. In addition, the change of the organisational culture and openness for diversity is crucial condition to create a truly international environment.

1. INTRODUCTION

The term internationalisation is on the agenda of most higher education institutions by now. However, the term is interpreted differently depending on many factors such as the national and regional framework affecting the institution as well as its internal settings and culture. Despite the fact that internationalisation is "one of the most ubiquitous terms" (Welikala 2011, 6) in the higher education area around the globe, there seems to be no definition or common understanding of its meaning. The perception of this term not only differs among higher education institutions from different countries but a variety of interpretation can even be spotted within an institution or amongst members of the same faculty.

This is remarkable as internationalisation is not a new trend; generating and spreading knowledge has always been a field of activity with an international dimension as "knowledge never showed much respect for juridical boundaries" (Marginson/van der Wende 2009, 18). In particular student exchanges, the phenomenon of students travelling to universities abroad for study purposes, in other words student mobility, was yet observed in the 7th and 8th century in Asia (Welikala 2011). Since then higher education systems became progressively more international leading to a boost in the 1990s. While the Bologna process was a major motive force in Europe, the implications in Asia, Africa and Latin America illustrate the cross-border effects of changing higher education systems (Vincent-Lancrin 2009). Despite the technical implications of cross-boundary activities, the organisational culture needs to be adapted with this approach as well.

2. FACULTY INTERNATIONALISATION STRATEGY

Having in mind the global challenges in the economical, societal, environmental and political areas that are more and more interlinked with each other, higher education institutions are socially obligated to seek for innovative solutions, to introduce the ability of appreciation of complex issues and to prepare members of society to cope with a changing environment. While the UNESCO does expect nothing less from universities than the contribution to "sustainable development, peace, well-being and the realisation of human rights, including gender equity" (Unesco 2009, 2), the actual drivers for the institutionalisation of internationalisation at higher education institutions may state its reasons in the demographic change, intensified competition with respect to students, academics and staff, as well as mere budgetary issues and the struggle to obtain funds.

Nonetheless, educational institutions are not only objects but also driving forces that have the opportunity to influence and lead the process, and to benefit from this development. Therefore, higher education institutions and their members are challenged to proactively look into the subject and to draft and implement the necessary steps to be equipped for international higher education management on institutional and personal level.

In order to internationalise the faculty and to convince and enable its members to cooperate on an international scale, a supportive organisational culture needs to be established. Internationalisation of higher education institutions as well as of faculties or departments is, in the first place, a management job and the responsibility of the respective leadership. Understanding that leadership is a set of mind, the responsibility of a dean is not only to act as the promoter of structured and planned cross-border activities of the faculty but the dean's actions should be indicative of internationalisation. Leading by example, the dean is the authority to initiate the development of a faculty-wide strategy to enhance the internationalisation of the faculty and its members.

However, there is no one-fits-all strategy and a copy-paste-mentality with respect to successful examples in other institutions is not productive. There are as many ways of internationalizing institutions as there are universities, all of them acting in a different framework of preconditions which need to be taken into account when developing a suitable strategy. Management and the evolution of institutional strategies as part of management tasks emerge from local traditions and operating experience (File/ Goedegebuure 2003). They need to be adapted to the needs, constraints and expectations in order to be suitable and effective.

The national, regional and institutional settings in which the institutions are embedded as well as the landscape of higher education institutions are diverse and leave room for manoeuvre within these frameworks.

However, differences can also be observed between neighbouring institutions in the same country. While the political, demographical, societal, and cultural characteristics may be similar, the organisational structure and the institutional culture vary. Although the strategies of other higher educational institutions may serve as an example, they cannot constitute more than a stimulus for the initiation of a strategy tailor-made to the needs of an institution. A concerted and planned action and a deliberate adjustment focused on international contents, methods, structures and persons is the base of a sustainable institutional internationalisation. The strategy cannot stand-alone but needs to be reflected in the overall vision, the mission statement, and the faculty plan. It is equally important that the internationalisation strategy is understood as the principle guiding all academic and administrative activities, e.g. the assessment, amendment or development of study programs, selection of students, Ph.D. candidates, researchers, lecturers and support staff, development and implementation of teaching methods, the establishment and continuation of partnerships and cooperation. Thus, first of all, a definition of the expected value of internationalisation, the reasons why and the willingness to invest needs to be considered; secondly, the status quo in other words the starting point of your strategic plans need to defined; thirdly, based on the aforementioned findings, a unique and adequate profile needs to be developed and the organisational change prepared.

3. THE PROCESS OF STRATEGY DEVELOPMENT

One cornerstone of internationalisation strategy development is to identify the stakeholders, their needs and expectations and to develop an overview of those directly or indirectly affected. There are, first of all, the current and potential students as well as researchers, lecturers, and professional staff. According to a survey conducted by the European University Association among its members, attracting students from abroad at all levels is given the highest priority with respect to internationalizing universities (European University Association 2013). The second highest priority is given to the internationalisation of teaching and learning followed by the aim to offer home students learning experience in a foreign country. Having in mind the Bologna goal to allow for 20% of the students experiencing studies in a foreign country, it is comprehensible that priorities are set as they are today. And, in fact, the study programs and curricula need to address international and intercultural aspects as the rationale behind internationalisation approaches is to provide for graduates that have gained the knowledge and skills needed to cope with international challenges and to develop the ability to live and work in international settings (Knight 2008).

These priorities, all focusing on students, can also be observed in non-European institutions. However, it should be emphasised that the mere enhancement of the number of foreign students does not suffice to meet the internationalisation objectives and that, despite the fact that students are one of the main stakeholders, internationalisation need to be considered from a broader perspective as internationalizing a faculty consists of many more components, e.g. mobility of scientific and professional staff, international experience of faculty members, joint research projects and publications, language abilities, etc.

The potential means and methods to be applied and the indicators of internationalisation have meanwhile often been assembled and examined (e.g. Brandenburg/Federkeil 2007; Beerkens et al. 2010) and, therefore, a principle toolbox is available. However, the instruments mainly have a technical focus, whilst the so-called soft skills are more difficult to define and to measure. An international open university needs an international atmosphere, in which the diversity of cultures, values and attitudes are understood and respected, and in which an intense exchange is actively fostered. In an environment, in which mainly national staff is employed, the awareness and ability to accept differences are a difficult task to achieve, and change management in line with the internationalisation strategy is a must.

Changing organisational behaviour is always a delicate task and developing a nationally oriented faculty into an internationally renowned one, is even more demanding having in mind the academic freedom of its members. The strategic approach therefore should be well thought out and implemented step by step. The cornerstone is laid by searching for and finding allies in the faculty who serve as positive role models and encourage others to follow their example. In order to demonstrate the importance of the cultural change, desired attitudes and conduct should be supported, rewarded and spread. Moreover, structures and practices need to be also slowly adapted in order to introduce new cultural values in the organisation and to facilitate the overall process.

A promising approach is holistic and includes not only academic programs and research activities but covers, in addition, the area of human resources management and development, organisational support structures and services. No matter whether the internationalisation activities are imposed by the leadership or jointly developed by university-wide working groups, whether the amount of internationalisation indicators and benchmarking activities are increased, whether the top-down or the bottom-up approach is applied – the success or failure of an internationalisation strategy depends on the people who are part of the university and faculty. The behaviour of people can, on the one hand, be lead by pointing out potential negative consequences if their performance does not coincide with the specifications announced and if expectations are not met. On the other hand, a much more promising leadership approach is to convince the faculty members of the university to support the internationalisation of themselves and their institution. In particular, in an environment that consists of manifold experts in a specific academic field and who are protected by and benefit from an enormous degree of professional freedom, it seems to be much more successful to convince than to oblige. Therefore, it is necessary to consider the adequate level and means of support that need to be provided in order to generate the favoured behaviour.

4. A CULTURAL CHALLENGE

Nowadays, cross-border contacts and collaborations are part of everyday life in almost every sector and thus, the receptiveness of different approaches, concerns and values is of high importance (Bergan 2011). This is also true for higher education institutions.

International activities, however, cannot be successfully conducted without intercultural knowledge. Successful cross-border cooperations and mobility activities are not only based on a technical level but on personal exchange activities of stakeholders from different cultural backgrounds. While globalisation and the intensification of international collaboration is a matter of fact, the development of a global culture that diminishes the differences is only occurring on the surface. In fact, the harmonisation of local and national cultures and the merging into a universally accepted culture is an unlikely event (Jakob 2003). Cultures are as diverse as the approaches to eventually define the term (Kluckhohn 1951; Hall 1959; Hofstede 1980; Trompenaars 1993; Adler 1997) and thus, the aim to fully understand the underlying cultural dimensions of all the stakeholders involved in higher education can realistically not be achieved.

However, in order to be successful in the management of international activities, a basic understanding of the different layers, characteristics, and dimensions of culture, including one's own, need to be cultivated on a personal and institutional level. These management prerequisite should not be underestimated as they not only include the capability to recognise but also to understand and interpret the behaviour of the respective counterpart. In addition, the aptitude to predict how certain attitudes, operations and ways of communication in cross-cultural cooperations might be perceived and its potential interpretation is crucial. It is nice to know the fact that Chinese business partners hand over their business cards with both hands and expect you to study it thoroughly. However, this knowledge serves no purpose if the importance and implied message of this behaviour, the underlying assumptions, and its cultural relevance are not understood. Although, there remains, of course, the risk of misinterpretation and cultural diversity should by no means be oversimplified, the ability to resort to a set of guiding principles enhances the likelihood of successful intercultural communication and minimises the risk of failed cooperations tremendously. Underestimating the value of cultural awareness might lead not only to discouragement and disappointment but constitutes a misdirected investment with respect to effort, time, and money. Moreover, via modern communication systems and social networks the unsuccessfulness will be highly visible and widespread and thus, is able to lead to a loss of reputation and might impede potential further collaborations. Therefore, it is crucial to acquire the capacity to consider the implications beyond the immediate horizon and to carefully weigh the consequences of international engagement also in the long run.

The successful internationalisation of faculties and departments is based on several preconditions. First of all, the fostering of intercultural sensitivity and knowledge is crucial.

A wholehearted commitment to recognition and promotion of diversity in the faculty is the basis for further activities. This includes the development of expertise in intercultural behaviour and foreign languages. The commitment must include the purposeful implementation of intercultural management models, support and training of scientific and professional staff and constant exchange of experiences and best practices among the scientific and professional staff of the faculty. It is, in particular, the dean's mission to ensure a climate of trust and understanding in order to provide for a fruitful exchange amongst the stakeholders, and to encourage all members of the faculty – professional staff included – to contribute to the assembling of intercultural knowledge and experience regardless of seniority, hierarchical level, and status. The recognition of different management models and the acceptance that colleagues and employees adjust to the respective situation and apply different management approaches when dealing with foreign cultures, is also necessary. Whilst specific training and seminars may be conducted, it is also a promising approach to create an internationally open campus and to learn from the foreigners studying and working at the faculty. Not only does this lead to a truly international atmosphere but also to a deeper cultural understanding and trust through mutual exchange. Therefore, the organisation should be aware of the fact that there might not be a need to book trainings, which are conducted in a sterile or at least artificial setting, if the cultural experts, such as lecturers, researchers and students from abroad, are yet within the faculty's grasp.

Initiating cultural changes and promoting internationalisation, however, must not be mistaken with imprudent standardisation of higher education systems across the globe. Higher education is each country's crucial resource to nourish social and economic development as well as an essential tool to convey its cultural diversity (Vincent-Lancrin/Pfotenhauer 2012). The development of intercultural management is based on the research in behavioural sciences and needs a strong and noticeable commitment of the faculty's leadership. Therefore, success or failures of international cooperation are closely linked to the way and means the faculty leadership advocate intercultural management approaches.

The intensity of expected leadership involvement in cross-culture relations vary and only after cultural sensitivity is gained can the extent of time and resources necessary to operate internationally in or with a country of interest be estimated. This includes the degree of personal contact necessary before a co-operation can even be considered, the

hierarchy level of those involved, the degree and value of formality, the extent to which uncertainty is sought to be avoided to name a few. Thus, to establish a long-lasting relationship it might not suffice to form a project team of highly knowledgeable faculty members if the sincere commitment of the dean or even the president is expected by the foreign partner. While investment in the training of academic and professional staff is needed in order allow for adaptation to varying teaching and learning techniques (Unesco 2009), the training of technical and methodological skills does not suffice the global challenges in higher education. Promotion and training of intercultural skills and competences is therefore not a luxury investment but a question of make or break and decisions for or against international collaboration should be based on that analysis. It is vital to consider the cultural implications that go far beyond technicalities to make a conscious decision.

5. CONCLUSION

Internationalisation strategies need to be developed for each university and faculty individually taking into consideration the national framework (e.g. political, economical and demographical aspects), the regional environment (economy, infrastructure, culture), and the institutional and cultural settings, (e.g. size of the institution, target groups, level of autonomy, low or high hierarchy level). There is no one fits all strategy. The development of an individual and tailor-made internationalisation strategy is vital, taking into account institutional particularities, the overall context in which the higher education institution or faculty is acting, and the respective target country.

Moreover, it is of utmost importance to strengthen intercultural competences in addition to subject-specific ones in order to be able to apply the latter adequately in complex and differing contexts. To achieve this ambitious goal, a sincere commitment by the leadership is necessary, including serving as an example and supporting faculty change.

REFERENCES

Adler, Nancy, International dimensions of organisational behaviour, Nashville (South-Western) 3. ed., 1997.

Beerkens, Eric/Brandenburg, Uwe/Evers, Nico/van Gaalen, Adinda/Leichsenring, Hannah/Zimmermann, Vera, Indicator projects on internationalisation – Approaches, methods and findings, A report in the context of the European project "Indicators for Mapping & Profiling Internationalisation", Gütersloh (IMPI) 2010.

Bergan, Sjur, Internationalization of higher education: A perspective of European values, in: *Martyniuk, Waldemar* (ed.), Internacionalizacia studiów wyższych, Warsaw (Fundacja Rozwoju Systemu Edukacji) 2011, 11-28.

Brandenburg, Uwe/Federkeil, Gero, How to measure internationality and internationalisation of higher education institutions, Indicators and key figures, in: CHE Working Paper 92 (2007), 1-42.

European University Association, Internationalisation in European higher education: European policies, institutional strategies and EUA support, Brussels (EUA) 2013.

File, John/Goedegebuure, Leo (eds.), Real-time systems. Reflections on Higher Education in the Czech Republic, Hungary, Poland and Slovenia, Brno (Brno University of Technology) 2003.

Hall, Edward T., The silent language, New York (Garden City) 1959.

Hofstede, Geert, Culture's consequences: International differences in work-related values, Thousand Oaks (Sage) 1980.

Jakob, Nina, Intercultural management, London (Kogan Page) 2003.

Kluckhohn, Clyde, The study of culture, in: *Lerner, Daniel/Laswell, Harold D.* (eds.), The policy sciences, Stanford (Stanford University Press) 1951, 86-101.

Knight, Jane, Higher education in turmoil, the changing world of internationalization, global perspectives on higher education, vol. 13, Rotterdam (Sense) 2008.

Marginson, Simon/van der Wende, Marijk, The new global landscape of nations and institutions, in: *OECD* (eds.), OECD higher education to 2030, volume 2, globalisation, Paris (OECD Publishing) 2009, 17-62.

Trompenaars, Fons, Riding the waves of culture, London (Nicholas Brealey) 1993.

Unesco, Communiqué World Conference on Higher Education: The new dynamics of higher education and research for societal change and development, Unesco, Paris, 5-8 July 2009.

Vincent-Lancrin, Stèphan, Cross-border Higher education: Trends and perspectives, in: *OECD* (eds.), OECD higher education to 2030, volume 2, globalisation, Paris (OECD Publishing) 2009, 63-88.

Vincent-Lancrin, Stèphan/Pfotenhauer, Sebastian, Guidelines for quality provision in cross-border higher education: Where do we stand?, OECD Education Working Papers 70 (2012), 1-62.

Welikala, Thushari, Rethinking international higher education curriculum: Mapping the research landscape. Universitas21 Position Paper, 2011.

Daniela Jänicke, international project manager and consultant, lecturer on culture & management, and intercultural trainer; experienced with developing and managing international projects and cooperations, e.g. the EU-funded 'China-EU School of Law' located in Beijing, PR China. She regularly evaluates international projects on behalf of the European Commission and the German Academic Exchange Service (DAAD).

Session 2

**Management of Faculties and Dean's
Competence Profile in Higher Education**

COMPETENCE DEVELOPMENT OF DEANS: A MENTORING APPROACH BASED ON THE STRATEGIC COLLABORATION MODEL

Anna Feldhaus

Chair for Human Resource Management and Organisational Behaviour, University of Siegen,
Hoelderlinstrasse 3, 57076 Siegen,
anna.feldhaus@uni-siegen.de

Deans as leaders in higher education are confronted with various facets, challenges and development opportunities of their faculty system. In order to cope with them, deans have to be well qualified. This paper focuses on the competence development of deans in the interplay of internal, external and personal career requirements. Some of these requirements can be influenced by the dean himself, others are set by the structures, systems, processes and culture of the faculty and university. The challenge for a dean competence development is to combine its requirements in a way that faculty members, stakeholders and the dean himself have a benefit. Applying a mentoring approach based on the strategic collaboration model, the contents and processes of experience and knowledge transfer from one dean to his successor will be examined.

1. INTRODUCTION

Faculties as dynamic and complex systems have to deal with different challenges in research and teaching. There are a lot of people being responsible for managing these challenges in order to secure the future of faculties and to make it contribute to various stakeholder interests. An important piece of this complex puzzle is the role of dean. The dean manages the faculty, represents the faculty in its external environment and needs to build up his [for improved readability, individuals are sometimes referred to in this article using solely the masculine form] own career (Bugaj/Beck-Krala 2010). The range of different requirements leads to conflicts within the role of the dean, in particular when the dean is expected to represent conflicting interests of stakeholders. The variety of tasks has the effect that deans are likely to run into the double bind dilemma (Sensing 2000). Therefore, it could be a useful strate-gy inspired by a professional human resource management to train and develop deans. A dedicated dean competence development is a challenge for faculties and universities in the future.

It is the objective of this article to identify how the internal, external and personal dean requirements can be matched within such a dean competence development, in particular considering that there usually is time pressure related to the (mostly) expiring dean position.

2. CONTENTS OF A DEAN'S COMPETENCE PROFILE

Internal Competence Requirements

Addressing the intra-faculty requirements first, managing a faculty means for a dean to pursue different goals and to fulfil various tasks that are defined from within the faculty. These goals and tasks make the role of a dean challenging. On the one hand, he has the responsibility for faculty staff and colleagues. On the other hand, the faculty has distinct expectations towards the dean's role. Alongside of managing human resources in team-related leadership approaches and influencing the culture among colleagues (Thompson/Harrison 2000), a dean has to deal with the strategic issues of the faculty.

In respect to team leadership, the competence requirements have to cover the diverse roles of faculty members. Harvey et al. (2006) identified a typology of faculty members from a dean's perspective with different roles and leadership challenges:

- Newcomers – new faculty members who want to acquire higher education. They are high potentials with limited accessibility but perfectly aware of future training opportunities. A dean is expected to provide substantial academic education and to support each newcomer in reaching goals and higher productivity.
- Fast-trackers – assistant professors or postgraduates who need to prove themselves. To work effectively they need resources. Therefore, the dean has to be suitable to manage the resource supply.
- Solid citizens – members of a faculty over a long period of time. They support the system of the faculty in time-consuming tasks and assume responsibility for different processes. The dean is expected to manage goal setting, encouragement and long-term motivation and to contribute to the individual needs of personal status.
- Achievers – members with responsibility who are important parts of the faculty. Often, they are not motivated to make further career within the faculty or to leave the faculty for a different job. In order to manage this supportive segment, deans have to be able to reward them by general recognition and monetary incentives.
- Minimalists – employees of a faculty which are not sophisticated enough for the academic system. Although they

have only little influence within the faculty, managing them requires systematisation, documentation and an open discussion in the sense of an at least partially confrontational management.
- Overachievers – senior members of the faculty who have no further benefit interests towards the faculty. Because of their enormous experience, deans are expected to manage those faculty members by giving them recognition, i.e. by installing them as mentors of young faculty members.

The different types of faculty members imply deans' competences in recruitment, training, development and leadership. As far as the dean's personality is concerned, the dean has to be loyal towards the colleagues in the faculty, solve problems and resolve conflicts at various levels (Harvey et al. 2006) and identify constantly changing needs of different groups inside the faculty.

In respect to strategic management, a dean has to be in a position to plan and implement a strategy and identify performance outcomes (De Boer/Goedegebuure 2009). In order to fulfil the strategic tasks, knowledge and competence in managing organisations will be absolutely essential for deans. Deans who are not capable of "number crunching" and understanding methods and contents of reports and analyses will have problems to cope with the administrative complexity of a faculty system. A study of Sarchami et al. (2012) supports the claim that beside leadership skills and information management, the knowledge of budget and fiscal management are important.

External Competence Requirements

Broadening the perspective to the faculty's external environment, a broad range of further obligations is imposed on the dean where support by a competence development could be helpful. Building up a competitive strategy will be necessary to ensure the future success of faculties (Gmelch/Miskin 1993). This means for a dean to be able to negotiate the faculty's position with external policy makers and to solve conflicts of interest. This includes negotiations with the university top management that is often following a centralistic approach and tends to overrule the faculty's interests from outside. Further issues of the increasingly demanding environment are that the evolving education market brings along a higher competition in national and international education and that there are increasing demands of becoming media-supported faculties with virtual-type cooperation. Those demands have also to be met in a flexible way (Gallos 2002).

Of course, deans are also facing financial restrictions for their faculties. The high competitive pressure in higher education makes it necessary to modify key performance indicators (KPIs) that are intended to measure efficiency and effectiveness of faculties. The reasonable application of KPIs should be linked to goals and strategies (Iveta 2012). The challenge is to have a faculty-specific combination of KPIs for internal and external needs, which puts a much stronger focus on the management of decentralised structures.

The scope of the dean's task broadens towards representing the faculty to the outside stakeholders (Bugaj/Beck-Krala 2010). In the face of international competition, faculties have to promote their interests even to international stakeholders, i.e. international communities and international providers of external funds. The situation of faculties resembles the situation of companies on a competitive market with a high necessity and responsibility for entrepreneurial thinking and action (Wagner Mainardes et al. 2010). In this context, a dean has to know the external stakeholders of the faculty, being a combination of international scientific community, industry, politics, the public sector and the general public (Jongbloed et al. 2007). Mitchell et al. (1997) identified three different kinds of stakeholders: depending on the influence of decision making, there are latent, expectant and definitive stakeholders. Their influence is characterised by the three attributes power, urgency, and legitimacy (Mitchell et al. 1997). The challenge for deans in this context will be to analyse the categories of stakeholders as

well as the increasing dynamics among them (Benneworth/Jongbloed 2009). Moreover, deans have to know how the reputation management of the faculty is to be optimised.

Personal Competence Requirements

Self-evidently, deans pursue personal career paths. There are two kind of deans: on the one hand, the elected deans who are academics from the faculty, taking over the job for a certain time and then stepping back into the ranks; on the other hand, the professional deans who perform deanship as a professional job. In the U.S., most of the deans had been promoted inside a university and half were external candidates (McTiernan/Flynn 2011). Analyses show that half of the future deans in the U.S. were faculty members and assistants of the dean; the others were working for a non-academic organisation before (Niederjohn/Cosgrove 2010). Although elected and professional deans have different career expectations, some of their personal motivations are similar.

One personal motivation of becoming a dean might be to climb the career leader and to increase the personal influence inside the faculty and the university. Some of the dean candidates see an opportunity to reach a higher status level within a short period of time (Sarros et al. 1998). Sometimes, intrinsic motivation comes from the expectation just to have a new challenge or to do something different. Mostly, the extrinsic motivation for the assumption of the dean position is related to the possibility to achieve higher incomes. Occasionally, no faculty member is willing to do the job of the dean and then candidates with the necessary skills are pushed into the position (Gmelch et al. 1999).

In order to match the personal motivation, there must be some added value for the dean. Becoming a successful dean has the need of a personal competence development in order to grow with the responsibility. Therefore, it will be necessary to prepare a dean for the position with its related challenge and chances.

One decisive personal competence of a dean is linked to "emotional intelligence" (Salovey/Mayer 1990) that can be categorised nto five components (Goleman 2004, 95):

- Self-awareness as the ability to recognise and understand moods, emotions, and drivers as well as their effect on others.
- Self-regulation as the ability to control or redirect disruptive impulses and moods and being able to think before acting.
- Motivation as a passion to work for reasons that go beyond money or status and a propensity to pursue goals with energy and persistence.
- Empathy as the ability to understand the emotional makeup of other people and the skills in treating people according to their emotional reactions.
- Social skill as the proficiency in managing relationships and building networks and the ability to find common ground and build rapport.

Emotional intelligence does not only help deans to manage faculty members but to develop their own personality. The best way to learn that is to practice the job and to be open for feedback from the affected environment. It can be discussed whether emotional intelligence is a necessary precondition to be a good leader. An emotionally intelligent dean could be a competitive advantage in faculty competition (Shuayto 2013). At the same time, it implies the responsibility for the election body to anticipate the challenges of the future in order to find the most appropriate dean in the given faculty environment.

3. A MENTORING PROCESS FOR DEANS

Procedural Concepts of Competence Development

The intelligent combination of the internal, external and personal requirements for a dean competence development represents a major challenge for the faculty. On the one hand, the existing competences have to be developed and extended, on the other hand, new skills and knowledge has to be acquired in order to succeed in the new role of a dean in a dynamic university organisation.

According to the broad range of competences associated with the role of the dean, there are different ways to develop those required competences. But in contrast to some companies where career paths imply a competence-related preparation for years, a dean does not have too much time to get used to his new position. To overcome difficulties rapidly, a dean ideally could be supported by the previous dean.

In order to transfer hard and soft skills of management, a situationally appropriate competence development concept has to be implemented (Haynes/Gosh 2008). One of these concepts is mentoring, which is a close and unique relationship between two persons who learn from each other but differ in the types of support (Eby et al. 2007). The less experienced person is the mentee and the mentor is the more experienced person. A former dean with the experience of the past dean's period can serve as the mentor and the new, incoming dean is the mentee (Kram 1985). While in companies a mentor generally has a higher organisational status than the mentee, in faculties, the mentor of a dean is on the same academic level as the mentee. Because of that, the mentoring relation is a networking-type or peer mentoring, which could even involve more than one mentor.

3.1 Effective Mentoring: Strategic Collaboration Model

In the following, the basic structure of the elaborated "strategic collaboration model" of mentoring (Wasburn/Crispo 2006) will be applied to the context of faculties and dean competence development (figure 1). It was developed in the context of succession planning. By this model, the whole dean mentoring process can be illustrated. It starts with a specific support structure:

- As *preconditions*, the faculty has to provide for some basic support, for example time and financial resources if necessary.
- The *strategic collaboration team* consists of the past dean (mentor) and the present dean (mentee), but also further potential deans as well as interested peers. Usually, a dean works together with several vice deans anyway. In a network structure, they all are supposed to form the team in which the relevant questions of competence development are to be discussed. This team has to go through the typical team building process.
- As *interpersonal skills training*, the team members have to increase their individual skills in communicating openly, giving constructive feedback and managing conflict.
- Mentor and mentee have specific expectations for their mentoring relationship. In form of a *strategic collaboration contract*, they agree on joint goals for themselves, but also on those for other peers and the faculty. Such a contract is mostly a psychological contract that implicates a perceived reciprocity of obligation between mentor and mentee (Eckerd et al. 2013). A formal contract is more useful to define objectives for the faculty and how they can be reached, such as a general strategy on competence development.

Up to now, these are preconditions and inputs for the strategic collaboration model.

In the effective mentoring phases called discovery, dream, design and delivery, mutual trust will be the crucial component:

- In the *discovery* phase, the internal, external as well as personal competence requirements are determined. The dean as mentee has to analyse the different strengths of resources which are available in the faculty, the different typologies of faculty members and their needs as well as the latent, expectant and definitive stakeholders. The mentor and the peers support this by sharing their experience. In this phase the mentor acts as an interface between faculty, stake-

holder and staff. The mentor is sharing his networking with the mentee. Conversations between mentor and faculty members or stakeholders give the mentee the ability to assess competences of every individual. The present dean can discuss his observations with the mentor. The culture of faculty can also be a part of the mentoring, which means that the mentor and mentee can share their experience and knowledge.

- The phase of *dream* means to develop a vision which could ensure the future of the faculty. The whole strategic collaboration team identifies possible ideas for the future in a kind of brainstorming.
- In the *design* phase, the mentee starts to encapsulate from the mentor but still has the opportunity to ask the mentor and the team of peers for advice. Based on the discovery and brainstorming with all strategic collaboration team members, the dean starts to create a faculty strategy, openly integrating personal career expectations and discussing them as well.
- The *delivery* phase implements both the faculty strategy as well as the career path of the dean.

Because of the cyclic design of the mentoring process, these mentoring phases are to be repeated continuously so that a dynamics of faculty development can be achieved.

The benefit of mentoring inside a faculty is the increasing self-reflection quality of the actors. The sharing of experience and knowledge among deans can help analysing and solving problematic and controversial issues. It also combines the internal, external and personal competence requirements. A side-effect is that based on the exchange of information, the faculty culture could be reshaped and changed (Zarovsky Levin 2010). The mentoring model can also overcome individual deficits such as the lack of some hard or soft skills (O'Brien et al. 2010). Furthermore, the mentoring relationship can encourage the dean to become more visible inside and outside the faculty (Zarovsky Levin 2010).

Figure 1: The Strategic Collaboration Model
for Dean Mentoring
(following Wasburn/Crispo 2006, 21)

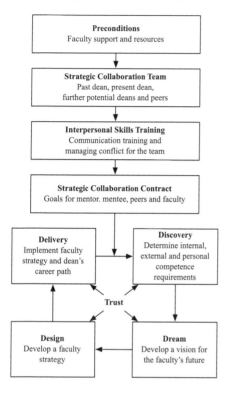

development. The experienced dean shares his experiences and information about faculty, members, stakeholders and environment (De Boer/Goedegebuure 2009). As presented in short, the benefit of mentoring based on the strategic collaboration model is a relatively fast development of deans. This model favours networking-type mentoring of a team, which shares knowledge and competences to ensure the future of the faculty. The strategic collaboration model does not only consider the needs of the dean and stakeholders, it also customises organisational needs (Wasburn/Crispo 2006).

Future work could analyse how competent deans who have gone through a mentoring process run their faculties and which effect their leadership has on faculty quality and success. Another research perspective is to debate which mentoring system is more suitable for faculties: formal, informal or a combination of both.

Finally, a study could focus on analysing the kind of effects mentoring has on culture and structure of faculties and universities. The most important insight, however, seems to be that the dean competence development has to combine its requirements in a way that faculty members, stakeholders and the dean himself have a benefit and that this will be transparently included in the strategic team collaboration of building up dean (and faculty) competences.

4. CONCLUSION

The result of the discussion of dean competences development is that they are caught between internal, external and personal competence requirements in academic leadership and their area of responsibility (De Boer/Goedegebuure 2009). This kind of challenge could be a problem for deans, faculties and universities.

To learn how to handle the complexity of the dean's role requires a multifaceted competence development. The challenge is to create and establish training for deans and in particular to decide which skills already exist and which are needed. Effective monitoring can serve as an approach to implement a faculty-specific dean competence

REFERENCES

Benneworth, Paul/Jongbloed, Ben W., Who matters to universities? A stakeholder perspective on humanities, arts and social sciences valorisation, in: Higher Education 59 (5/2010), 567-588.

Bugaj, Justina/Beck-Krala, Ewa, Dean's competencies after the transformation in Poland, in: http://www.srhe.ac.uk/conference2010/abstracts/0224.pdf, accessed 07 January 2014.

De Boer, Harry/Goedegebuure, Leo, The changing nature of the academic deanship, in: Leadership 5 (3/2009), 347-364.

Del Favero, Marietta, The social dimension of academic as a discriminator of academic dean's administrative behaviors, in: The Review of Higher Education 29 (2/2005), 69-96.

Eby, Lillian T./Rhodes, Jean/Allen, Tammy, Definition and evolution of mentoring, in: Allen, T.D./Eby, L.T. (eds.) Blackwell handbook of mentoring, Oxford (Blackwell Publishing), 2007.

Eckerd, Stephanie/Hill James/Boyer Kenneth K./Donohue, Karen/Ward, Peter T., The relative impact of attribute, severity, and timing of psychological contract breach on behavioural and attitudinal outcomes, in: Journal of Operations Management 31 (2013), 567-578.

Gallos, Joan V., The dean's squeeze: The myths and realities of academic leadership in the middle, in: Academy of Management Learning and Education 1 (2/2002), 174-184.

Gmelch, Walter H./Miskin, Val D., Understanding the challenges of department chairs. Bolton, MA (Anker) 1993.

Gmelch, Walter H./Wolverton, Mimi/Wolverton, Marvin L./Sarros, James C., The academic dean: An imperiled species searching for balance, in: Research in Higher Education 40 (6/1990), 717-740.

Goleman, Daniel, What makes a leader? in: Harvard Business Review 82 (1/2004), 82-91.

Harvey, Michael G./Novicevic, Milorad M./Sigerstad, Thomas/Kuffel, Thomas S./Keaton, Paul N., Faculty role categories: A dean's management challenge, in: Journal of Education for Business 81 (4/2006), 230-236.

Haynes, Ray/Gosh, Rajashi, Mentoring and succession management: An evaluative approach to the strategic collaboration model, in: Review of Business 28 (2/2008), 3-12.

Iveta, Gabcanova, Human resources key performance indicators, in: Journal of Competitiveness 4 (1/2012), 117-128.

Jongbloed, Ben/Enders, Jürgen/Salerno,Carlo, Higher education and its communities: Interconnections, interdependencies and a research agenda, in: Higher Education 56 (3/2008), 303-324.

Kram, Kathy E., Mentoring at work: Developmental relationships in organizational life. Glenview, IL (Scott Foresman) 1985.

McTiernan, Susan/Flynn, Patricia M., "Perfect Strom" on the horizon for women business school deans?, in: Academy of Management Learning & Education 10 (2/2011), 323-339.

Mitchell, Ronald K./Agle, Bradley R./Wood, Donna, Towards a theory of stakeholder identification and salience: Defining the principle of who and what really counts, in: Academy of Management Review 22 (4/1997), 853-886.

Niederjohn, M. Scott/Cosgrove, Sarah B., The economist as dean: An investigation of the academic training of business school deans, in: Eastern Economic Journal 36 (2/2010), 217-228.

O'Brien, Kimberly E./Biga, Andrew/Kessler, Stacey R./Allen, Tammy D., A meta-analytic investigation of gender differences in mentoring, in: Journal of Management 36 (2/2010), 537-554.

Salovey, Peter/Mayer, John D., Emotional intelligence, in: Imagination, Cognition and Personality 9 (3/1990), 185-211.

Sarchami, R./Asefzadeh, S./Ghorchian, N./Rahgozar, M., Selection criteria for the position of dean in medical schools: A competency approach, in: Middle-East Journal of Scientific Research 12 (6/2012), 899-905.

Sarros, James C./Gmelch, Walter H./Tanewski, George A., The academic dean: A position in need of a compass and clock, in: Higher Education Research & Development 17 (1/1998), 65-88.

Satter, Andrew, M./Russ, Diane, E., Why don't more senior leaders mentor? And how they are mortgaging their company's future in the process, in: Journal of Management Inquiry 16 (4/2007), 382-390.

Sensing, Tim, The role of the academic dean, in: Restoration Quarterly 45 (1/2000), 5-10.

Shuayto, Nadia, Management skills desired by business school deans and employers: An empirical investigation, in: Business Education and Accreditation 5 (2/2013), 93-105.

Thompson, John. E./Harrison, Jeanette, Competent managers? The development and validation of normative model using the MCI standards, in Journal of Management Development 19 (10/2000), 836-852.

Wagner Mainardes, Emerson/Alves, Helena/Raposo, Mário, An exploratory research on the stakeholders of a university, in: Journal of Management and Strategy 1 (1/2010), 76-88.

Wasburn, Mara H./Crispo, Alexander W., Strategic collaboration: Developing a more effective mentoring model, in: Review of Business 27 (1/2006), 18-25.

Zarovsky Levin, Shelly, Deans of career and technical education: Charting the course to senior administration, Dissertation at National-Louis University (2010).

Anna Feldhaus is research assistant for Human Resource Management and Organisational Behaviour at the University of Siegen. Her research focuses on the empirical analysis of the dynamics of mentoring in organisations. She received her M.Sc. degree in Management of Small and Medium Enterprises from the University of Siegen in 2011.

THE EVOLUTION OF PERFORMANCE MEASUREMENT SYSTEMS FOR FACULTIES IN AUSTRALIAN UNIVERSITIES

Julie Wells

RMIT University, 124 La Trobe St, Melbourne, Australia 3000
julie.wells@rmit.edu.au

Performance measurement systems in higher education is a diverse research field, several countries are employing different approach. In this paper the evolution of the Australian approach will be observed. From the starting point in the late 1970s to the Dawkins Revolution, reforms led towards a centralised and unified national system today. Such system was followed by different adaptations to improve the quality and uphold the competition among universities. Subsequently in 2007 reforms of the government introduced the Tertiary Education Quality and Standards Agency (TEQSA) and implements new quality standards, evolution processes and tools that are necessary to review the quality of todays universities in Australia.

1. INTRODUCTION

In Australia, higher education performance measurement and quality assurance has become highly centralised. The state has taken a strong role in determining how academic quality is measured, and more recently established "threshold standards" for registration of universities and other higher education institutions. Just as institutions respond to other determinants of performance that drive reputation and access to resources, so too has this shaped the culture of review.

In charting the 'evolution' of performance review of faculties in Australia, I am essentially concerned with three intersecting themes: the relationship between universities and the state and how it has shaped evaluation of faculty performance, the significance of structural reforms of Australian higher education and consequent changes in internal governance structures and processes, and the more recent shift in emphasis from external quality assurance to external registration and compliance.

Performance measurement systems in universities are very much a product of their time and place. Rather than reflecting objective or uncontested views about the quality of academic outcomes and how they should be measured, they can express a range of ideas about the public benefit delivered by higher education, and of the university's place in a society.

Gavin Moodie observes how marked changes to higher education funding, governance and administration typically provoke doubts about its quality, which then frequently result in new forms of quality assurance (Moodie 2013). This is a useful lens through which to consider the evolution of performance measurement systems in Australian universities, which have developed largely in response to external change, coupled with the desire of academic staff and university leaders to better understand and promote the quality of their work.

Therefore, this reflection on the evolution of performance measurement systems for faculties (which I define as academic

77

organisational groupings of significant scale, organised by discipline) is largely a reflection of the recent evolution of Australian higher education itself, and the ideas about 'quality' that have shaped academic review and evaluation. The trends it describes are similar to those experienced world-wide: however, they have a particular resonance in the Australian higher education system, reflecting its history and its relationship to government, its rapid transition from providing elite to mass to universal access to higher education, and its increasing reliance on non-government revenue.

In common with their counterparts globally, Australian governments (both state and national) have devoted significant attention to how they might measure and evaluate the performance of the sector, and of the individual institutions within it. State governments classify universities as public bodies, and prescribe their governance arrangements, regulation and reporting requirements in legislation. The Australian national government, which is the largest single source of institutional funding, also regulates and influences outputs, through conditions attached to funding and targeted performance-based funding mechanisms.

The strong involvement of the state in the governance and management of universities, and its development of measures of their effectiveness and efficiency – many tied to the machinery of funding and regulation – has thus created strong incentives for university leaders to use these measures to allocate resources within their own institution. So, in relation to the evaluation of faculty performance in Australian higher education, there are two different, but intersecting, processes to consider: on one hand, formal mechanisms for academic review and evaluation, involving a mix of qualitative and quantitative analysis and frequently informed by academic expertise external to the institution; and on the other, the regular measurement of faculty performance by university management for the purpose of performance reporting and for determining the allocation of funding for research and teaching activity. The latter process usually comprises only quantitative measures: the number and volume of research grants won by faculty members, student satisfaction as measured through questionnaires, completion rates and attrition, and student demand, for example. Some will go to measures of 'efficiency' – the use of floorspace, the ratio of students to teaching staff, and the margin on teaching revenue. While the former process is widely recognised as important from a developmental and reputational perspective, it is the latter which can shape the flow of resources to a faculty or department. This essay considers the relationship between mechanisms which drive funding and ideas about quality review and evaluation as it has involved in the Australian higher education sector.

2. ACADEMIC QUALITY COMES UNDER THE SPOTLIGHT: FROM WILLIAMS REVIEW TO DAWKINS REFORM (1979-1987)

A good starting point for an examination of these themes is the late 1970s, when Australian universities, like many of their counterparts around the world, faced increased enrolments, decaying infrastructure, and stagnating funding. This in turn sparked concern about quality: feeling the pinch of increased competition for public funding, universities were under pressure to demonstrate the quality of their work at the same time as government sought to improve the returns on public investment. Quality concerns were exacerbated by participation and graduate completion rates that were significantly lower than those in comparable OECD nations.

In 1977, the federal government commissioned a report into the national education and training system (Williams Committee 1979). It found that measures or processes for systematically reviewing the quality of university work were largely invisible or non-existent. It proposed a number of factors to be considered in evaluating the operational effectiveness of higher education institutions, revolving around governance structures, administration and the induction, promotion and development of staff. Interestingly, the only student-related indicator proposed was attrition rates. For institutions conducting research (universities), it proposed additional elements relating to the administration and allocation of research resources and the support available for research staff (Williams Committee 1979, 212-213).

Implicit in these recommendations was concern about the way universities were governed and managed, and the belief that in order to improve quality, one had to be able to measure it. This was echoed in a review of the efficiency and effectiveness of higher education in 1986 undertaken by the Commonwealth Tertiary Education Commission (CTEC, the statutory agency established to advise government on tertiary education funding and provision). CTEC noted a lack of accountability for expenditure of public funds and variability in the outcomes universities produced, linked in part to the different mission, history and resource base of institutions. It argued that linking universities' triennial funding to strategic plans, and the development of outcome measures for the sector, would lead to improved outcomes and greater accountability.

Not surprisingly, these two landmark reviews fuelled interest in the development of performance indicators within disciplines and within academic organisational units. The Williams Review argued for stronger institutional oversight of faculty performance, suggesting that because actual delivery of academic programmes and research were devolved to Academic Boards, faculties and departments, there was no way for the governing body to maintain an appropriate line of sight on academic quality. It recommended that the Australian Vice-Chancellor's Committee consider the need for more detailed information about the performance of disciplines and academic units, noting that this would strengthen the evidence base for internal resource evaluation and decision-making. In another report commissioned by Government, Bourke (1986) also found no evidence of systematic approaches to review at a faculty level. He suggested that a focus on student, faculty and administrative outcomes, input variables, group structures and processes, environmental constraint and support would provide a suitable framework for assessment of academic units. Bourke also noted the drivers of performance measurement in other countries, most notably the UK, where government and administrators exerted considerable influence, and the US, with more of a tradition of self-review and reporting. He argued the case for the development by universities of a recognisably Australian culture of academic self-review, one that would create a bulwark against government interference in the autonomy of universities while improving the quality of their outputs (Bourke 1986, 24-26; DEET 1993).

Both CTEC and the Australian Vice-Chancellor's Committee undertook a series of discipline reviews between the mid-1980s and the early 1990s. They were time-consuming exercises which revealed significant disparities in the research outputs and teaching qualities of departments (Moodie 2013). Such attempts to explore academic outputs in a systematic fashion at an organisational level revealed the inherent problem of seeking to evaluate quality within a disparate and uncoordinated higher education sector, in which there were significant differences in resourcing and history and no consensus on the evidence base to be deployed. According to Ashenden (2012), these reviews revealed the "collegial system" to be 'person-dependent, erratic and amateurish', producing wonderful outcomes in some faculties but not in others, and lacking overall transparency and accountability.

These attempts to demonstrate quality and conceptualise faculty review in Australia were in some respects responding to declining levels of funding per student and pressures to reform. This was reflected in the first substantial academic text devoted to performance measurement in Australian universities, 'Reviewing Academic Performance' (Roe/MacDonald/Moses 1986). Its authors acknowledged that 'worries about declining standards' provided impetus to their work. They nonetheless focused on positive arguments for review, linking it to improvement and quality:

"'The pursuit of excellence' is a currently popular phrase. It suggests that quality or excellence does not just happen, does not permanently reside in this or that individual academic or course of study. It must be pursued; it must be continually sought, questioned, stimulated, refreshed, renewed. The review process, both self-evaluation and scrutiny by others, makes a significant contribution; not because it is primarily judgmental in the negative sense, or fault-finding, but because it leads to improvement, to development, to new ideas and extended horizons. In the last analysis, institutions (and in particular their leaders) have a moral obligation to provide developmental opportunities for their departments and for their staff. A key argument for review systems of any kind is that they pave the way for institutions to discharge that moral obligation effectively." (Roe/MacDonald/Moses 1986, 105).

Consistent with these principles, their analysis focused on formative, rather than summative, review with a goal of promoting organisational and professional development. It drew a clear distinction between evaluation and review, describing evaluation as relating only to measurement against key performance indicators. Review was described as broader conceptually, possibly including evaluation, but then as a tool to support more wide-ranging discussion of departments characteristics, history, and disciplinary links. For instance, the authors criticise University of Uppsala (Sweden) departmental research evaluation because its 'one weakness is that it focuses on quantitative data'. But it was nevertheless reproduced as an example of a review panel using quantitative input to inform its work.

3. THE CREATION OF A UNIFIED NATIONAL SYSTEM AND ITS IMPACT ON QUALITY REVIEW

Such analyses of performance evaluation at a discipline and organisational unit both responded to and fuelled the impetus for reform, not least because they exposed the problems of sustaining quality across a sector where coordinating mechanisms were weak and institutions were resourced differently. The major structural reform of Australian higher education that started with the publication of a Government Green Paper (Dawkins 1987) implemented many of the ideas which had emerged in the Williams and CTEC reports. It sought to address the fragmented nature of Australian higher education, merging universities and colleges of advanced education to create a 'unified national system' where each university reached a threshold enrolment level (5,000 students) and all were funded under a common set of formulae. CTEC was abolished and its functions absorbed within the Australian Government department, giving the Minister a much more direct say in the affairs of universities. Funding was contingent upon the preparation of a Strategic Plan and the development of institutional profiles and enrolment targets which would be negotiated with government and reviewed annually.

The reform programme included the introduction of an income contingent loans scheme (HECS) and the lifting of restrictions on enrolling international fee-paying students. This led to significant expansion of the system. Between 1988 and 1992, the number of students in Australian universities rose from 394,000 to 560,000 (DEET 1993). According to 2013 Department of Innovation statistics in 2013 it stands at 1.2m, and approximately 27% are international students, studying Australian university programmes delivered in Australia and around the world.

These reforms thus set out to address the problems of increasing student participation while improving institutional productivity, quality and efficiency as highlighted in earlier reviews. They also mirrored the pro-gramme of microeconomic reform of the public sector in Australia and other parts of the world, resulting in more centralised management structures and greater devolu-tion of management powers from governing bodies to vice-chancellors, all in the name of improving the responsiveness and efficiency of universities.

The quality of the new system needed to be measured. The Government commis-sioned its newly formed advisory body, the Higher Education Council, to conduct a review of quality in the sector. A working party on performance indicators comprising vice chancellors was established, and rec-ommended a suite of KPIs which have since informed a plethora of performance reports at an institutional level (for example Linke 1991; DEET 1993; Martin 1994; McKin-non/Walker/Davis 1999). Government re-porting requirements have increased year on year, such that a recent analysis of reporting and regulatory requirements in Australian universities undertaken by Universities Aus-tralia – much of it focused on the collection and reporting of benchmarkable data – esti-mated the annual cost to the sector to exceed $280m (Universities Australia 2013). While universities' increasing use of quantitative measures for internal review has been driven by government, it has also been reinforced by the changing nature of university govern-ance linked to these reforms. In line with the reforms' focus on efficiency and accounta-bility, university governing bodies are now smaller (22 is the nationally agreed bench-mark but in some states membership is low-er), comprise a majority of members external to the university, and are focused on institu-tional sustainability and productivity. It is no coincidence that most Australian universities now produce 'business plans' including suites of performance indicators which pur-port to measure operational efficiency and academic quality.

4. QUALITY AND COMPETITION

At the time it launched these reforms, the Australian Government did not seek to im-mediately prescribe mechanisms for quality assurance or review at a faculty or institu-tional level. Indeed, during much of the 1990s the quality assurance and performance evaluation process was driven largely by universities themselves, albeit responding to the performance imperatives imposed by reforms. Between 1993 and 1995, universi-ties voluntarily participated in three thematic rounds of quality review – one focusing on research, one on teaching and one on com-munity engagement – overseen by a commit-tee led by vice-chancellors and resourced by the federal government. Controversially, the results of these thematic reviews were pub-lished, ranking universities into three 'bands' of performance. Some have mar-velled that universities participated so readi-ly in a process with obvious impacts on reputation, but one incentive was access to $70m in discretionary funding each year tied to performance in the quality rounds. (Aitkin 1996; Harman 2006). According to at least one Vice-Chancellor at the time, the process also provided a strong stimulus to the devel-opment of internal procedures for self-assessment and quality assurance (Penington 2001).

The election of a conservative federal government in 1996 presaged a new stage in the evolution of the sector and with it, new arrangements for quality assurance. Through a programme of fee deregulation for domes-tic students, along with funding cuts and the opening up of more public funding to private higher education providers, the government encouraged a more commercial and competi-tive landscape for Australian higher educa-tion. This in turn sparked fresh concerns about 'standards' and whether the quality of the sector as a whole was being undermined by the admission of new providers and the rush to bolster revenue with fee-paying stu-dents. Such concerns were heightened by the fact that states and territories, which con-trolled the accreditation of private providers, applied different and sometimes dubious criteria. This was illustrated when the Norfolk Island administration accredited as an 'Australian university' Greenwich University, a private provider accredited in the US state of Hawaii but with little academic credibility, infrastructure or resources.

The ensuing outcry encouraged the Ministerial Council on Employment, Education Training and Youth Affairs (a committee of state and federal ministers of education) to agree a set of protocols for the accreditation of higher education providers, including universities. This provided a basis for the harmonisation of state legislation governing the accreditation of private providers, and underpinned the foundation of a new body devoted to assuring quality: the Australian University Quality Agency (AUQA), formed in 2000.

AUQA's objective was: "to be the principal national quality assurance agency in higher education, with responsibility for quality audits of higher education institutions and accreditation authorities, reporting on performance and outcomes, assisting in quality enhancement, advising on quality assurance; and liaising internationally with quality agencies in other jurisdictions, for the benefit of Australian higher education." No funding was attached to its outcomes, and while it was required to report significant problems of quality to the Minister, it had no power to enforce penalties or sanctions in its own right. It reviewed universities and private providers on a five-year cycle, and its audit committees comprised 'experts' from the university sector. While it was frequently criticised for the costs it imposed on the sector and its focus on process rather than output (Matchett 2011) it nevertheless had an impact on internal quality assurance processes. This was partly because of its reports were published, which ensured some reputational impact for universities under review and prompted reflection on what might constitute good quality review and evaluation processes (AUQA published a database on 'best practice' drawn from review reports). It cultivated a class of 'quality assurance specialists' in Australian universities through an 'Australian Universi-

ties Quality Forum', which met annually (AUQA 2011). Its impact was also evident in its methodology: AUQA required institutions to carry out an exhaustive self-review against a comprehensive suite of administrative and academic functions and measures, which were then validated by an external panel with reports providing commendations and recommendations. At the conclusion of the first round of AUQA audits, more than half of those institutions reviewed were running a systematic cycle of organisational reviews (at faculty, department or administrative unit level). Many of them adapted elements of the AUQA methodology for these purposes. These internal reviews often functioned as 'training grounds' for AUQA audits as well as opportunities for internal quality review, development and improvement, although a substantial number of them relied only on internal members rather than external expertise (Jarzabkowski 2009). As such, AUQA reinforced the close connection between national systems for sectoral and institutional evaluation and those applied internally to faculties, departments and other organisational units.

5. FROM REVIEW TO REGISTRATION

In 2007, following a change in the national Government, yet another review of the higher education sector and its capacity to meet national needs was commissioned. Responding to national workforce needs, the Bradley Report (Bradley et al. 2008) resulted in a lifting of restrictions on publicly-subsidised undergraduate places. Henceforth, government funding would follow student enrolments. The proposed increase in participation predictably sparked a further round of discussions about 'standards'. The Bradley Review also noted the growth in the number of private providers of higher education in Australia registered to receive government assistance. Together, these changes have introduced a further dynamic into the culture of performance measurement in Australian universities: the imperative to safeguard sectoral quality and reputation by ensuring there is a baseline of performance which every higher education provider must meet in order to be recognised. The Tertiary Education Quality and Standards Agency (TEQSA) had its origins in recommendations of the Bradley review, and was established in 2011 as a statutory body charged with overseeing compliance with a set of threshold standards relating to governance, financial sustainability, research and teaching. All higher education providers, ranging from large self-accrediting universities to small, recently established private providers must now be registered as compliant with these standards in order to operate in Australia. Unlike AUQA, TEQSA has teeth: the power to remove course accreditation, self-accrediting authority, or in extreme cases remove registration.

TEQSA has to date only conducted a few registration reviews of universities, and unlike AUQA does not publish its reports on individual institutions. So, it is too soon to tell its impact on internal review and quality assurance processes. However, TEQSA's standards-based approach may encourage a compliance- oriented approach to quality review processes, as standards need to be assessed and monitored at a faculty or school level. At the same time, there is growing concern about the role of a regulator in reviewing quality and potentially establishing benchmarks, especially as threshold standards provide only a baseline (Lee Dow/ Braithwaite 2013).

6. CONCLUSION

The period under discussion here has been characterised not only by rapid expansion and change in Australian higher education, but also by significant tensions between the imperatives towards efficiency and accountability characteristic of new public sector management and principles of academic autonomy. The emphasis on quantitative measurement to drive internal allocation of resources exists uneasily alongside a less systematic commitment to formative review described by Roe et al. nearly thirty years ago.

I started this essay with Moodie's reflection how change in higher education can heighten concerns about quality. As Moodie goes on to argue, such concern is not necessarily founded in evidence: it can simply be a reflection of the failure of government or of institutions and academic leaders themselves to demonstrate robust measures of review in times of change. This in itself contributes to a centralised or managerialist approach to quality review.

Evaluation processes and tools are widely acknowledged to be, in certain hands, political instruments, used in different ways to achieve and legitimise particular institutional or sectoral outcomes (Harman 2006). The Australian experience shows how successive governments have promoted particular models of quality review and evaluation to support their broader policy objectives. Debate continues in Australia about the functions and purposes of review and evaluation, its links to managerialism and the impact of the language and practice of performance measurement on the academic enterprise (Ashendon 2012; Gaita 2012).

These debates have continuing relevance in the current global environment for academic activity. Despite the inevitable tensions between managerialist imperatives and academic autonomy embedded in review processes, they may nevertheless yet prove to be a powerful force for demonstrating public benefit and so winning public support in times of declining government revenues and increasingly competitive markets. Higher education is now manifestly a global enterprise, and national systems will increasingly compete internationally for the best academic staff and students, based at least in part on the quality and differentiation of their outputs. If evaluation and review can be linked meaningfully to the aspirations and expertise of those students and staff, as well as to the requirements of government and other stakeholders, they may yet support the ongoing quality of those systems and the academic work that underpins them.

REFERENCES

Aitkin, Don, Victory of Coalition heralds end of quality round, in: *Times Higher Education Supplement* (1 July 1996).

Australian Universities Quality Agency, Good Practice Database, 2000-2011, in: http://pandora.nla.gov.au/pan/127066/201108 26-0004/www.auqa.edu.au/gp/index.html, accessed June 2013.

Ashenden, Dean, Decline and Fall?, in: *Inside Story,* in: http:/inside.org.au/decline-and-fall, 22 November 2012, accessed 26 November 2013.

Bourke, Paul, Quality Measures in Universities, Canberra (Commonwealth Tertiary Education Commission) 1986.

Bradley, Denise/Noonan, Peter/Nugent, Helen/Scales, Bill, Review of Australian higher education: Final report, Canberra (Department of Education, Employment and Workplace Relations) 2008.

Dawkins, John, Higher Education: A green paper, Canberra (Australian Government Publishing Service) 1987.

DEET (Department of Employment, Education and Training), National report on Australia's higher education sector, Australian Government Publishing Service, Canberra 1993.

Department of Education, Training and Employment (Williams Committee), Report of the Inquiry into Education and Training, (The Williams Report), Canberra (Australian Government Publishing Service) 1979.

Gaita, Raimond, To Civilise the City? Speech given at the University of Melbourne, in: http://meanjin.com.au/articles/post/to-civilise-the-city/, 2012, accessed October 2013.

Harman, Grant, The politics of quality assurance: The Australian quality assurance program for higher education 1993-1995, in: Australian Journal of Education (01/08/2001).

Jarzabkowski, Lucy, The place of the internal reviewer in internal reviews, Proceedings of Australian Universities Quality Forum 2009, in: Internal & External Quality Assurance: Tensions & Synergies, in: http://www.auqa.edu.au/files/publications/auq f%20proceedings%202009.pdf, 2009, accessed June 2013.

Lee Dow, Kwong/Braithwaite, Valerie, Review of higher education regulation: Report, Australian government, in: http://www.innovation.gov.au/highereducation /Policy/HEAssuringQuality/Documents/Final ReviewReport.pdf, 2013, accessed October 2013.

Linke, Russell D., Performance Indicators in Higher Education. Report of a Trial Evaluation Study Commissioned by the Commonwealth Department of Employment, Education and Training, Volumes I and II, Australian Government Publishing Service, Canberra 1991.

Martin, L. M., Equity and general performance indicators in higher education. Canberra (Australian Government Publishing Service) 1994.

Matchett, Stephen, AUQA over and out, in: The Australian Higher Education Supplement (25/8/2011).

McKinnon, Ken R./Walker, Suzanne. H./Davis, Dorothy, Benchmarking. A manual for Australian universities, Department of Education, Training and Youth Affairs, Higher Education Division, Canberra (Commonwealth of Australia) 1999.

Moodie, Gavin, Quality, in: *Croucher, Gwilym/Marginson, Simon/Norton, Andrew/Wells, Julie* (eds.), The Dawkins Revolution – 25 years on, Melbourne (Melbourne University Press) 2013.

Penington, David, Managing quality in higher education institutions of the 21st century: A framework for the future in: Australian Journal of Education (01/08/2001).

Roe, Ernest/MacDonald, Rod/Moses, Ingrid, Reviewing academic performance: Approaches to the evaluation of departments and individuals, St. Lucia (University of Queensland Press) 1986, xv.

Universities Australia, Submission to the coalition's deregulation reform discussion Paper, in: http://www.universitiesaustralia.edu.au/ resources/4/1580, April 2013, accessed June 2013.

Julie Wells was appointed University Secretary at RMIT in April 2009. She heads the Governance and Planning Office, which provides integrated support for governance and strategic and business planning. She has extensive experience in tertiary education administration and management and expertise in public policy. She has taught in schools, universities and TAFE colleges and held senior administrative and policy positions at RMIT since April 2002. Between 1998 and 2002 she was the Policy and Research Coordinator in the National Office of the NTEU. She has also worked as an adviser to Commonwealth and State parliamentarians and in the Australian Public Service. She is a former member of the Board of the Council of the Humanities, Arts and Social Sciences.

GENDER AS A CHALLENGE FOR FACULTIES IN JAPANESE PRIVATE UNIVERSITIES

Eriko Miyake

Faculty of Contemporary Social Studies, Doshisha Women's College of Liberal Arts,
Kodo, Kyotanabe City, Kyoto, 610-0395 Japan
emiyake@dwc.doshisha.ac.jp

When we look at how colleges and universities are managed from a gender point of view, we see that in most parts of the world, women are not equitably represented, particularly in upper-level leadership positions such as dean and president. This paper examines the university management process of Doshisha Women's College of Liberal Arts (DWCLA) in Japan as a case study. Separating the count data of faculty and staff members of DWCLA by gender revealed a striking under-representation of women in university management positions. Such gender imbalance in the management process shuts out diverse perspectives from women and minority members and affects the democratic accountability of university education. Future deans could play a critical role, particularly in the area of faculty development, including hiring and promotion, by taking steps towards more equitable university management. Colleges and universities need to make a long-term commitment to achieve the global trends of incorporating diversity in the organisational structure.

1. LOW PROFILE OF JAPANESE WOMEN IN ACADEMIA

The gender gap is certainly a challenge that we face in almost all sectors in Japan. The World Economic Forum reports that the ranking of the gender gap index of Japan is 101st out of 135 countries, while that of Germany is 13th. The gender gap index is measured by scales in four different sectors: economic participation and opportunity, educational attainment, health and survival, and political empowerment. What brings the Japanese ranking so low is the significantly small percentage of women managers in private corporations and of women in the Diet (Japan's parliament), and the gender gap in estimated earned income. On the other hand, the health sector on its own ranks 34th, the education sector 81st. However, those rankings do not give complete pictures of those sectors. For example, when we take a closer look at the scale of educational attainment, although female literacy rates and enrolment in primary and secondary education rank at the top, enrolment in tertiary education ranks 100th (Hausmann/Tyson/Zahidi 2012, 216). This means that while almost 100% of Japanese women graduate from high school, women's enrolment rate in higher education is significantly lower in Japan than in other countries.

Furthermore, the gender gap built into the institutional structure of higher education, such as the low percentage of woman presidents and deans, is not taken into account in the index; doing so would further lower the international ranking of Japan's education sector. In Japan, there are 666 coeducational universities and 81 women's universities. About 80% of all students attending colleges and universities are enrolled in private institutions. The gender gap in the institutional structure of Japanese universities can be seen in the following percentages. As of 2011, female university presidents constituted 8.5% of the total, female professors 13%, associate professors 20.8%, lecturers 29.1%, assistant professors 25.4%, and research assistants 54.2%. As the occupational ladder goes up, the rate of women's participation goes down. The overall ratio of women researchers is 13.8% in Japan – the lowest among the developed countries – and 24.9% in Germany. Of researchers working in a university setting, 24.3% are female in Japan and 34.7% in Germany. The top four reasons given for Japanese women's low participation in research fields are the difficulty in juggling work and family, difficulty in returning to work after nursing, the disadvantage associated with evaluation due to the burdens of childcare and elderly care at home, and preference given to male researchers by the evaluators (Cabinet Office 2012, 114-117).

Having presented the low profile of Japanese women in academia in general, this paper will use Doshisha Women's College of Liberal Arts (DWCLA hereafter) and one of its faculties, the Faculty of Contemporary Social Studies, as a case study to illustrate the dean's role in the management of faculty at a private university. This case study attempts to examine how the low profile of female faculty and staff members in the decision-making process affects university accountability. The main purpose of this paper is to present the notion of gender equity in university management as an area for expansion of the dean's role in the university of the future.

2. THEORETICAL FRAMEWORK

Improving Gender Equity in Higher Education

Women-friendly corporations have recently been receiving media attention in Japan, particularly since Prime Minister Shinzō Abe announced in May 2013 that women should be strategically incorporated into the workforce to promote economic growth. Also, the International Monetary Fund

(IMF) urges Japan to fully utilise women as a productive human resource, suggesting that more active participation of women in the workforce would increase Japan's GDP by 5% (Steinberg/Nakane 2012). However, Japanese colleges and universities seem to be slow even to realise that there is a global campaign towards a "woman-friendly academy" (Martin 2000, 182).

By examining gender equity issues in college and university settings in a variety of contexts in the United States, Cooper et al. (2007) report a significant under-representation of women in upper-level leadership positions such as dean, president, or chancellor despite women's recent advancement to lower level administration. Recommendations to improve gender equity in higher education include the following: the long-term commitment of colleges and universities to ensure equity at all levels for women in all positions, including hiring practices, equitable pay, and equitable promotion; consideration of parental leave policies and accommodation of productivity gaps associated with childbirth in tenure-clock modifications; use of gender equity institutional self-assessment and an equity scorecard that would foster organisational learning; and promotion at the institutional level of self-reflection leading to conversations among colleagues, including the voices of women, about current practices and policies (Cooper et al. 2007, 648-649).

The United States, which ranks 22nd among 135 countries in its gender gap index (GGI), strives to implement a more gender-equitable management system in its universities. In the case of American universities, in addition to gender equity, equity among diverse racial and ethnic groups and among people of different sexual orientations has become an issue. Therefore, rather than "gender equity" or "gender equality" the term "diversity" is more commonly used in organisational practice.

Let us turn to the example of a more gender-equitable country. In Norway (ranking 3rd in GGI), women occupy 43% of teaching posts in higher education, but only 17% of full professor positions (Cabinet Office 2009, 86-87). This data indicates that women may not be equitably represented in university management in Norway, either. Soyland et al. (2000) describe a mentor project initiated to increase the number of women occupying leading administrative positions at the Norwegian Natural Science and Technology University. In the mentor project, senior faculty members (mostly men) and junior colleagues (all women) were paired, with specific goals set for the project, the mentors, and the junior colleagues so that junior colleagues would receive coaching about the organisational culture and support for their professional development. The final outcome was not reported in the paper, but the junior colleagues in the project had positive experiences. In Norway, the independent but government-funded Center for Gender Equality works to influence people's attitudes, and the Gender Equality Ombudsman enforces the Equal Opportunity Act. Furthermore, the University Act revised in 1995 seems to encourage action towards gender equity in university management (Soyland et al. 2000, 147-151).

With regards to leadership, there are no fundamental differences in leadership capabilities between men and women because there are no gender differences in the personal traits (e.g. Adair 2011, 48) required to exercise effective leadership. However, some differences in leadership style among men and women are reported. For example, women leaders' decision-making process tends to be more participative and democratic, and women leaders tend to be interpersonally-oriented rather than task-oriented (Eagly/Eagen 2004, 1658). In addition to such leadership style differences, it is reported elsewhere that women leaders tend to give weight to issues and values that are low priority for male leaders, such as care, environment, safety, human rights, and social justice.

As postsecondary educational institutions work to achieve gender equity, some women's colleges in the United States have demonstrated significant achievement in producing women leaders and creating an effective educational environment and teaching methods for female students. One of the lessons that those women's colleges provide is the importance of ensuring that women are equitably represented in every management level among faculty and staff members, so that female students see them as positive role models (Tidball et al. 1999, 98-99).

In the process of developing feminist perspectives since the late 1960s, new perspectives such as "women's way of knowing" (Belenky et al. 1997) and the discourse of gender have added a new dimension to the politics of knowledge (Weiler 2011). And one of the key concepts that would empower women is "agency", with which women as autonomous members actively and critically engage in reconstruction of knowledge (Horn-Kawashima 2000, 60-63). Where women stand today in terms of knowledge production has shifted from exclusion or subordination to inclusion or integration. Thus women's movements and gender perspectives have influenced the global trend in academia towards a more woman-friendly environment. If universities are to internationalise their management systems, gender equity and diversity will be a critical component of such reform.

In any institution in society, the power relationship between men and women that has persisted in society at large is symbolically reflected in management structure and organisational culture. Therefore, despite the global trend in academia towards a more woman-friendly environment, we in Japan inevitably are confronted by a male-dominated management structure and organisational culture in colleges and universities. Women's colleges and universities may not be exceptions to the rule. From the educational point of view, however, they are less likely to be influenced by the gender relationship and gender biases of society at large, because faculty members can focus on educating women seriously instead of on educating male students and paying less attention and giving less support to female students (Miyake 2012). In that sense, women's colleges and universities can use their institutional arrangements to their advantage in their educational practices.

For example, Ewha Womans University in Seoul, Korea is a unique example of a women's university with the purpose of liberating and empowering Korean women. Its university management system symbolises gender equity in postsecondary education by having women leaders, managers, and faculty members in a gender-equitable distribution (Chang 2008). The success of Ewha Womans University with 20 departments and 23,000 students may have resulted from a holistic accountability comprised of the five aspects of professional accountability, democratic accountability, functional accountability, responsive accountability, and market accountability.

Higher Education Policies and Reform in Japan

In many parts of the world, post-secondary education reform is underway with the partial intention of increasing a nation's competitiveness in the global economy. Based on the four different types of university management culture – collegium, bureaucracy, corporation, and enterprise – Ehara (2011) argues that the overall nature of university management is shifting from the collegial and bureaucratic types to the corporate and entrepreneurial types worldwide, drawing on his examination of university management practices in the United Kingdom, the United States, and Japan. This shift has to do with trends such as neo-conservatism, deregulation, decentralisation, and privatisation that have taken place in those three countries since the late 1980s (Ehara 2011, 342-347).

These categories help us to understand overall patterns in the ways universities are managed. However, it is conceivable that there must be significant differences among universities beyond overall patterns, depending on each university's type, size, and historical development. Furthermore, in addition to diversity in university management styles, Weiler (2005) argues that universities entail a quality of "ambivalence" in their organisational culture and manifest contradictory elements in their organisational behaviours in the following realms: institutional autonomy vs. individual professor's autonomy; institutional change vs. resistance to change; inclusion vs. exclusion of different kinds and traditions of knowledge; and university identity as national vs. international institutions. These elements of ambivalence are likely to camouflage some aspects of university management that the dominant perspectives failed to interpret. Therefore, let us delve into a case study that would present a challenge to the existing "ambivalent" patterns of university management.

In Japan, a series of university reforms started taking place in the early 1990s after the University Council was established in 1987. In 1991, university regulations were reformed, and self-reviews and outcomes assessment of university education were introduced. In 1999, the university regulations were reformed again, and self-reviews and outcomes assessment became mandatory. In the same year, the National Institute for Academic Degrees and University Evaluation was created. In the 2000s, further reforms took place. In 2003, the National University Corporation Law was enacted and in 2004, national universities were incorporated. Also in 2004, a certified evaluation system by the Japan University Accreditation Association was introduced and became mandatory. These changes are in line with the government's policy to control and raise the quality and accountability of university education.

As part of this series of educational changes made since the 1990s, an educational funding project that focused on women researchers was implemented for the first time in 2006. With the goal of increasing the number of women researchers in the natural sciences in particular, the government provides funding (22 million yen a year per organisation for up to 3 years) to about 10 universities and research institutions annually to support women researchers involved in child-raising and elderly care (Ministry of Education, Culture, Sports, Science and Technology 2013a). This was the first attempt to incorporate gender equity issues into human resources development by the Ministry of Education. In relation to gender equity issues, women members of the Higher Education Division of the Central Council on Education gradually increased over time.

The current Higher Education Division consists of 33 members, of whom 26 (79%) are men and seven (21%) are women. Of the seven women members, six are university employees, and only one is a gender specialist (Ministry of Education, Culture, Sports, Science and Technology 2013b). In regard to higher education policy-making, women's issues were of low priority, and women members were significantly under-represented in the decision-making process until recently.

Accountability of Educational Institutions

Fujita (2000) categorises "accountability" from five different aspects as a concept that legitimises different demands by the recipients of public service by incorporating Mann's notions of accountability (Mann 1991). The five different aspects of accountability are professional accountability, democratic accountability, functional accountability, responsive accountability, and market accountability. Professional accountability asks whether the obligation is carried out in accordance with professional ethics and norms. Democratic accountability asks whether public service or educational activities represent people's interest and are administered in an adequate and equitable manner. Functional accountability examines whether educational and public institutions fulfil their goals. Responsive accountability measures the extent to which public or educational organisations respond adequately to the inquiries, requests, and administrative procedures of the clients. Finally, market accountability asks if the service provided by the educational and public institutions fulfils the personal interests of the clients (Fujita 2000, 246-247).

Fujita (2000) further elaborates that there are distinctive differences in nature among these five aspects. For example, democratic, functional, and responsive accountability require external monitoring and regulations with respect to activities carried out by public and educational institutions, while professional accountability requires autonomous monitoring and regulation of the persons in charge. On the other hand, market accountability has a tendency to transform educational services into a private commodity where free market competition takes place. However, as the term "market accountability" includes the four other aspects of accountability by connotation, it works as a rhetorical device for shifting education from public service to private consumption (Fujita 2000, 247-248).

The 2004 reform requiring certified evaluation by the Japan University Accreditation Association was intended to increase the functional and professional accountability of higher education in Japan. Issues such as women's involvement in university management relate to democratic accountability. Nonetheless, the university evaluation prescribed in the 2004 reform does not include women's participation in university management among its criteria. This means that democratic accountability that would require external monitoring as mentioned above is not included in the criteria for university evaluation. Therefore, issues of gender gap in academia become less visible and more challenging to break through.

3. A CASE STUDY OF A GENDER GAP IN THE MANAGEMENT SYSTEM OF DOSHISHA WOMEN'S COLLEGE OF LIBERAL ARTS (DWCLA) IN JAPAN

Historical Background of DWCLA

This section presents a brief overview of the historical development of DWCLA since its inception in 1876, preceding "3.2. Decision-making structure at DWCLA".

DWCLA is a part of the integrated educational system of the Doshisha. The Doshisha consists of ten educational institutions: Doshisha University, Doshisha Women's College of Liberal Arts, four middle schools, one international middle school, one elementary school, one international elementary school, and one kindergarten. Joseph Hardy Neesima, after ten years of self-imposed exile and study in the United States, founded the Doshisha in 1875 with the vision of creating a liberal arts university based on Christian education. In the Meiji era, men and women were educated separately. One year later, in 1876, Neesima, his wife Yae, an American missionary, and others opened a school for young women. Doshisha Girls' School provided an unconventional liberal arts curriculum for Japanese young women, for whom only primary education or finishing school was commonly provided at the time.

In the democratisation process and educational reform after World War II in Japan, Doshisha Girls' School was promoted to a four-year women's college. Doshisha Women's College of Liberal Arts (DWCLA) started initially with three departments under one faculty with an educational philosophy characterised by a liberal arts education combined with Christianity and internationalism. DWCLA now has ten departments under five faculties and four graduate schools, with 6,500 students in total.

The postwar development and transformation of DWCLA can be divided into four different periods. The first period, from 1949 to 1966, can be described as a foundation-building period with a steady increase in the number of students, progressing from 86 graduates in 1952 to 400 in 1966. The second period, from 1967 to 1985, can be characterised as an expansion period, a time of further increasing the enrolment, constructing buildings and facilities, and creating research organisations in each department. This period coincided with a nationwide increase in university enrolment (Miyake 2013, 24-26), from 17.9% (women: 13.4%, men: 22.2%) in 1967 to 37.6% (women: 34.5%, men: 40.6%) in 1985 (Ministry of Education, Culture, Sports, Science and Technology 2013c).

During the third period, from 1986 to 1999, DWCLA opened a second campus in the southern part of Kyoto, and moved the Music Department to the new campus. It also opened a two-year junior college of English and Japanese programmes. The curriculum was reformed and departments were restructured. Because of laws deregulating universities in 1991, during this period, a number of new private universities were opened, new departments were created, and admission quotas were significantly increased, particularly among private universities (Miyake 2013, 26-27).

The fourth period, from 2000 to 2012, was a period of transformation from small-size to mid-size university by adding five new departments. During this period, DWCLA added the departments of Social Systems Studies (2000), Information and Media Studies (2002), Contemporary Childhood Studies (2004), Pharmaceutical Sciences (2005), and International Studies (2007). The junior college closed in 2003. This was also a period when a series of university reforms were carried out and organisational transformation took place in such areas as accreditation, faculty development, diploma policy, class evaluation, quality accountability, and expansion of graduate schools (Miyake 2013, 28-30). Since its inception in 1876, DWCLA has graduated about 59,500 students up to March 2013.

Decision-Making Structure at DWCLA

The decision-making process starts with the president and the presidential advisory council, consisting of five deans and the directors of 11 division offices, three of whom are administrative staff. Though those five deans and 11 directors of division offices can suggest some agenda to the president, the president has the power to decide which agenda to initiate for university management. The presidential advisory council members, who sit with the president, are the core decision-making group, and they function as a kind of board of vice-presidents. Out of 17 presidential advisory council members including the president, only two are women. All members of the presidential advisory council are initially appointed by the president.

After discussion by the presidential advisory council, agenda items relating to education, research, curriculum, admission, graduation, university regulations, faculty hiring, and promotion are proposed to the faculty meeting, where 119 tenured faculty members from all departments participate. (Including contract teachers, we have 105 male faculty members and 73 female faculty members.) Out of 119 tenured faculty members, 73 are men and 46 are women. Each faculty member has one vote and the final decision is made at the faculty meeting. The agenda concerning faculty promotion is discussed and approved at faculty meetings of full professors only. Some selected agenda items such as university regulations or the creation of a new department are consequently brought up to the board of trustees of the Doshisha for overall coordination.

The agenda items that relate to administrative matters, budget, facility, and staff hiring have to be discussed and approved at the administrative council. The council members consist of the president, 16 presidential advisory council members, 10 department chairs, and five professors elected in the faculty meeting, forming 32 members all together. Of the current 32 members, six are women, which is the highest rate of women's participation to date. Some selected agenda items such as employment regulations, pay scheme, appointment of deans and directors, facility budget, and large-scale construction, after being approved at the administrative council, are brought up to the board of trustees of the Doshisha for overall coordination.

The board of trustees of the Doshisha is the highest decision-making body, and it consists of 15 members including the chancellor, the president of Doshisha University, and the president of DWCLA. Only one of the trustees is a woman. It is said that the board of trustees of the Doshisha normally does not overturn decisions made by the DWCLA presidential advisory council, administrative council, and faculty. One characteristic aspect of the decision-making process at DWCLA is that critical departmental matters are discussed and decided at the faculty meeting attended by tenured members of all the faculties; thus, each department or faculty does not function as an autonomous governing body as is the case with most national and public universities in Japan.

The Role of the Dean

Regarding the decision-making process within the department/faculty, the dean calls for the departmental meeting and department-specific issues such as curriculum, hiring of faculty members, and departmental budget are discussed and decided. Decisions that relate to curriculum and hiring then have to be brought up at the general faculty meeting to be approved and finalised. This process might obscure the dean's prominence. However, as mentioned earlier, the dean is a member of both the administrative council and the presidential advisory council, which together form a core decision-making group with the president. Also, as supervisor of the department/faculty, the dean has power extending to endorsing all kinds of administrative papers, reports, and applications submitted by the department faculty members.

Unfortunately, there is no job contract or description of the dean's responsibilities at DWCLA. Based on current practice, the dean's responsibilities include such areas as strategic planning, developing policy, chairing meetings, networking within the university, participating in meetings, developing organisational process, and budget negotiation. These task areas overlap with many of those listed by Scott/Coates/Anderson (2008). What is missing and critical in the dean's role seems to be the formulation of a faculty strategy and construction of a faculty with competitive strength by taking the notion of gender equity into consideration.

At DWCLA, deans are appointed by the president. The term is two years, and can be extended for another two years. The Faculty of Contemporary Social Studies, for example, with 37 faculty members (28 tenured, 9 contract teachers), has had five deans since its creation in 2000, and all five have been men. As stated in the Initial Statement for the Conference, deans have some room to influence faculty management and perfor-mance, particularly in respect to faculty strategy development and faculty leadership (Scholz/Stein 2013, 12), and to take gender equity into consideration in those areas. For example, among 28 tenured faculty members of the Faculty of Contemporary Social Stud-ies, 18 are men and 10 are women. Of the 18 tenured men, 15 (83.3%) are full professors and 3 (16.7%) are associate professors. Of the 10 tenured women, five (50.0%) are full professors and five (50.0%) are associate professors. These numbers indicate that women are likely to take longer to be pro-moted to full professor. Here in this area of gender gap comes the dean's leadership to provide career development opportunities to both men and women faculty members in a gender-equitable way. Since deans are ap-pointed from among full professors, there remain fewer women candidates for deans if no such career development opportunities are provided.

The case of DWCLA demonstrates the necessity of implementing a university-wide policy for gender equitable faculty develop-ment, including promotion and hiring, and the inclusion of women at all levels of man-agerial positions in a gender-equitable way.

Gender Gap in University Management at DWCLA

This section sums up the gender gap statis-tics regarding the faculty and staff members in managerial positions at DWCLA. The implications for university management are discussed in the section following.

The chancellor of the Doshisha and the president of DWCLA are men (100.0%) and not women (0.0%). In the 137 years of its history, the Doshisha has had no woman chancellor, and DWCLA has had only two woman presidents to date. Of the 15 mem-bers of the board of trustees of the Doshisha, 14 (93.3%) are men and only one (6.7%) is a woman. Of 17 presidential advisory council members, 15 (88.2%) are men and only two (11.8%) are women. Of 32 administrative council members, 26 (81.3%) are men and six (18.8%) are women. Out of five deans of

faculties, four are men (80.0%) and one is a woman (20.0%). Out of 10 department chairs, seven (70.0%) are men and three (30.0%) are women. Out of 119 faculty meeting participants, 73 (61.3%) are men and 46 (38.7%) are women. These gender ratios are listed from the highest decision-making level to the faculty meeting deci-sion-making level. As the percentages indi-cate, as the ranking level goes down, the women's participation rate increases – from 0.0% to 6.7%, 11.8%, 18.8%, 20.0%, 30.0%, and 38.7% thus illustrating the male-dominated hierarchical decision-making structure at DWCLA.

As mentioned above, as of 2013, of 119 tenured faculty members who sit at the fac-ulty meeting, 73 (61.3%) are men and 46 (38.7%) are women. However, a recent trend is that the number of tenured faculty posi-tions has gradually decreased and the num-ber of contract positions has increased. Pro-portionately, there are more female contract teachers than female tenured faculty mem-bers. There are 59 contract teachers who do not participate in the faculty meeting. Of those 59 contract teachers, 32 (54.2%) are men and 27 (45.8%) are women. Also, as reference, there are 626 part-time lecturers who do not participate in the decision-making process of the university manage-ment, of whom 328 (52.4%) are men and 298 (47.6%) are women. This further indi-cates that in accordance with the male-dominated hierarchical decision-making structure, nearly half of the lowest teaching positions at DWCLA are occupied by wom-en.

The gender ratios of tenured faculty members in the five faculties are as follows: Pharmaceutical Sciences, 89.5% men and 10.5% women; Liberal Arts, 66.7% men and 33.3% women; Contemporary Social Stud-ies, 64.3% men and 35.7% women; Culture and Representation, 52.2% men and 47.8% women; and Human Life and Science, 36.4% men and 63.6% women. These ratios also closely represent the gender segregation in different academic disciplines that are observed in Japanese academia.

Though the focal point of the conference is the role of the dean, in the case study of

DWCLA, the gender gap among staff members needs to be mentioned as they are coworkers in university management. Of the staff members at DWCLA, 74 are full-time and 177 are contract and part-time employees. Of the 74 full-time staff members, 51 (68.9%) are men and 23 (31.1%) are women. Of the 177 contract and part-time staff members, 3 (1.7%) are men and 174 (98.3%) are women. As these numbers indicate, the low-paying, short-contract staff positions are occupied almost exclusively by women. There are five high-level managerial positions, such as the directors of administrative divisions, all five of which are occupied by men. There are 15 mid-level managerial positions, such as the section chiefs of administrative divisions, of which 13 (86.7%) are occupied by men and only two (13.3%) by women. This means that the women staff members who occupy managerial positions at DWCLA constitute around 10% of the whole, which is on a par with the ratio of woman managers in most other private corporations in Japan.

Regarding the gender gap in university management, DWCLA is not an exception among private and national/public universities in Japan. If there were some differences between private and even national/public universities, national/public universities with good sized graduate schools are more likely to acquire funding from the Ministry of Education for women's faculty development in science fields, through the funding project mentioned above ("2.2. Higher education policies and reform in Japan"). Among private universities, some exceptions would be a few women's universities where faculties of gender studies have a solid foundation and exercise influence over the university management policies and mission.

4. IMPLICATIONS – CURRENT GENDER GAP CHALLENGES IN UNIVERSITY MANAGEMENT

Breaking the number of faculty members in managerial positions into men and women sheds light on the imbalanced gender situation of university management and the extent to which women are excluded from important decision-making processes. The gender ratio of DWCLA tenured faculty members is 61.3% men to 38.7% women. If other gender ratios were proportionate to the gender ratio of tenured faculty members, among presidential advisory council members there should be six to seven women instead of two, in the administrative council there should be 12 women instead of six, and in the five dean's positions there should be two women instead of one.

What the case study of DWCLA demonstrates is that future deans need to exercise leadership roles in shaping faculty development strategy, including promotion and hiring, in a gender-equitable way. Such strategy and leadership will increase the number of women candidates for future deans, which will result in more gender-balanced representation in university management positions.

Because faculty members have autonomy in teaching and research, the gender gap in university management is less likely to be overtly felt or visibly observed in daily educational practices. It is further hidden by the fact that the Japan University Accreditation Association does not include gender gap issues in university management in its accreditation criteria. The criteria for university accreditation are university mission, organisation of research and education, organisation of teaching members, curriculum, diploma policy, teaching methods, educational effects, admission policy, student support, adequate educational facilities and environment, social contribution, and management and financing (Japan University Accreditation Association 2013).

Management policies that would change the inequitable work conditions and curriculum content that would teach students the inequitable situation in society are less likely to be adopted when men monopolise the decision-making structure, because men's and women's priorities are likely to be different.

Regarding the criteria of management, the most recent guidelines of the university accreditation association aim to clarify the decision-making mechanism, define the power and responsibilities of a faculty meeting, university president, and deans, and create validity in the screening system of university president and deans. It is possible to interpret "validity" as including gender equity in selecting university president and deans. However, the previous DWCLA report submitted to the Japan University Accreditation Association in 2007 has no mention of gender equity in university management. The previous 2007 report explains about the presidential advisory council as an assisting body to the university president for speedy decision-making to respond swiftly to the changing environment and society. In contemporary Japan, notions of gender and gender roles are becoming less traditional, and people's values are diversifying. The question arises whether the current presidential advisory council with just 11.8 percent women is adequately equipped to respond to the needs rising from such social transformation.

Ehara (2011) argues that when a university is in a steady growth cycle, the collegial style of university management works well. DWCLA has had a steady growth cycle in the past 12 years with a stable financial foundation receiving AA+ from Rating and Investment Information, Inc. Yet the trend in recent faculty meetings is for the given agenda to be unanimously approved without much debate. In a way, this management style may be shifting closer to the corporate style in which the president and the presidential advisory council can more readily exercise decision-making power. In that case, faculty members are likely to feel isolated and excluded from the important decision-making process, rather than feeling they are legitimate participants in the final stage of decision-making.

In that context, the under-representation of women in the central decision-making bodies means the lack of input from diverse perspectives, and that affects the shaping of the university mission, research agenda, curriculum, hiring patterns, campus design, and many other aspects. The risk of not including women equitably in important decision-making in the university management is the sacrifice of democratic accountability by giving priority to market accountability and functional accountability. Universities can maximise their accountability when the five aspects of accountability – professional, democratic, functional, responsive, and market – are well balanced.

5. CONCLUSION

In analysing the challenges that university management face from gender equity perspectives, this paper used Doshisha Women's College of Liberal Arts (DWCLA) and one of its faculties, the Faculty of Contemporary Social Studies, as a case study to illustrate the decision-making process of a private university in Japan. Separating the count data of faculty and staff members of DWCLA by gender revealed a striking under-representation of women in the university management system. Such gender imbalance erodes the democratic accountability of university education and shuts out the valuable input from diverse perspectives that would come from women and minority members of the university.

What this study suggests is that the deans could play a critical role particularly in the area of faculty development, including hiring and promotion, by taking steps towards more equitable university management with gender equity and diversity in mind. Thu,s the Conference Communiqué of the 2013 KORFU Conference "The Dean in the University of the Future" reads, "… a broad understanding of diversity will be important in the university of the future". "[D]eans should assume the following important roles" such as "educator(s) empowering faculty, staff, and students." (printed in these Conference Proceedings).

Women have come a long way from the era of exclusion from academia to the era of a "woman-friendly academy". We are well into an age when women have joined men to actively exercise their autonomy in knowledge production. The Conference Communiqué proposes the new role of "The Dean in the University of the Future" that would contribute to creating a more equitable environment of organisational culture in higher education.

REFERENCES

Adair, John, John Adair's hundred greatest ideas for effective leadership, Chester, West Sussex (Capstone Publishing Ltd.) 2011.

Belenky, Mary/Clinchy, Blythe/Goldberger, Nancy/Tarule, Jill, Women's ways of knowing, New York (Basic Books) 1997.

Cabinet Office, Danjyo Kyodou Sankaku Hakusho [White Paper on Gender Equality] Tokyo (Cabinet Office) 2012.

Cabinet Office, Shogaikoku ni okeru seisaku houshin kettei katei eno jyosei no sankaku ni kansuru chousa [Research on women's participation in policy-making process in foreign contries] internal documents prepared by the Cabinet Office, Japan, available online. 2009.

Chang, Pilwha, Feminist consciousness and women's education: The case of women's studies, Ewha Womans University, in: Asia Journal of Women's Studies 14 (2/2008), 7-29.

Cooper, Joanne/Eddy, Pamela/Hart, Jeni/Lester, Jaime/Lukas, Scott/Eudey, Betsy/Glazer-Raymo, Judith/Madden/Mary, Improving gender equity in postsecondary education, in: Klein, Susan/Richardson, Barbara/Grayson, Dolores A./Fox, Lynn H./Kramarae, Cheris/Pollard, Diane S./Dwyer, Anne (eds.), Handbook for achieving gender equity through education, Mahwah, NJ (Lawrence Erlbaum) 2007.

Eagly, Alice H./van Engen, Marloes L., Women and men as leaders, in: Goethals, George/Sorenson, Georgia/Burns, James

(eds.), Encyclopedia of leadership, vol. 4, London (Sage Publications) 2004, 1657-1663.

Ehara, Takekazu, Daigaku no kanriunei kaikaku no seikaiteki doukou [Global trends of university management], in: Yonezawa, Akiyoshi (ed.), Daigaku no Management: Shijyou to Soshiki [University Management: Market and Organisation] Tokyo (Tamagawa Daigaku Shuppanbu) 2011, 327-356.

Fujita, Hidenori, Kyouiku Seiji no Shin Jidai [New Era for Politics of Education], in: Fujita, Hidenori/Shimizu, Koukichi (eds.), Hendou Shakai no naka no Kyouiku Chishiki · Kenryoku [Education, Knowledge, and Power in Social Transformation] Tokyo (Shinyo-sha) 2000.

Hausmann, Ricardo/Tyson, Laura/Zahidi, Saadia, The Global Gender Gap Report 2012, Geneva (World Economic Forum) 2012.

Horn-Kawashima, Yoko, Feminism riron no genzai: America deno tenkai o chushin ni [Feminist thought: From modern to postmodern] in: Gender Kenkyu [Gender Studies] 3, Tokyo (Ochanomizu University) (2000), 43-66.

Japan University Accreditation Association, Daigaku hyoka handbook [Handbook for university accreditation] a handbook prepared by the Japan University Accreditation Association, 2013.

Mann, Pamela, School boards, accountability, and control, in: British Journal of Educational Studies 39, (2/1991), 173-189.

Martin, Jane, Coming of age in academe, New York (Routledge) 2000.

Ministry of Education, Culture, Sports, Science and Technology, http://www.mext.go.jp/a_menu/jinzai/lifeevent, accessed 09 June 2013.

Ministry of Education, Culture, Sports, Science and Technology, http://www.mext.go.jp/a_menu/shingi/chukyo/chukyo4/meibo/1302376.htm, accessed 09 June 2013.

Ministry of Education, Culture, Sports, Science and Technology, http://www.mext.go.jp/a_menu/toukei/001/08121201/1282588.htm, accessed 12 June 2013.

Miyake, Eriko, Danjyo kyoudou sankaku shakai ni okeru jyoshi koutou kyouiku no konnichiteki kadai [Today's challenges in educating women in higher education in gender equitable society] in: Journal of Contemporary Social Studies 9 (2013), 16-38. Kyoto (Association of Contemporary Social Studies, Doshisha Women's College of Liberal Arts).

Miyake, Eriko, Koutou kyouiku ni okeru gender [Gender in higher education] in: Kawashima, Noriko/Nishio, Akiko (eds.), Asia no naka no Gender [Gender in Asia], Kyoto (Minerva Shobo) 2012, 131-154.

Scholz, Christian/Stein, Volker, The dean in the university of the future: Challenge for an academic conference, initial statement for the international academic conference "The dean in the university of the future. Learning from and progressing with each other", June 26-28, 2013 in Saarbrucken/Germany.

Scott, Geoff/Coates, Hamish/Anderson, Michelle, Learning leaders in times of change: Academic leadership capabilities for Australian higher education, Sydney (University of Western Sydney/Australian Council for Educational Research) 2008.

Soyland, Ann/Skarsbo, Anne-Marit/Amble, Nina/Christensen, Lise/Olnes, Anna, Strategies for achieving gender equality in higher education and research in Norway, in: Higher Education in Europe 25 (2/2000) 147-153.

Steinberg, Chad/Nakane, Masato, IMF Working Paper: Can Women Save Japan? Washington, D.C. (International Monetary Fund) 2012.

Tidball, M. Elizabeth/Smith, Daryl/Tidball, Charles/Wolf-Wendel, Lisa, Taking women seriously: Lessons and legacies for educating the majority, Phoenix, Arizona (The Oryx Press) 1999.

Weiler, Hans, Knowledge and power: The new politics of higher education, in: Journal of Educational Planning and Administration 25 (3/2011), 205-221.

Weiler, Hans, Ambivalence and the politics of knowledge: The struggle for change in German higher education, in: Higher Education 49 (2005), 177-195.

Eriko Miyake is an Associate Professor at Doshisha Women's College of Liberal Arts in Kyoto, Japan. She earned her doctorate in comparative and international education at Stanford Graduate School of Education in 1994. Her research interests are gender and education, women and leadership, and higher education policies.

MATCHING INDIVIDUAL CAREER DEVELOPMENT WITH INSTITUTIONAL GOALS: A CASE STUDY

Edgar H. Vogel[1] and Pablo A. Reyes[2]

[1]Facultad de Psicología, Universidad de Talca, Avenida Lircay S/N, Talca, Chile
[2]Universidad Católica del Maule, Talca, Chile
[1]evogel@utalca.cl, [2]preyes@ucm.cl

This paper presents a case study that summarises a Dean's action plan for the development of a high-performance team in a newly created Faculty of Psychology at a public Chilean University. In the construction of this plan, three stages were followed: Theoretical analysis, diagnostic, and implementation. The result of the theoretical analysis suggested that a highly productive team would be achieved by increasing the level of job satisfaction, which in turn is mediated by a number of labour conditions such as collegiality, autonomy, mentoring, recognition, workload, meaning and sense of competence. The initial diagnostic revealed that low productivity and low job satisfaction in the team is associated with poor indicators of collegiality, mentoring, recognition and workload. An action plan attempting to enhance these aspects was developed.

1. INTRODUCTION

Globally, universities are faced nowadays with progressively increasing demands upon productivity at multiple levels such a teaching, research and knowledge transfer. Universities, Faculties, schools and academic staff are constantly subjected to productivity assessments and their performance is more than often translated into quantitative indicators and quality rankings. Moreover, in the case of many institutions, predominantly state universities, allocation of funds depends, at least in part, on the results of these assessments.

This tendency towards academic productivity has recently reached developing countries. In the Chilean case, the financing of universities is becoming more a more dependent on performance indicators, especially those associated to scientific production. Accordingly, Universidad de Talca, one of the 16 public universities in Chile, has developed an ambitious strategic plan to fulfil the requirements of this new scenario and to keep being recognised as one of the leading universities in the country. Among the major goals of this strategic plan are to substantially increase the volume and impact of the scientific production of the academic staff and to transfer relevant knowledge to the community. For this, a number of individual and collective incentives have been established and career development and academic promotion have become strongly tied to such indicators.

The Faculty of Psychology at University of Talca was recently created and a relatively young body of academic personnel was hired. At the present time, it offers only one undergraduate programme and one master degree in Psychology, and has no doctoral programmes. As expected, the underdevelopment of postgraduate programmes is correlated with low indicators of scientific productivity. Likewise, the professors are in the early to medium stage of their career and their transfer activities are limited to a few individual efforts.

The institutional demands for high productivity may have a number of collateral consequences for the people that work on it. Indeed, it has been reported a progressive impoverishment in the quality of life and satisfaction at work on universities and that this may be the result of the increment in the demands for academic productivity (e.g. Johnsrud 2002). Furthermore, it has been shown that productivity is directly related to job satisfaction, and that these variables are less related to intrinsic incentives such as awards and earnings than to intrinsic factors such as the social climate at work. Apparently, faculties are sensitive to the degree to which the institution provides them with the appropriate conditions to have a meaningful job and with support for their career development. Thus, the extent they perceive that the goals of the institution lead to personal career development may be a powerful motivator to increase productivity.

This situation poses a dilemma for the Dean of the faculty who must find an adequate equilibrium between individual and institutional goals. It seems reasonable that some of the undesirable outcomes of the stress that may suffer a recently formed team subjected to great demands can be partially overcome by potentiating intrinsic rewards that would emerge from working in highly collaborative teams. In this paper we describe the first steps taken by the directives of the faculty to solve this puzzle.

2. BACKGROUND

Considerable theoretical and empirical research has focused on understanding the organisational and psychological processes involved in job productivity in different types of institutions, and academia is not the exception (e.g. Bender/Heywood 2006; Levin/Stephan 1991; Hagedorn 1996; 2000; Hesli/Lee 2013; Smart 1990). In this section, instead of reviewing exhaustively theories and empirical findings, we focus on a sample of the most important variables and on the theoretical organisation that they seem to call for. The assumption is that over the years some insight has been gained about a

few critical aspects of working in academia that are necessary for any action plan addressing the development of a high performance team in a context of institutional demands for high productivity.

The model depicted in figure 1 summarises the basic structural elements found in the majority of theoretical approaches, which for the sake of simplicity, are assumed to be organised into a net of three conceptual layers. In the input layer, there is a set of independent or input variables, representing intrinsic motivators, extrinsic motivators and personal attributes. In the intermediate or meditational layer, there is a single variable called "job satisfaction" and in the output layer are the dependent variables in the form of "behavioural outputs" (productivity and intent to remain) and "consequences" (career development and promotion). The directional links connecting variables represent positive relationships among them.

A good number of theories have been put forward in this tradition; each with mayor or minor differences in their architectures, focusing in somewhat different subset of phenomena, and supported by different degrees of statistical sophistication and empirical testing (e.g. Hagedorn 2000; Volkwein/Zhou 2003). In the majority of these proposals, productivity, normally measured as the rate of publications (Levin/ Stephan 1991) and intention to remain in academia (e.g. Ryan/Healy/Sullivan 2012; Smart 1990) are the critical variables to be explained. In these approaches, authors normally have made the simplistic but reasonable assumption that greater productivity and stronger intention to remain in academia are associated with greater work satisfaction (Akerlof et al. 1988; Hagedorn 1996; Hesli/ Lee 2013, Ryan/Healy/Sullivan 2012; Smart 1990). Consistent with some observations in the literature, the schema assumes that productivity may influence turnover (e.g. Ryan/Healy/Sullivan 2012). But also, as showed in figure 1, the behavioural outcomes may recursively influence job satisfaction.

Figure 1: A simplified model of the variable involved in the study

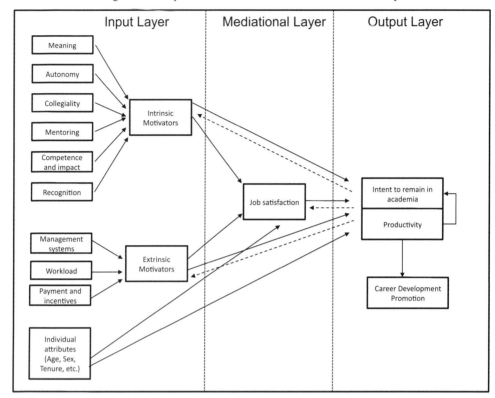

As shown in figure 1, behavioural outcomes are also assumed to depend on extrinsic motivators, such as financial rewards or release from administrative load, and on intrinsic motivators, such as the perceived meaning of research itself (e.g. Deemer/Martens/Buboltz 2012; Deemer/Mahoney/Ball 2010; Levin/Stephan 1991). In the figure, these factors are supposed to influence directly the behavioural outcomes, or indirectly via mediation by job satisfaction. Finally, the literature also indicates that a number of personal attributes, such as gender, tenure status, and age, are also influential in determining job satisfaction and performance (Bozeman/Gaughan 2011, Carmichael 1988; Ponjuan/Conley/Trower 2011; Rosser 2005; Sabatier 2012).

The influence of extrinsic factors and rewards on performance and job satisfaction has been examined with considerable interest in the academic milieu (e.g. Kim/Oh 2002; Manolopoulus 2006). The major extrinsic motivators are those associated to economic rewards and fair pay (Bender/Heywood 2006; Hagedorn 1996) but other factors such a workload and management systems are also frequently cited (Hagedorn 1996; Olsen 1993; Volkwein/Zhou 2003). Although some authors have suggested that extrinsic motivators are less important than intrinsic motivators for academic job satisfaction and performance (e.g. Cangur et al. 2009), there is relative agreement in that both types of motivators should be regarded as complimentary (Lawler 1981; Murddok 2002).

There is a less clear agreement in the literature with respect to what constitutes an "intrinsic motivator" in academic work life. Here we follow Ryan/Deci's (2000) approach that indicates that human beings have three types of intrinsic needs: autonomy, competence and relatedness. The literature addressing job satisfaction in academia provided substantial evidence of the importance of this sort of variables in predicting job satisfaction and productivity. Figure 1 summarises some of these variables, which include autonomy, meaning, competence and impact, collegiality, mentoring and recognition (Bozeman/Gaughan 2011; Cangur et al. 2009; Chung/Kowalski 2012; Dreher/Ash 1990; Hagedorn 2000; Hesli/Lee 2013; Porosnky 2012; Spreitzer 1995).

It should be recognised the simplistic nature of the model cartooned in figure 1, in which it is assumed that the variables in one layer are positively related to the variables in the next layers and that the variables belonging to the same layer do not interact among themselves. Undoubtedly, this is not always the case, but instead that under different labour circumstances these variables interact in complex ways. We have adopted this oversimplified approach as an attempt to capture the predominant relations among the most relevant variables. Given the exploratory nature of the study, we keep this model as an appropriate heuristic to conduct the diagnosis of our team group.

3. ASSESSMENT

Assessment Methodology

In order to conduct a diagnostic of the Faculty of Psychology, a survey was constructed that attempted to assess the majority of variables depicted in figure 1. The items that comprise the survey were based on several published questionnaires (Deemer/Mahoney/Ball; Chen 2011; Hesli/Lee 2013; Smart 1990). As shown in table 1, a total of 41 items were constructed which belong to the following 9 dimensions: autonomy (4 items), meaning (4 items), competence and impact (5 items), collegiality (5 items), mentoring (4 items), recognition (5 items), payment and incentives (5 items), funding and management systems (5 items), and workload (4 items).

In the first part of the survey, information on gender, age, rate of publications over a 5-year period, and percent of research and teaching workload during the last year was collected. In the second part, the importance of each item was assessed trough a scale ranging from 1 (extremely low importance) to 7 (extremely high importance). In the third part, participants judged the degree to which the concept represented in each item was present in their job over the last year, using a scale ranging from 1 (extremely low degree) to 7 (extremely high degree). Finally, participants responded 4 items addressing how frequently in the last year they "have felt satisfied with their position", "have felt satisfied with their career development", "had the intention to leave academia", and "have the sense of failing institutional expectations". The scale ranged from (1 extremely low frequency) to 7 (extremely high frequency).

The survey was responded by all faculties (n=16) except for one case who was out of the country at the time of the study.

The University and the Faculty

The Universidad de Talca is one of the 16 public universities in Chile. It was founded in 1981, and has about 9,000 students (of which 7,600 are undergraduate and 1,500 belong to master, doctoral or specialisation programmes). There are 23 undergraduate and 27 postgraduate programmes (21 master and 6 doctoral). The academic organisation of the university comprises 7 faculties and 5 institutes.

The Faculty of Psychology was founded in 2007 and offers one undergraduate programme in Psychology (with three minors in Clinical Psychology, Social-organisational Psychology and Social-community Psychology), one master programme in Social Psychology, and 5 short specialisation courses. The academic staff is composed of 17 full time professors (14 doctors and 3 masters). There are two secretaries, two research assistants and two administrative collaborators. It serves approximately 500 undergraduate and 40 graduate students.

Results

Figure 2 presents the mean scores of importance and satisfaction of each of the 9 dimensions measured. Firstly, the figure indicates that the majority of the dimensions were regarded as very important by the participants (mean scores above 5.5). Conversely, the level of satisfaction was comparatively low in the majority of the dimensions. Specifically, while the dimensions "meaning", "competence and impact" and "autonomy" were relatively well evaluated by the faculties, other intrinsic motivators associated with the social environment, such as "mentoring", "recognition" and "collegiality" were poorly evaluated. Especially notorious is the case of "collegiality" that got only a mean of 4.7 in satisfaction while it was deemed as one of the most important factor by the professors (6.2). Those dimensions involving extrinsic factors, such as "payment and incentives", "workload" and "management systems" also received low qualifications.

Figure 2: Mean importance and satisfaction of the 9 dimension of the faculty survey

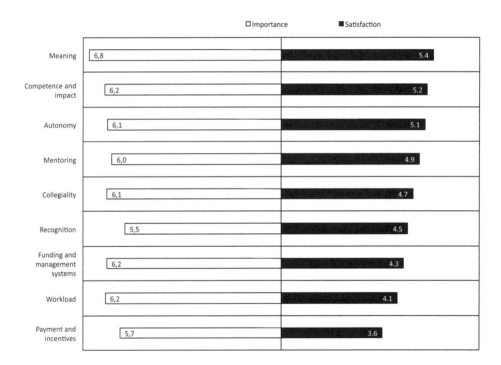

In order to examine the behaviour of specific aspects underlying each dimension, table 1 presents the mean scores of importance and satisfaction for the 41 items of the survey that were used to calculate the scores in each dimension. The overall mean for importance and satisfaction were 6.07 (SD =0.51) and 4.59 (SD=0.89), respectively. It can be seen that the distribution of the importance scores was very homogeneous with the majority of items above 5, a maximal of 6.8 (autonomy to decide my research) and a minimal of 5.1 (being recognised by the students, being recognised by the colleagues, and provision of financial incentives for outstanding professional work with the community). On the other hand, the distribution of the satisfaction scores was quite variable, ranging from a maximal of 6.1 (autonomy to decide my research) and a minimum of 2.3 (provision of financial incentives for outstanding teaching).

Table 1: Mean importance (Ȳimp) and satisfaction (Ȳsat) of the 41 items of survey

Attribute	Dimension	Ȳimp	Ȳsat
Autonomy to decide what to teach	Autonomy	5,8	4,6
Autonomy to decide research	Autonomy	6,8	6,1
Autonomy to decide to do professional	Autonomy	5,9	5,3
Autonomy to distribute my workload	Autonomy	6,1	4,3
Opportunity to develop new ideas	Meaning	6,7	5,2
To have a challenging and stimulation work environment	Meaning	6,8	5,1
To do work that is important and meaningful to me	Meaning	6,9	5,9
Job demands congruent with career development	Meaning	6,7	5,3
Opportunity to make a significant contribution to the discipline	Competence/impact	6,3	4,7
Impact of my work on the achievement of the goals of the unit	Competence/impact	6,0	5,3
To feel confident about my ability to do my job	Competence/impact	6,6	5,8
To feel that my achievements lead to my career development	Competence/impact	6,6	5,3
To feel that my performance satisfies institutional expectations	Competence/impact	5,6	4,7
Tolerance of diversity	Collegiality	6,4	5,2
Knowledge sharing with the group	Collegiality	6,4	4,2
Existence of working teams with common goals	Collegiality	5,7	4,9
Climate of respect and cordiality	Collegiality	6,7	4,9
Encouragement of group rather than individual productivity	Collegiality	5,6	4,1
Supervisors involvement in my career development	Mentoring	6,1	5,4
Being mentored	Mentoring	6,3	5,2
To have the opportunity to mentoring others	Mentoring	6,0	4,3
Presence of colleagues serving as role models and mentors	Mentoring	5,4	4,6
Being recognised as a teacher	Recognition	5,7	3,2
Being recognised as a researcher	Recognition	5,8	4,2
Being recognised by the students	Recognition	5,1	5,0
Being recognised by the colleagues	Recognition	5,1	4,8
Being recognised for the job well done	Recognition	5,8	5,1
To have a fair salary	Payment/incentives	6,6	5,4
Provision of financial incentives for outstanding management	Payment/incentives	5,4	3,1
Provision of financial incentives for outstanding teaching	Payment/incentives	5,4	2,3
Provision of financial incentives for outstanding research	Payment/incentives	5,8	4,6
Provision of financial incentives for outstanding professional work with my community	Payment/incentives	5,1	2,3
Institutional financial support for research	Funding/ management systems	5,7	4,4
Institutional financial support for travelling to conferences	Funding/ management systems	5,6	5,1
Availability for research and teaching assistants	Funding/ management systems	6,0	5,0
Objective criteria for academic assessment and promotion	Funding/ management systems	6,9	3,6

Academic assessment takes into account the wide range of dimensions of my job	Funding/ management systems	6,6	3,5
Availability of time to pursue most desired tasks	Workload	6,1	3,9
Adequate administrative workload	Workload	6,3	3,7
Supervisors with reasonable expectations about my performance	Workload	6,1	5,3
Availability of time for leisure and family life	Workload	6,4	3,5

In order to define specific areas of improvement, a performance control matrix was constructed using importance and satisfaction standardised scores (Chen 2011; Hung et al. 2003; Lambert/Sharma 1990). Figure 3 depicts the resulting matrix in which the importance scores are plotted in the Y-axis and satisfaction scores in the X-axis. Following Lambert and Sharma (1990), the matrix was divided into the nine cells that resulted of dividing each axis into a low scores zone (between -3 and -2 standard deviation from the mean), a medium scores zone (between -2 and 2 standard deviation from the mean) and a high scores zone (between 2 and 3 standard deviation from the mean). On the one hand, the items located proximal to the top left cells are those that need to be improved since they are regarded as more important and are less well evaluated. In this condition are "objective assessment", balanced assessment", "time for leisure", "administrative workload", "recognition as a teacher", "challenging work", "new ideas", "respect", "congruent demands" and "salary". On the other hand, the items "meaningful work", "autonomy of research" and "sense of competence" are important aspects that enjoy of good levels of satisfaction, and therefore should be regarded as strengths that must be maintained.

The results of the performance control matrix provide a useful tool to define the improvement priorities based on the importance and satisfaction reported by the faculties. In this respect, the results clearly indicate that a matter of worry for the directives of the unit is that the professors perceive that some extrinsic motivators associated with their career development are not working as well as they would like. On the other side, the perception of competence, meaning and autonomy in the workplace are functioning at relatively satisfactory levels.

However, the performance control matrix clearly tells only one part of the history. It may very well be the case that faculties perceive as less important some aspects that may be decisive to improve their performance and job satisfaction. This may the case of several items associated to the dimension of collegiality and mentoring that are poorly evaluated (e.g. "encouragement of group rather than individual productivity" and "presence of colleagues serving as role models") but that are not regarded as important as others and that have been emphasised in the literature and that count with high absolute scores of importance. In this respect, it may be useful to look at the results in each dimension as a function of job satisfaction, intention to remain in academia and productivity, which provide an independent assessment of the importance of the dimensions.

For this, an index of productivity, based on the rate of publications over the last 5 years was calculated for each faculty. The values ranged from 0.2 to 1.8 with a mean of 0.775 (SD=0.543). This index can be interpreted as low to medium productivity considering that the 2015 goal for the faculty is to reach a rate of 1.5 publications per professor.

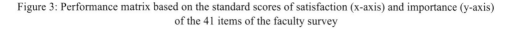

Figure 3: Performance matrix based on the standard scores of satisfaction (x-axis) and importance (y-axis) of the 41 items of the faculty survey

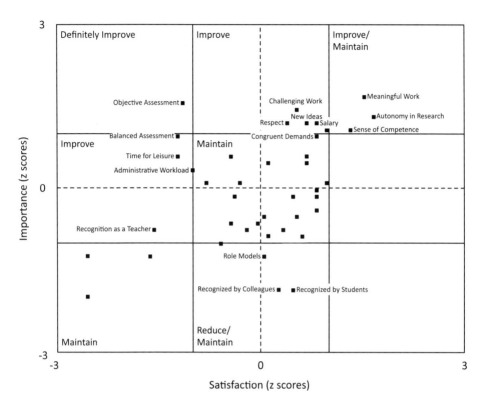

The index of productivity was used to create three groups: The high productivity group was formed by those faculties that produced more than 1 publication per year (n=4); the medium productivity group was formed by those that published more than 0.5 and less than 1 paper per year (n=4), and the low productivity group was formed by those that published less that 0.5 paper per year.

Figure 4 presents the indicators of satisfaction of these three groups. Since the midpoint of the scale is 4, the results indicate a modest level of "global satisfaction" (total mean equal 5.06) and of "satisfaction with career development" (total mean 4.88). Interestingly, these two components of job satisfaction were substantially better evaluated in the low productivity group that in the other two groups. This may be the result of the fact that more productive workers are more aware of the need of increasing their performance than are the less productive faculties and, as a consequence of this, they are more stressed.

Figure 4: Mean global work satisfaction (left-hand plot) and mean satisfaction with career development (right-hand plot) as a function of faculty productivity

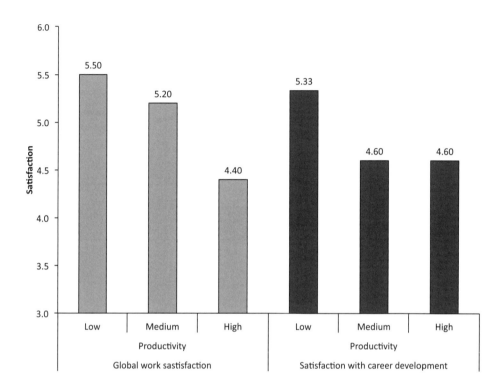

Figure 5 presents the results of the other two output variables measuring how frequently the faculties "had the intention to leave academia" and "had a sense of failing institutional expectations". The global results lead to mean scores of 3.50, and 3.38, which indicate that these are not common worries among faculties. Unsurprisingly, however, these concerns are more marked among those that exhibit lower productivity.

Beyond the differences between the three productivity groups, the data of figures 4 and 5 clearly show that there are several areas that must be improved in order to get people more satisfied and productive. Some aspects of the actual labour conditions may help to understand this pattern. This is exemplified in table 2, which presents a general charac-terisation of the three groups in terms of the several variables measured in the present study. A general inspection of the table indicates that the less productive professors are comparatively of older age, have less research workload, more administrative workload, and similar teaching workload than their more productive counterparts. On the one hand, the high teaching and administrative workload in the three groups may explain the low level of productivity in the entire team and the poorer job satisfaction of the more productive group. On the other hand, the table shows that the three groups have a similar perception of the intrinsic and extrinsic motivators in their workplace.

Figure 5: Mean judged frequency of "intention to leave" (left-hand plot) and of "sense of failing institutional expectations" (right-hand plot) as a function of faculty productivity

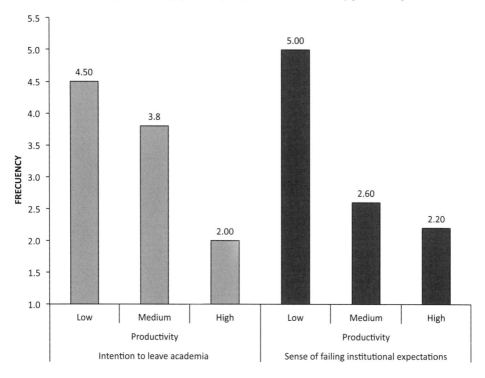

Table 2: The three productivity groups compared

Variable		Productivity		
	Total	Low	Medium	High
Mean Age	38.63	41.67	34.20	39.40
Mean percent of teaching workload	42.62	39.64	44.24	44.61
Mean percent of research workload	30.64	23.26	37.17	32.97
Mean percent of administrative workload	22.79	28.05	17.96	21.31
Autonomy	5.06	5.42	5.10	4.60
Meaning	5.38	5.67	5.05	5.35
Competence and impact	5.15	5.10	5.04	5.32
Collegiality	4.65	5.17	4.48	4.20
Mentoring	4.88	4.83	5.10	4.70
Recognition	4.45	4.40	3.84	4.45
Payment and incentives	3.56	3.30	3.60	3.84
Funding and management systems	4.31	4.58	4.28	4.04
Workload	4.09	4.33	3.50	4.45

4. DEVELOPMENT OF AN ACTION PLAN

The results of the quantitative diagnosis presented above combined with the initial qualitative observations that motivated this study suggest the following conclusions: First, the faculty counts with a majority of junior professors, with excellent and diverse postgraduate education and a high sense of competence and meaning at work. Very few have ever considered leaving academia. However, their research is incipient and has no clear focus yet.

Second, autonomy is a highly valued attribute of the unit. Although this is positive, some caution concerning individualism should be considered. Some indicators such collegiality and mentoring were poorly evaluated in the team. Moreover, these attributes were not recognised as the most important among the professors. This is consistent with the fact that there is little systematic collaborative work in the unit. Likewise, there are very little formal and informal mentoring activities among the faculties.

Third, the risk of individualism is consistent with the government policy of allocation of funds to public institutions, which is based on outcome indicators. The performance of the professors is progressively becoming more dependent on external indicators. In this respect, there is some concern that the professors are not completely satisfied with the assessment, promotion and career development system in the university. Their teaching and administrative workload is comparatively much higher than their formal research load. Since, currently there is a sort of disentanglement of research, teaching, and transfer to the community activities, there may be an additional source of stress that could explain, in part, the relative dissatisfaction among faculties.

Based on this diagnostic, our strategy regards, as first step, to get a conceptually unified project of development of the faculty that is accepted by the academic staff. The initial analysis leaded to three major working areas or conceptual domains in which team has its major strengths. Second, it will be attempted to regard each domain as being embodied into three action lines: Education, Research and transfer to the community. Then, the faculties will be encouraged to form collaborative working teams in each domain and to set goals for the faculty in each domain X action lines. For this, it will be necessary to negotiate with the rector for additional resources needed for the goals. The next step is to tie individual career development of the professors with faculty goals.

One of the most critical aspects of this action plan is to get the professors involvement. For this, at the beginning of each year, the professors should propose a working plan including his o her contribution to the achievement of the goals of the faculty. This implies some degree of negotiation with the dean. Then, the professors will be encouraged to integrate one of working teams based on their research, teaching and transfer interests. Publications and research grants will be regarded as a team result, instead of individual results.

Each working team should define actions to contribute to the goals of the faculty in the three action lines: education, research and transfer. The leader of each working team will define mentoring activities based on successful mentoring programmes instantiated elsewhere (e.g. Tsen et al. 2011). Each group will be encouraged to contribute to the development of a project for a doctoral programme and to seek for funds for the recruitment of postdoctoral positions.

The Dean, in conjoint with each professor will examine the matching between individual career development and faculty goals. Since some professors are at an initial stage of their respective careers, they would need first orientation and support. This situation should progressively change and more autonomy will be required. Next, the strategy in the majority of cases will be one of persuasion and negotiation rather than direction and support.

5. CONCLUSION

In this paper, we reported a case study that illustrates the first steps taken by the directives of a recently created academic unit towards maximizing productivity as well as job satisfaction of the academic asset. The study combined quantitative measures, qualitative observations and a literature review to define an action plan addressing the harmonisation of institutional an individual expectations.

The basic idea was to form a highly productive and highly satisfied team. Our conclusion was that this could be achieved by enhancing several intrinsic components of the social environment at work. Clearly, this is an on-going process that will require a mid-term evaluation and further adjustments.

REFERENCES

Akerlof, George A./Rose, Andrew K./Yellen, Janet L., Job switching and job satisfaction in the US labor market, in: Brookings Papers on Economic Activity 1988 (2/1988), 495-582.

Bender, Keith A./Heywood, John S., Job satisfaction of the highly educated: the role of gender, academic tenure, and earnings, in: Scottish Journal of Political Economy 53 (2/2006), 253-279.

Bozeman, Barry/Gaughan, Monica, Job satisfaction among university faculty: Individual, work, and institutional determinants, in: The Journal of Higher Education 82 (2/2011), 154-186.

Cangur, Sengul/Yilmaz, Veysel/Ediz, Bulent/Kan, Ismet, How motivation, communication-cooperation and reward system affect faculty members' job satisfaction in a developing country, in: The New Educational Review 17 (1/ 2009), 154-164.

Carmichael, H. Lorne, Incentives in academics: Why is there tenure?, in: Journal of Political Economy 96 (3/1988), 453-472.

Chen, Shun-Hsing, A performance matrix for strategies to improve satisfaction among faculty members in higher education, in: Total Quality & Quantity 45 (1/2011), 75-89.

Chung, Catherine E./Kowalski, Susan, Job stress, mentoring, psychological empowerment, and job satisfaction among nursing faculty, in: Journal of Nursing Education 51 (7/2012), 381-388.

Deemer, Eric D./Martens, Matthew P./Buboltz, Walter C., Toward a tripartite model of research motivation: Development and initial validation of the research motivation scale, in: Journal of Career Assessment 18 (3/2010), 292-309.

Deemer, Eric D./Mahoney, Kevin T./Ball, Jacqueline H., Research motives of faculty in academic STEM: Measurement invariance of the research motivation scale, in: Journal of Career Assessment 20 (2/2012), 182-195.

Dreher, George F./Ash, Ronald A., A comparative study of mentoring among men and women in managerial, professional, and technical positions, in: Journal of Applied Psychology 75 (5/1990), 539-546.

Hagedorn, Linda S., Wage equity and female faculty job satisfaction: The role of wage differentials in a job satisfaction causal model, in: Research in Higher Education 37 (5/1996), 569-598.

Hagedorn, Linda S., Conceptualizing faculty job satisfaction: Components, theories, and outcomes, in: New Directions for Institutional Research 2000 (105/2000), 5-20.

Hesli, Vicki/Lee, Jae, Job satisfaction in academia: Why are some faculty members happier than others? In: PS: Political Science and Politics 46 (2/2013), 339-354.

Johnsrud, Linda K., Measuring the quality of faculty and administrative worklife: Implications for college and university campuses, in: Research in Higher Education 43 (3/2002), 379-395.

Kim, Bowon/Oh, Heungshik, Economic compensation compositions preferred by R&D personnel of different R&D types and intrinsic values, in: R&D Management 32 (1/2002), 47-59.

Lambert, Douglas M./Sharma, Arun, A customer-based competitive analysis for logistics decisions, in: International Journal of Physical Distribution & Logistics Management 20 (1/1990), 17-24.

Lawler, Edward E., Pay and organizational development, Reading, MA (Addison-Wesley) 1981.

Levin, Sharon G./Stephan, Paula E., Research productivity over the life cycle: Evidence for academics scientists, in: The American Economic Review 81 (1/1991), 114-131.

Manolopoulos, Dimitris, What motivates R&D professionals? Evidence from decentralized laboratories in Greece, in: The International Journal of Human Resource Management 17 (4/2006), 616-647.

Murdock, Kevin, Intrinsic motivation and optimal incentive contracts, in: Rand Journal of Economics 33 (4/2002), 650-671.

Olsen, Deborah, Work satisfaction and stress in the first and third year of academic appointment, in: Journal of Higher Education 64 (4/1993), 453-471.

Ponjuan, Luis/Conley, Valerie/Trower, Cathy, Career stage differences in pre-tenure track faculty perceptions of professional and personal relationships with colleagues, in: The Journal of Higher Education 82 (3/2011), 319-346.

Poronsky, Cathlin B., A literature review of mentoring for RN-to-FNP transition, in: Journal of Nursing Education 51 (11/2012), 623-631.

Rosser, Vicki J., Measuring the change in faculty perceptions over time: An examination of their worklife and satisfaction, in: Research in Higher Education 46 (1/2005), 81-107.

Ryan, Richard M./Deci, Edward L., Intrinsic and extrinsic motivations: Classic definitions and dew Directions, in: Contemporary Educational Psychology 25 (1/2000), 54-67.

Ryan, John F./Healy, Richard/Sullivan, Jason, Oh, won't you stay? Predictors of faculty intent to leave a public research university, in: Higher Education 63 (4/2012), 421-437.

Sabatier, Mareva, Does productivity decline after promotion? The case of French academia, in: Oxford Bulletin of Economics and Statistics 74 (6/2012), 886-902.

Smart, John C., A causal model of faculty turnover intentions, in: Research in Higher Education 31 (5/1990), 405-424.

Spreitzer, Gretchen M., Psychological empowerment in the workplace: Dimensions, measurement and validation, in: Academy of Management Journal 38 (5/1995), 1442-1465.

Tsen, Lawrence C./Borus, Jonathan, F./Nadelson, Carol C./Seely, Ellen, W./Hass, Audrey/Fuhlbrigge, Anne L., The development, implementation, and assessment of an innovative faculty mentoring leadership program, in: Academic Medicine 87 (12/2012) 1757-1761.

Volkwein, James F./Zhou, Ying, Testing a model of administrative job satisfaction, in: Research in Higher Education 44 (2/2003), 149-171.

Edgar H. Vogel is the Dean of the Faculty of Psychology at Universidad de Talca, Chile (2010-2016). His research focuses on theoretical and empirical analyses of Pavlovian conditioning and habituation. Vogel received his B.A. degree in Psychology from Universidad de Chile in 1993 and his Ph.D. degree in Behavioural Neuroscience from Yale University in 2001.

Pablo Reyes is the Chair of the Compensations and Well-Being Department at Universidad Católica del Maule, Chile. His research focuses on career development, organisational development, personnel selection and compensations. Ryes obtained a B.A. degree in Psychology from Universidad de Talca in 2008.

Session 3

Faculty's Autonomy in Higher Education

THE EFFECTS OF NEW PUBLIC MANAGEMENT ON THE AUTONOMY OF FACULTIES IN JAPAN

Kiyoshi Yamamoto

Graduate School of Education, University of Tokyo, 7-3-1 Hongo, Bunkyo-Ku, Tokyo, 101-0033 Japan
ykiyoshi@p.u-tokyo.ac.jp

This paper examines the actual impact on university governance through corporatisation of national universities in Japan. The corporatisation was influenced from the new public management like in other nations. Using three surveys, we show that presidents generally feel positive effect on incorporation in terms of efficiency and improving quality, although deans acknowledge negative effects on administrative efficiency and research. At the same time, academic deans feel themselves more being exercising leadership and stronger roles after corporatisation. On the other hand, faculties still have significant power in decision making on faculty issues. Three scenarios explain these findings: transitional phrase into new governance, milder budget cut and insufficient competition among universities.

1. INTRODUCTION

Higher education institutions (HEIs) have changed its governance and management since the 1980s around the world. The transformation is driven by the globalisation and neo-liberal ideology. Now higher education is considered a promoter or an engine of economic growth and global competitiveness of the state. HEIs are asked to improve performance and become more competitive through a market mechanism and business management tools. Corporatisation is a policy instrument for transforming the sheltered organisation into more a business entity. It is an organisational reform based on the new public management (NPM) or managerialism (Deem 2001; Reed 2002). Of course corporatisation, as many scholars indicate, introduced the corporate governance and management of the private sector into HEIs. Also as some scholars insist, NPM is not new, but is considered adoption of old management model in the early 20th century called scientific management or Taylorism (Currie 2004; Lucas 2006): top management

has a strong power in decision making, strategic planning and control. It means that HEIs are centralised and more hierarchical. Accordingly incorporation has caused the tensions and conflicts with collegial governance model, especially in faculties. Some commentators (Marginson/Considine 2000; Neumann/Guthrie 2002) criticised that academic autonomy has deteriorated through NPM or corporatisation. However there are few studies on effects and impacts, while a lot of research using institutional theory or neo-institutional sociology was done on changing or corporatizing process. In addition, recently a new approach from organisational theory or ambidexterity indicates the contrasting view, which the tensions and trade-offs could be reconciled and further successful universities or units would achieve the balance between opposing and conflicting demands.

From this perspective, national universities in Japan transformed into corporation in 2004 are a good example to examine the effects through the corporatisation owing to its character of maintaining academic autonomy (Arimoto 2011) and nine-year practices in new governance. This paper intends to answer the following questions. How the disciplines of NPM have adopted in university management and resulted in the intended or unintended outcomes after incorporation? What are different in decision-making and behaviour between president and academic deans? To what extent do faculties have autonomy in decision-making? Finally, which theory would better explain the actual practices and reality in the corporatised national universities?

Accordingly the next section briefly explains the corporatisation and system for Japanese national universities. The third section reviews the previous studies then shows the theoretical framework. In the fourth section the research methods and data are described. The fifth section analyses the results and their implications are discussed. Finally, conclusions and future issues are shown.

2. CORPORATISATION OF NATIONAL UNIVERSITIES AND NPM

Background

National universities in Japan were transformed into national university corporations (NUCs) in 2004. From their former status as just a branch of the Ministry of Education, Culture, Sports, Science and Technology (MEXT), each national university became an independent public body separated from the central government. The transition was implemented through the National University Corporation Act, which was effectively the enactment of the report entitled "New Vision for National University Corporations" (MEXT 2002). The report indicates three aspects for reform: identifying the missions and goals of universities, defining the management responsibility and giving considerable autonomy in operations through the adoption of business management tools, and introducing a mechanism to stimulate competition between universities in addition to more respecting the needs of students and business world. The basic idea is quite similar to NPM in other developed countries, where the focuses are on results and being customer-oriented, the market mechanism and devolution or decentralisation (Hood 1991; Pollitt 1993).

The corporatisation, as Yamamoto (2004a) indicated, contains a considerable element of public sector reform, although MEXT mentions it as educational reform (Toyama 2004). In fact, the basic regulatory framework for the Independent Administrative Institutions (IAIs), which are semi-autonomous public bodies implementing public services (Yamamoto 2004b), has been applied to the NUCs. Further the system of NUCs introduced a competitive mechanism among universities by contrast to IAIs having varied functions. Therefore, the incorporation has dramatically changed the governance and management system of national universities.

Governance

In the former system, as mentioned earlier, national universities were internal organisations within the government granting them academic freedom. As a result, there were two different structures or a dual system depending on the academics and administration involved. Decision-making on academic issues was undertaken by the Academic Council whose members came from faculties and headed by president. On the other hand, administration issues were managed by the administrative head as an accounting officer of MEXT in compliance with government regulations.

Corporatised universities became independent public bodies. Consequently the president now holds decision-making power on academic and administration issues. In other words, the president's role changed from the chief academic officer to the chief executive officer for the university. He or she controls the administrative bureau which was previously under the control of administrative head. The board of directors consisting of the president and several directors is the executive body for managing university. Since the president appoints the directors, the president can exercise strong leadership.

Management

In accordance with NPM based principles, much flexibility in management was given to NUCs in exchange of strengthening accountability for the results through the medium-term plan, which is approved by MEXT. NUCs are required to set targets to enhance the quality of teaching and research, and to improve their operation and efficiency. Of course, owing to the specific nature of universities, external evaluation is to be based on self-evaluation by the university.

Corporatisation changed the status of staff from civil servants to non-civil servants. Academic and administrative staffs are no longer public employees. The personnel system gradually transformed from seniority to more performance or competency based. In addition, some part of life-long employment has been replaced by contracted or tem-employment.

In financial management, operating grant which is a sort of block grant in a lump sum is delivered to NUCs. By contrast to line item control in the former system, the president has full discretion in resource allocation of the grant. The operating grant unspent is able to be carried over to the next year.

Facilities are owned by NUCs, by contrast to national property or assets in the previous system. However, there are significant constraints in facilities management. Capital expenditure is basically funded by the government through the capital expenditure subsidies, which are separated from operating grants (no depreciation). Accordingly the focus is on maintenance and use of facilities.

3. THEORETICAL FRAMEWORK

Literature Review

There are three types of research on NPM including corporatisation in higher education. What are driving forces of NPM? How has NPM been implemented or adopted into

the public sector or related sectors like higher education? What are the outcomes by adopting NPM? This paper examines the effects and impact on faculties through corporatisation of national universities in Japan. So we focus on the research in implementation and results of corporatisation.

Previous studies on corporatisation are basically divided into rational approach and institutional approach. Agency theory is a rational approach in which each actor would seek his or her benefit or utility. The relations between government and university, president and deans, dean and faculty members are considered a contract having an incentive system. Accordingly, it gives the guidance for designing governance and management system. The rational approach presumes that faculties as the agent would behave in alignment with the incentive system in which executives as the principal will encourage faculties to make their effort towards intended outcomes. There is so far little research on the outcomes and whether the intended outcomes have been caused is not definitely (Lewis/Ross 2011): some studies rather found negative effects (Auranen/Nieminen 2010; Furedi 2012) or did not support the presumed assumptions that performance schemes would improve teaching and research activities (Leisyte et al. 2009; Wilkesmann/Schmid 2012). In other words, agency theory can prescribe for improving performance while taking account of academic autonomy. However, the evidence that the prescriptions have worked well is few and sometimes is contrary to them.

On the other hand, new institutional theory is most used in institutional approach. A lot of articles indicate that NPM has transformed the traditional values of universities into the corporate, enterprising values. Institutional theory presumes that organisations pursue legitimacy, approval and funding from the society and their environment (Meyer/Rowan 1977; Euske/Euske 1991; Stone 1991). In case of corporatisation, initially universities responded to coercive pressures from the government in compliance with the rules and regulations (DiMaggio/Powell 1983; Scott/Meyer 1991). Secondly, they took mimetic isomorphic behaviours since they have to compete with other HEIs in higher education market induced by the government. These isomorphic behaviours cause the tensions between new centralised power by management and traditional collegial power by academic staff. In other words, academics take strategies of alignment with formal structures through centralised and strengthening accountability, while they take a strategy of decoupling from the formal institution like corporatisation or regulations. Alignment and decoupling coexists in responses to corporatisation of universities (Parker 2011). Institutional theory explains that the trade-offs within universities will gradually been transformed into new corporate forms and institutionalised. Consequently traditional academic autonomy also would deteriorate.

However, recently a different view from the above two streams has emerged. It is the idea of ambidexterity in organisational theory (Duncan 1976; Tushman/O'Reilly 1996). Organisations are always to some extent facing conflicting demands like in efficiency and flexibility or cutting costs and improving quality. Successful organisations reconcile them, although the trade-offs can be not completely eliminated.

Structural ambidexterity is a method to cope the conflicts through separating organisation into units for specific need. It is setting up autonomous business units in corporate management, which was imported as agencification or "hiving of" (Pollitt/Talbot 2004) into the public sector. Accordingly structural ambidexterity has an idea common to corporatisation. Another type of ambidexterity, contextual ambidexterity was developed by Gibson/Birkinshaw (2004). It is seen as a meta-level capacity for alignment and adaptability (Gibson/Birkinshaw 2004).

By contrast to rational theory and institutional theory having the commonality shifting for alignment, organisational ambidexterity seeks to achieve both of alignment and adaptation whether structural or contextual. In higher education studies, adopting the idea of ambidexterity in the case study, Tahar/Niemeyer/Boutellier (2011) analysed the transfer of business management in higher education from the view that universities can be perceived as ambidextrous organisations. They found there were two different organisational structures of faculties and administrations resulting in a dilemma of efficiency and creativity.

We have therefore three approaches in analysing the outcomes by corporatisation.

Model

Corporatisation of universities significantly changed the governance and management. The relations between government and universities have become more contractual: indirect control from the government while strengthening accountability for results. Performance management and management leadership are also promoted. This means that president in senior executives, deans in faculties, and heads of administrations have definite roles in their leadership. Especially professional management groups in administrations have greater power in contrast to before corporatisation. As a result, our model explicitly takes account of not only external relations between government and universities, but also internal relations among executives, administrations and deans including faculties (see figure 1).

When we relate three theoretical streams to the model, firstly rational approach, especially agency theory, focuses on hierarchical relation between executives and deans/faculties or administrations. Second, institutional theory focuses on the relation between government and universities: universities would respond to government policies and directives, take mimetic behaviour each other. Third, ambidexterity pays attention to the decision-makings of organisational level. The focus is on internal responses within organisation. As shown in literature review, each theory has some limitations and lacks in sufficient data to validate. Therefore we examine which approach could better explain the relations and responded behaviour.

Figure 1: Conceptual Model

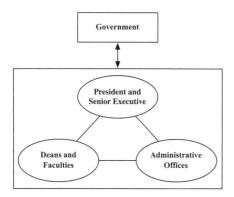

4. METHOD AND DATA

In order to examine the impact on universities by organisational unit, we have to collect the data on changing figures and their outcomes after incorporation. As the previous section described, academic autonomy as the specific nature of universities is associated with the relationships between faculties, executives and government. In addition, it is noteworthy that president and dean are respectively spanning the boundary between HEI and government, executives/administrators and academic staff. Also it should be considered the experience effects: it takes time to cause some impacts whether intended or unintended outcomes. The most adequate method in this case is using a survey traced for the same person or groups composing executives, faculties, administrators of national universities and government before and after corporatisation.

However, there is no systemic survey on governance and management just before the incorporation for those groups in Japan. Consequently three kinds of survey in which the author involved are used: two are implemented in retrospective way with reference to corporatised time and the other was cross sectional type for faculties in three sectors. The first is the questionnaire for all presidents of national universities (N=86) in 2006. The second is the questionnaire for all presidents (N=86) and deans of national universities (N=372) in 2009. Both surveys are a census and their items were designed to be comparable each other and be able to trace the trend after incorporation for presidents, while for deans it was just a retrospective method. The third survey is for faculties or academic staff and randomly extracted from national, public and private universities (total=4,000, sample number is 698, 244, 3,058 respectively). Although this is a cross-sectional survey, it might be useful in analysing the impact for faculties which the influence by NPM is most likely found in national universities by contrast to public and private universities. Because the governance and management for NUCs adopt a more business like model indiscriminately. Corporatisation of public universities also began in 2004, however, the decision lies in each governor or mayor holding the universities. As a result, the rate of corporatisation is 28% in 2006 and 55% in 2009, not 100%. Besides, private universities set up their medium-term plan or strategic plan were just 25% in 2006 and 55% in 2009. So it is supposed that faculties in national universities have been more affected by the NPM and their implementation.

The respective questionnaire was sent to presidents, deans and faculties through postal mails. The response rates for presidents in 2006 and 2009 were 97.6% (=84/86) and 98.8% (85/86) respectively. Also there was a 70.2 percent response rate with effective 261 returns in case of deans in 2009. Further 1,689 of 4,000 (42.2 percent response rate) in case of faculties were returned.

5. FINDINGS AND DISCUSSIONS

Implementation and Outcomes

The vision for corporatisation was closely enacted as the National University Corporation Law. The result orientation and flexibility in operations are reflected in operating grants and balanced by strengthening accountability for results. The competition among universities was also introduced in evaluation system linked to funding for operating grants. In this regard, the corporatisation in case of national universities is considered institutionalisation of NPM based organisation reform in higher education. Of course the adoption of NPM principles differs from the inherited idea in flexibility and accountability. For example, the discretion in resource allocation was limited in personnel costs in accordance with the government request for cutting the costs. Besides the linkage between evaluation results and funding was marginalised (Goldfinch/Yamamoto 2012) despite insisting competition among universities in the vision statement.

According to the survey for presidents in 2009, the basic principle that more discretion in exchange of strengthening accountability would improve performance was generally acknowledged. More than seventy percent of the presidents felt the improvement of the management through increased flexibility. The net effects deducting the percentage of respondents answered "disagree" or "somewhat disagree" from those answered "agree" or "somewhat agree" were found in all four sub-management systems: organisation (87.0%), personnel (72.9%), financial management (82.4%) and planning (84.7%).

Relations between Presidents and Deans

The above results give a support that he intended outcomes have been caused by the corporatisation. However, if we look at the views of other major player in universities, the contrasted figures are shown. Let the net effects through incorporation measure the difference between the percentage of positive respondents answered "agree" or "somewhat agree" and that of negative respondents answered "somewhat disagree" or "disagree" in major functions. The net effects on efficient administration and research were negative for deans, –22.9% and –28.3% respectively in 2009, by contrast to being greater positive for presidents in both surveys of 2006 and 2009. More than eighty percent of presidents felt the positive effect on efficient administration and research by the corporatisation.

In addition, in case of teaching, there are significant differences in the recognised effect between deans and presidents (9.5% and 94.6% respectively). Presidents greatly support incorporation, compared to less support from deans except for public services.

The findings might be explained by the presidential power and changing relations between presidents and deans after incorporation. The president now holds a greater power on whole issues and has discretion in resource management given the regulation and medium-term goals. The former position was just a chief academic officer having no authority in financial management which was responsible to the head of administration. The president is responsible to academics and administration, while academic deans still have authority over faculty issues. This means that president has more dominant position to deans after incorporation. The corporatised universities have a decentralised system in which autonomy or flexibility in management is granted to faculties and administration offices provided the medium-term goals by faculty or department and accountability for results. Therefore new governance asks academic deans to exercise their leadership in faculty management, while the former was a collegial way. In other words, it is presumed in NUCs that deans will become more powerful and need a leadership in decision making than those in previous system at least faculty issues. In practice, the survey for deans in 2009 indicated that deans felt power shift from deans to executives or presidents. More than seventy percent of deans acknowledged rising influence from the president (79.8%) or executives (73.9%) over faculty issues. At the same time, 47 percent of deans perceived increasing nature in their role and 60 percent felt increase in leadership of decision making.

Taking into the deans' negative or less positive perception to the corporatisation, it is presumed that deans have been facing the conflict between exercising their leadership and loyalties to the president and senior executives. Deans believe that the more they become loyal to the executives through exercising their leadership, administrative efficiency and research activities in the faculty level will deteriorate.

Faculties

The survey for faculties in 2013 shows the actual figure in Japanese higher education institutions. Faculty control over decision in national, public and private sector, which is calculated by the percentage of respondents answered 'significantly' and 'to some extent' involvement, is still great in content of curriculum (91.6, 88.5 and 91.5% respectively), appointment and promotion of faculty (82.4, 80.2 and 76.4%), and selecting deans (94.2, 69.5 and 53.5%). In particular faculties of national universities have highly influence in selecting deans comparing to public and private universities. On the contrary, the level of faculty participation of national universities in resource management is not large: 49.9 percent perceived in sizes of the faculty, 28.6 percent in resource allocation, 38.3 percent in planning.

When we turn into the faculty knowledge on changes and conditions, which is measured by the percentage of respondents answered "agree" and "somewhat agree", we find mixed results with reference to or critics to NPM and corporatisation in case of national universities. 31.7 percent of faculties acknowledged that pressures from the executives constrain autonomous decision-making in faculty meeting. 29.3 percent felt the tight control from administrative offices. Also 30.7 percent believed good communication between faculty and executives. By contrast, 89.0 percent felt that deans have exercised their leadership, and 42.7 percent satisfied the activities by executives and president. These results show that faculties in national universities still maintain autonomous position, while they felt greater leadership from deans and executives. However, fiscal stress of the government has affected feeling of the faculties on austerity of resources. 86.9 percent agreed that downsizing faculty or decreasing academic staff is an issue in faculties, and 93.7 percent acknowledged budge cut in faculty issues. This is partly caused by the austerity of national government.

6. DISCUSSIONS AND CONCLUSION

This paper examined the actual impact on university governance through corporatisation in Japan. The corporatisation was influenced from NPM like in other nations. Using three different surveys, we showed president generally felt positive effect on incorporation in terms of efficiency and improving quality, although deans acknowledged negative effects on administrative efficiency and research. At the same time, academic deans felt themselves more being exercising leadership and stronger roles after corporatisation. On the other hand, faculties still have significant power in decision making on faculty issues, while budgeting and future planning have been traditionally implemented by executive or administrative offices. Consequently so far little changes were found in faculty issues.

These findings show that the effects of corporatisation differ by organisational unit, executives, deans and faculties. It also indicates academic autonomy in faculties or collegial culture has still been maintained and is not transplanted by centralised business management system endorsed by NPM. The situation could be explained by a transitional phrase into new governance, milder budget cut for national universities, and insufficient competition among universities or higher education market place. From the viewpoint of three theoretical streams identified, the first factor is related to institutional theory: decoupling of collegialism and NPM and alignment with NPM coexists until now, however alignment would gradually dominate to decoupling. The second factor is associated with ambidexterity. Presidents and faculties seem to succeed at coping to the corporatisation, which demands accountability for results and improving efficiency due to a slight budget cut (1,241 billion yen for FY2004 to 1,152 billion yen for FY2011). By contrast, deans felt conflict between academic activities and NPM based management. The third factor is related to rational theory which competition, even though potential based, would produce higher performance and efficiency improvement using incentive system like performance based funding. The practical linkage between evaluation and funding was quite marginal (Yamamoto 2011), partly consistent with survey result for deans (efficient administration is negative). It is therefore early to determine the effects, causes of the corporatisation, in addition to which theory is most appropriate to explain the impacts.

Accordingly we have to further investigate corporatisation of universities in more longitudinal way, international comparison and organisational unit.

REFERENCES

Arimoto, Akira, Japan: Effects of changing governance and management on the academic profession, in: *Locke, William/Cummings, William K./Fisher, Donald* (eds.), Changing governance and management in higher education: The perspectives of the academy, Dordrecht (Springer) 2011.

Auranen, Otto/Nieminen, Mika, University research funding and publication performance – an international comparison, in: Research Policy, 39(2010), 822-834.

Currie, Jan, The neo-liberal paradigm and higher education: A critique, in: *Odin, Jaishree K./Manicas, Peter T.* (eds.), Globalization and higher education. Honolulu (University of Hawaii Press) 2004.

Deem, Rosemary, Globalisation, new managerialism, academic capitalism and entrepreneurialsim in universities: Is the local dimension important? in: Comparative Education, 1(2001), 7-20.

DiMaggio, Paul/Powell, Walter, The iron cage revisited: Institutional isomorphism and collective rationality in organizational fields, in: American Sociological Review, 48(2/1983), 147-160.

Duncan, Robert, The ambidextrous organization: Designing duals structures for innovation, in:

Kilman, Ralph H./Pondy, Louis R./Slevin, Dennis P. (eds.), The management of organization. Vol.1. New York (North-Holland) 1976.

Euske, Nancy/Euske, Kenneth, Institutional theory: Employing the other side of rationality in Non-Profit Organizations, in: British Journal of Management, 2(1/1991), 81-88.

Furedi, Frank, Satisfaction and its discontents, in: Times Higher Education, 8 March, (2012), 36-40.

Gibson, Cristina/Birkinshaw, Julian, The antecedents, consequences, and mediating role of organizational ambidexterity, in: Academy of Management Journal, 47 (2/2004), 209-226.

Goldfinch, Shaun/Yamamoto, Kiyoshi, Prometheus assessed? Research measurement, peer review and citation analysis, Oxford (Chandos Publishing) 2012.

Hood, Christopher, A public management for all seasons, in: Public Administration, 69(1/1991), 3-19.

Leisyte, Liudvika/Enders, Jürgen/de Boer, Harvy, The balance between teaching and research in Dutch and English universities in the context of university governance reforms, in: Higher Education, 58 (2009), 619-635.

Lewis, Jenny/Ross, Sandy, Research funding systems in Australia, New Zealand and the UK: Policy settings and perceived effects, in: Policy and Politics, 39 (3/2011), 379-398.

Lucas, Lisa, The research game in academic life, Buckingham (Open University Press) 2006.

Marginson, Simon/Considine, Mark, The enterprise university: Power, governance and reinvention in Australia, Cambridge (Cambridge University Press) 2000.

MEXT, New vision for national university corporation, Tokyo (MEXT) 2002.

Meyer, John and Brian, Rowan, Institutionalized Organizations: Formal Structures as Myth and Ceremony, in: American Journal of Sociology, 83(2/1977), 340-363.

Neumann, Ruth/Guthrie, James, The corporatization of research in Australian higher education, in: *Critical Perspectives on Accounting*, 13 (5&6/2002), 721-741.

Parker, Lee, University corporatisation: Driving redefinition, in: Critical Perspectives on Accounting, 22 (2011), 434-450.

Pollitt, Christopher, Managerialism and the public services, Oxford (Blackwell) 2. ed.,1993.

Pollitt, Christopher/Talbot, Colin, Unbundled government: A critical analysis of the global trend to agencies, quangos and contractualisation. London (Routledge) 2004.

Reed, Michael, New managerialism, professional power and organisational governance in UK universities: a review and assessment, in: *Amaral, Alberto/Jones, Glen A./Karseth, Berit* (eds.), Governing higher education: National perspectives on institutional governance. Dordrecht (Kluwer Academic Publishers) 2002.

Scott, Richard/Meyer, John, The organization of societal sectors: Proposition and early evidence, in: *Powell Walter/DiMaggio, Paul* (eds.). The new institutionalism in organisational analysis, Chicago (The University of Chicago Press) 1991.

Stone, Melissa, The propensity of governing boards to plan, in: Non-Profit Management & Leadership, 1 (3/1991), 203-215.

Tahar, Sadri/Niemeyer, Cornelius/Boutellier, Roman, Transferral of business management concepts to universities as ambidextrous organisations, in: Tertiary Education and Management, 17 (4/2011), 289-308.

Toyama, Atsuko, University reform in Japan to usher in century of knowledge, in: JSPS Quarterly, 9 (2004), 2-7.

Tushman, Michael/O'Reilly, Charles, Ambidextrous organizations: Managing evolutionary and revolutionary change, in: California Management Review, 11 (1996), 71-87.

Wilkersmann, Uwe/Schmid, Christian, The impacts of new governance on teaching at German universities: Findings from a national survey, in: Higher Education, 63 (2012), 33-52.

Yamamoto, Kiyoshi, Corporatization of national universities in Japan: Revolution for governance or rhetoric for downsizing?, in: Financial Accountability and Management, 20 (2/2004a), 153-181.

Yamamoto, Kiyoshi, Agencification in Japan: Renaming or revolution?, in: *Pollitt, Christopher/Talbot, Colin* (eds.), Unbundled government: A critical analysis of the global trend to agencies, quangos and contractualisation, London (Routledge) 2004b.

Yamamoto, Kiyoshi, Educational and public accountability of higher education institutions in case of national universities in Japan, in: The Journal of Management and Policy in Higher Education, 1 (2011), 1-19.

Kiyoshi Yamamoto is a Professor of Financial Management at the University of Tokyo, Japan, and was formerly the Research Director for the Center for National University Finance and Management. His areas of interest include university governance and management, public sector reform. Dr. Yamamoto has published widely in leading academic journals.

Session 4

External Relations of Faculties in Higher Education

MIDDLE MANAGEMENT IN THE UNIVERSITY OF THE FUTURE – AN AUSTRALIAN PERSPECTIVE

Leo Goedegebuure[1] and Marian Schoen[2]

[1,2]*LH Martin Institute, Level 1, 715 Swanston Street, University of Melbourne, Australia*
[1]*leo.g@unimelb.edu.au*, [2]*m.schoen@unimelb.edu.au*

Universities operate in an environment that will become more competitive, that will integrate more stakeholders, that will show an increasing diversity of the student body and that will be affected by rapid technological changes. In this paper, the implications of these environmental changes and pressures for university middle management, in particular in Australia, will be explored. Constant reorganisation and restructure bring along current and future challenges that university middle management will have to address, which will include an emphasis on professional development. These challenges will be translated into an action agenda of what needs to be accomplished in the short to medium term if Australian universities are to successfully accommodate the change that is upon them, covering some opportunities and threads.

1. INTRODUCTION

When discussing what middle management will be like in the 'university of the future' the first question to deal with, obviously, is what this future will be and what kind of a university we are talking about. With respect to the future, we can be sure that it will be different from what we currently experience in terms of the environment in which universities operate. There is little doubt that it will be an environment that is more competitive, with private providers entering the domain that previously was the prerogative of relatively protected public universities. It will be an environment where even more stakeholders than originally predicted by Neave (2002) will want something out of universities thus furthering the 'demand overload' that is already there. There is no doubt that with a further expansion into universal tertiary education systems, it is a future where the student body becomes increasingly diverse with all the challenges that brings in

terms of preparation and expectations. And there is no doubt that the future will be shaped by further rapid change in technology, affecting all aspects of our institutions. It is not very difficult to extrapolate this from what we currently are witnessing and experiencing.

The extent to which these trends will result in the gloom and doom predicted by global consultancy firms such as Ernst & Young (2012) and policy think tanks such as IPPR (Barber/Donelly/Rizvi 2013), however, is far from a foregone conclusion. Obviously, we need to be concerned about the traction these kinds of reports get with senior university executives and peak body representatives. These are merely marketing strategies to sell the next fad with respect to organisation structure (or restructure, see further), business re-engineering, and mergers and acquisitions. In this respect, it would be helpful to take into account the far more rigorous work done by e.g. Kennie and Price (2012a; 2012b) in their analysis of what has happened with professional services firms compared to universities, and their take on the new ecology of higher education. Contrary to what one may have thought in the face of increasing global competition, universities have proven to be far more resilient than professional services firms, and truly global universities with campuses across the continents – as is the case for the major five consultancy firms – are yet to emerge. Yet, in the face of the trends identified above, it is equally unlikely that the ecology of our systems will not change. Mergers without a doubt are on the table, as are strategic alliances and partnerships, public and private, and co-opetition increasingly will form an integral part of institutional strategy (Goedegebuure 2012).

In this paper we explore the implications of these environmental changes for university middle management. We do so from an Australian perspective as this is our frame of reference, certainly empirically, but also partly conceptually as we will elaborate upon below. We deliberately use the 'middle management' terminology rather than 'the dean' as we believe the 'university of the future' will be managed in a mixed mode of 'academic' and 'professional' management, an assumption we also will further substantiate below. We begin by a brief sketch of what tertiary education, and more particular universities, are like in Australia in 2013, and what pressures they face. This will lead us to reflect on the one constant that can be found across all Australian universities, the wonderful world of reorganisation and restructure. From this we will discuss the current (and future) challenges that middle management will have to address, which will include an emphasis on professional development. We will translate these challenges into an action agenda of what needs to be accomplished in the short to medium term if our universities are to successfully accommodate the change that is upon us, and we will discuss some of the issues that accompany this.

2. AUSTRALIAN TERTIARY EDUCATION IN 2013

Australia is a relatively new nation and its university sector is young compared to those in Europe and North America. Its first universities were established when 'Australia' was still a set of British colonies; the inauguration of Australia as a nation didn't occur until 1 January 1901. The 'model' followed by Australia's universities was distinctly British. In fact, it has been suggested that the early universities were established 'to recreate the social order and the institutions of the Mother Country' (DEET 1993, 1), rather than as a response to student demand. This also meant that the Australian university system had all the characteristics of an elite system along the classic British lines, and it followed the same path as England in establishing a binary system in the 1960s to deal with the expansion of the system through its Colleges of Advanced Education (CAE).

The year 1989 represents a 'natural' point for analysing change in Australian higher education. This was the first year of the so-called 'Dawkins reforms', through which the then education minister, the Hon. John Dawkins, sought to increase the opportunity for university attendance among people previously 'excluded' from higher education (Dawkins 1987). These reforms are perhaps best remembered because of the reintroduction of tuition fees for domestic students ('HECS', the Higher Education Contribution Scheme), the dismantling of the binary system through institutional mergers and the changes in the way research was funded.

Creating a Unified National System through institutional mergers meant the end of the Colleges of Advanced Education. Government statistics for 1988 list 44 CAEs and 19 universities (DEET 1988, Table 3). These institutions morphed into 35 universities in a relatively short period, through a combination of mergers and take-overs (Goedegebuure/Meek 1991). Few of the existing institutions managed to avoid the considerable pressures to merge (Goedegebuure 1992).

Notwithstanding Dawkins' concept of the "Unified National System", universities are not all the same, and perhaps the biggest point of departure from the 'average' university is the proportion of total research undertaken by a small number of them, locally known as the Group of Eight (Go8), which are the classic pre-Dawkins sandstone research universities. They account for approximately 75% of all competitive research funding available across the university sector. The Go8 would be followed by a second group of research universities comprising another 8 university, though with far less success in attracting competitive research funding, whilst another two groups can be discerned that have little (11 universities) to virtually no (14) competitive research grants income (Pettigrew/Bentley, forthcoming). Thus, research intensiveness is the distinguishing feature in the sector despite the fact that by the very definition used in Australia, all universities are considered to be research universities.

The Australian higher education sector in 2013 is radically different from the one just twenty or so years ago. The major change worth elaborating on has been the massive growth in the sector. Student numbers increased from about 441,000 to over 1,000,000 in the period from 1989 to 2007, an increase of something approaching 130 per cent. The largest growth segment within that came from fee-paying overseas students to compensate for the decline in government expenditure over the same period. Australia has become one of the major destinations for foreign university students after the USA and Britain. In Australia, foreign students' proportion of all enrolments increased from less than 6 percent in 1989 to over 26 percent in 2007.

The current 'higher education' sector comprises 37 multi-disciplinary 'public' universities, a few single discipline public non-university higher education institutions, two private universities and myriad small private providers, many of which can scarcely be described as 'higher education'. We mention these because they feature in government statistics and reports somewhat indiscriminately, along with traditional universities.

When a Labour government returned to power in 2007 a further expansionist policy was adopted aimed at a 40% participation rate for bachelor level study, resulting in a so-called 'uncapping' of student places and the introduction of a demand-driven system. This basically implied that universities could enrol as many students as they could attract and would obtain Commonwealth funding for them. Current enrolment figures have surpassed the 1.2 million mark which has raised two serious policy issues. This first is whether Australia can sustain this level of expenditure on higher education, with the most likely answer being "no". The second is whether universities now are admitting students that would have been better off in Australia's vocational education and training sector, with the most likely answer being "yes".

3. A SECTOR IN CONTINUOUS RESTRUCTURE

Our snapshot of forty odd years of higher education policy making presented above already hints at some of the issues confronting the sector. They can be summarised as follows. For the last twenty years, the Australian university sector has been a sector 'in stress'. Benign neglect turned to serious funding cuts over the Coalition government reign during the 1990s-2000s. A brief reinvestment occurred during the initial Labour reign from 2007 onwards, but this recently has taken a turn for the worse with proposed significant budget cuts in combination with delays in promised expenditure increases – one of the preferred policy options in Australian politics. A more detailed analysis of this can be found in (Goedegebuure/Hayden/Meek 2009; Marginson 2013).

Australian universities have responded to these challenges in two ways. The first has been to further professionalise and maximise the attraction of fee paying international students. And the institutions have been extremely successful in this (Davis/Mackintosh 2011). International education has become the country's third export industry, after coal and iron ore, generating some B$15 (AUD). Having a quarter of an institution's student body coming from outside of Australia no longer is considered remarkable, university campuses have been transformed as have been their surrounding cafes and eateries and local communities, with all sorts of challenges emerging for a truly 'international experience' for foreign students (Arkoudis/Baik/Richardson 2012; Arkoudis et al. 2013). There is common agreement across the sector that if it weren't for the international students, Australian universities would be in very serious financial problems. This makes the sector vulnerable to fluctuations in its two primary markets, China and India, as spouts of ethnic violence against Indian and Chinese students have demonstrated in 2012, raising the question of the sustainability of this dependency and the need for diversifying revenue streams.

The second way Australian universities have responded to the financially challenging environment has been by continuous internal restructure. One would be hard pressed to find one university in Australia that currently (June 2013) isn't experiencing or has just gone through, a significant organisational restructure. This ranges from proposed merger (Central Queensland University with Central Queensland Institute of TAFE), campus closure (Swinburne University of Technology) or campus 'transfer' (Monash University's Gippsland campus to the University of Ballarat), to all forms of faculty restructure, administrative repositioning, internal efficiency drives, and full programmatic restructure, both in the teaching and research domains. In addition, outsourcing and partnering with public and private education providers are the order of the day. And some Australian universities would be engaged in most if not all of the above at the same time.

Managing the major change programmes that these restructures require is both an issue in terms of the volume but also in terms of the internal capability to actually implement and embed change, i.e.: (i) the capability to deal with the necessary project management during the implementation phase, (ii) the capability to than move to sustainability of the implemented change(s), and (iii) the capability to maintain change readiness across the organisation in the context of continuous change .

This raises a different form of the 'demand overload' referred to earlier (Neave 2002). How much restructure can an institution, and more pertinent its constituent parts of academic and professional staff, students, and middle and senior executives, bear before it becomes dysfunctional or, even worse, before it results in disengagement of staff? Ultimately this is an empirical question that for Australia, at least yet, still has to be answered. So far, tolerance has been remarkable if one is to go by the results of the VOICE surveys carried out across the sector (Langford 2010). Although contrary views are expressed through the National Tertiary Education Union channels (cf. NTEU 2012), overall staff satisfaction remains high as demonstrated by these staff surveys (Bentley et al. 2013; Langford 2010). But there is little doubt that this has further raised the management and leadership challenges associated with continuous change (Kotter 2012).

4. MIDDLE MANAGEMENT IN THE UNIVERSITY OF THE FUTURE: TWO FUNDAMENTAL CHALLENGES

An earlier comparative study on university middle management identified Australian deans as a group of professional academic managers (Meek et al. 2010) who find themselves somewhat 'caught in the middle'. They are, in general, part of the senior executive of their university yet also consider themselves to be 'academics at heart'.

Deans are also at the intersection where the institutional strategy is delivered, which today in Australia includes industry engagement, fundraising, and innovation in addition to the usual foci of teaching and learning and research. They must implement and drive strategic change at the faculty level and hence require the capabilities for that as well as for performance in the delivery of corporate targets. We use 'corporate' on purpose as the university enterprise in Australia in 2013 prevalently is seen in these terms by both the Senior Executive and the Governing Boards of our institutions.

Using empirical data collected by Scott et al. (2008), de Boer/Goedegebuure (2009) reconfirm this increasingly complex picture. Today's Australian dean no longer is the 'lone operator' that he or she once was, nor the 'first among equals' that for a long time has been the leading principle. It would be fair to say that in the vast majority of Australian universities the dean now leads the Faculty Management Team. This team normally would consist, in addition to the Dean, of a number of Associate Deans (Teaching & Learning, Research and International), the Faculty General Manager and depending on local circumstances, possibly a Financial Manager and a Human Resource Manager. The Faculty Office would be home to a substantial group of professional staff that work in supporting roles, ranging from student administration to research administration, from finance to human resources, and from strategy and policy to engagement. In short, Australian universities have seen the emergence of professional middle management that complements a similar structure at the central university level. And like in the US, this professionalisation of university administration has been accompanied by growth in the number of professional associations and the size of their membership, which in Australia include the Association of Tertiary Education Managers (ATEM), the Australian Research Management Society (ARMS), the International Education Association of Australia (IEAA), and the Association of Australasian Institutional Research (AAIR).

Despite these obvious indicators of increased professionalisation of university middle management the concept of 'parallel universes' also exist: Australian universities very much are constituted around academic and administrative domains or realities. As the Australian data from the Changing Academic Profession (CAP) study clearly shows (Bentley et al. 2013), Australian academics consider their administrative structures cumbersome and have little love for their management embodied in the structures outlined above. Whilst this may be a reflection of the general disdain academics feel for all things non-academic in universities, Australian academics are more outspoken in this respect than many of their international colleagues (Coates et al. 2011). Quite possibly this is a reflection of the rather dramatic changes that have been let loose on the sector over the past twenty years and that we have briefly summarised earlier. But it most likely also reflects the true nature of management and administration in universities, that by its very nature is contested terrain. It is not for nothing that those in management positions characterise their job as 'herding cats' (Garret/Davies 2010) whilst for many academics 'managerialism' still constitutes the 'dark side'.

A key issue for Australian universities and therefore for its middle management is to what extent these two parallel universes interact or not. No empirical data to answer this question exists to our knowledge, and anecdotal evidence is inconclusive. Much of the issues discussed in the workshops and leadership and management programmes that we have run over the past five years one way or another focus on the 'two worlds' of academe and administration. Most of the observations made are that academics don't (want to) understand why particular strategies, policies, and management as such are necessary, and that administrators fail to understand that their principal role is to support the academic enterprise, not to stifle it. Slow progress is being made in bridging this divide, which makes it a key issue for middle management in the University of the Future, particularly from an Australian perspective.

This is further compounded by the increased blurring of roles between academic and professional staff, the emergence of a so-called 'third space' (Whitchurch 2013) that blends traditionally separate roles, and changes in roles. We will have a more multi-generational workforce, with younger generations seeking more flexible working arrangements, and greater clarity about career paths and futures. For both academic and professional staff there is likely to be an expansion and diversification of roles – reflecting an increasing variety of broad functions required in the future. For example, the expectation that academics and professional staff engage with different stakeholders will require business and commercial capabilities such as negotiation, intercultural awareness and collaborative leadership. At the same time, there will be a further specialisation and division of roles e.g.: reflected in the professionalisation of areas that are developing their own career paths and norms and standards, with professional associations referred to above – student services, international offices, as well as the areas of finance, and HR. As core functions for jobs are becoming more specialised, more general capabilities will also be required – such as the management of multiple functions in a complex environment, delivering a wide transformational agenda, conducting a bridging role with external partners, organisational skills, capacity to create, navigate and lead networks and alliances locally and internationally across sectors, and with business and governments.

There is no doubt that the Australian University of the Future will be a professionally managed institution, if only for the very simple fact that we are talking about large, complex organisations that are required to do substantially more with at best stable resources, but most likely with less resources. This can only be done if our institutions become more agile, with an increased emphasis on effectiveness and efficiency: do we deliver the right outcomes for our various stakeholders and do we do this at the lowest possible costs in a timely manner? This second challenge can only be adequately addressed if the first one – bridging the academic and administrative divide – is dealt with. At the middle management level this implies tailoring institutional imperatives to academic realities for it is within Faculties and Schools that the actual outputs of universities in terms of teaching and learning, research and engagement are being created. It is this tailoring that requires an action agenda if these challenges are to be met in the University of the Future.

5. AN ACTION AGENDA FOR MIDDLE MANAGEMENT – OPPORTUNITIES AND THREATS

In no particular order we see the following operational strategies as essential to effective middle management meeting the challenges outlined above. First, a true professionalisation of the administrative processes at Faculty level is necessary. By this we mean serious professional development that empowers professional staff to truly master their jobs, to take responsibility for their actions and to seek the boundaries of what can be done rather than rigidly stick to prescribed policies and procedures. This implies clear autonomy and accountability principles to be implemented at Faculty level. Whilst some Australian universities are quite exemplar when it comes to continued professional development for its professional staff, for the majority of institutions this remains an area of concern. As is the case for any organisation, unless staff are adequately equipped to undertake their role substandard performance will be the result. This mastery of function in an academic environment needs to be complemented with an understanding of what it is that makes academics 'tick', for it is only then that the bridging we discussed above can actually take place. This 'lived professionalism' is an essential ingredient for the University of the Future and it is here that 'leading by example' is crucial for our middle management teams.

The trend in having academics manage administrative functions at the university level is also an interesting one as is for example demonstrated by shifts in executive portfolios from e.g. the Vice Principal Administration to the DVC Engagement who will have no background in managing such major functions as IT, HR, and Marketing or the technical skills required to strategically drive those functions in a complex organisation and dynamic environment.

Second, an agile organisation requires minimizing bureaucracy, something at which Australian universities do not particularly excel. Admittedly, they cannot be blamed for every bit of paper that needs to be shuffled. A recent study by PhillipsKPA (2012) clearly indicates that there is an overly demanding external regulatory environment that forces universities in duplicating compliance requirements. But equally, our universities are good at self-inflicted compliance and reporting as well. In part this is the resultant of not well equipping staff for their respective roles and tasks identified above, resulting in risk avoidance and 'playing strictly to the hymn sheet' which ought to be remedied if the true professionalisation is realised. In part, however, it also requires a cultural change to truly bring new public management to the fore, rather than an 'over-managed and under-led corporate culture' (Kotter 2012, 28-33).

Third, performance management for academic staff needs to be fully implemented to complement performance management for professional staff. Too often academics are able to 'duck the bullet' because their direct supervisors are not willing or not able to both mentor their staff in an appropriate manner suited to the 21st century (for an extended discussion of this, see Coates/Goedegebuure 2012). This transparency is crucial if the divide is to be bridged for in any organisation – and therefore equally in the University of the Future – it cannot be the case that different rules apply to different groups of employees. This will only reinforce stereotypes that are truly unhelpful.

Fourth, distributed academic leadership needs to be taken seriously. As is the case for professional staff, unless one is equipped to do what needs to be done, underperformance will be the nature of the game. Whilst universities require from their academic staff a proven competency in terms of teaching and learning, no such thing exists when it comes to management. Course coordinators

generally 'learn on the job' and in that process can be forced into all sorts of problematic behaviour. Managing an increasing number of casual/sessional staff is no mean thing, yet preparing academic staff for these challenges is virtually non-existent. If the academic career of the future is to be a career of choice rather than a last resort, increasingly younger academic staff need to be invested with responsibility, and for this they need to be adequately prepared.

Fifth, the future will require a focus on workforce planning and productivity, as well as talent management and capacity development that currently is underdeveloped. Strategic workforce management will be critical and must be a priority that involves determining the institutional capabilities needed to establish and sustain both market position and identity and business strategy. This in turn means defining the skills, capacity, relationships and behaviours required of staff in academic and professional roles as discussed earlier. For example, some academic, enterprise and professional roles will require specific skills in cross-disciplinary collaboration or building institutional collaboration, or managing complex partnership as well as more general need for continuing development across all roles such as a high-level confidence with e-learning and e-business technologies. At the Faculty level we will need leadership, management and governance capabilities, with leaders who can set direction for the future, drive the implementation of strategy, manage uncertainly, deal with complexity and effectively manage risk – and deal with complex finance, people and change management issues. Administrative leaders will need high-level skills in dealing with business uncertainty, risk and ambiguity, through internal development as well as the recruitment of business experience from outside HE. The heads of business support functions will need to ensure greater alignment of their functions with institutional goals, and higher levels of professionalism – seeing a shift from a transactional focus to a more strategic approach to business services, more strategic business partnering model.

The performance and reputation of the University of the Future will be determined by the quality of staff including professional staff – hence a source of competitive advantage – it will become a key differentiating capability between institutions. And since most of the workforce of 2015 and 2020 is already employed in the sector and or the institution, this will require substantial staff development – the pace of workforce change will need to increase to meet these challenges.

REFERENCES

Arkoudis, Sophie/Baik, Chi/Richardson, Sarah, English language in higher education: From entry to exit, Camberwell (ACER) 2012.

Arkoudis, Sophie/Watty, Kim/Baik, Chi/Yu, Xin/Borland, Helen/Chang, Shanton/Lang, Ian/Lang, Josephine/Pearce, Amanda, Finding common ground: Enhancing interaction between domestic and international students, in: Teaching in Higher Education 18/3 (2013), 222-235.

Barber, Michael/Donelly, Katelyn/Rizvi, Saad, An avalanche is coming; Higher education and the revolution ahead, London (Institute for Public Policy Research) 2013.

Coates, Hamish/Dobson, Ian R./Goedegebuure, Leo/Meek, V. Lynn, Across the great divide: What do Australian academics think of university leadership? Advice from the CAP survey, in: Journal of Higher Education Policy and Management 32 (2010), 379-387.

Coates, Hamish/Goedegebuure, Leo, Recasting the academic workforce: Why the attractiveness of the academic profession needs to be increased and eight possible strategies for how to go about this from an Australian perspective, in: Higher Education 64 (2/2012), 875-889.

Davis, Dorothy/Mackintosh, Bruce (eds.), Making a difference – Australian International Education. Sydney (NewSouth Publishing) 2011.

Dawkins, John, Higher Education: A green paper, Canberra (Australian Government Publishing Service) 1987.

de Boer, Harry/ Goedegebuure, Leo, The changing nature of the academic deanship, in: Leadership 5 (3/2009), 347-364.

DEET (Department of Employment, Education and Training), National report on Australia's higher education sector, Australian Government Publishing Service, Canberra 1993.

DEET (Department of Education, Employment and Training), Standard report 16, Canberra (Australian Government Publishing Service) 1988.

Ernst & Young, University of the future; a thousand year old industry on the cusp of profound change. (Ernst & Young) 2012.

Garret, Geoff/Davies, Graeme, Herding cats; Being advice to aspiring academic and research leaders. Axminster (Triarchy Press) 2010.

Goedegebuure, Leo/Hayden, Martin/Meek, V. Lynn, Good governance and Australian higher education: An analysis of a neo-liberal decade, in: *Huisman, Jeroen* (ed.), International perspectives on the governance of higher education, New York & London (Routledge) 2009, 145-159.

Goedegebuure, Leo/Meek, V. Lynn, Restructuring higher education. A comparative analysis between Australia and The Netherlands, in: Comparative Education 27 (1/1991), 7-22.

Goedegebuure, Leo, Mergers in higher education. A comparative perspective, Utrecht (Lemma) 1992.

Kennie, Tom/Price, Ilfryn, Leadership and innovation lessons from professional services firms. London (Leadership Foundation for Higher Education) 2012a.

Kennie, Tom/Price, Ilfryn, Disruptive innovation and the higher education eco-system post-2012. London (Leadership Foundation for Higher Education) 2012b.

Kotter, John, Leading change. Boston (Harvard Business Review Press) 2012.

Langford, Peter, Benchmarking work practices and outcomes in Australian universities using an employee survey, in: Journal of Higher Education Policy and Management 32 (1/2010), 41-53.

Marginson, Simon (ed.), Tertiary education policy in Australia. Melbourne (Centre for the Study of Higher Education) 2013.

Meek, V. Lynn/Goedegebuure, Leo/Santiago, Rui/Carvalho, Teresa (eds.), The changing dynamics of higher education middle management. Dordrecht (Springer) 2010.

National Tertiary Education Union (NTEU),Advocate [various articles] 19 (1/2012).

Neave, Guy, On stakeholders, cheshire cats and seers: Higher education and the stakeholder society. Enschede (Universiteit Twente Inaugural Lecture) 2002.

Pettigrew, Alan/Bentley, Peter, An analysis of research block grants 2001-2013. Melbourne (LH Martin Institute), forthcoming.

PhillipsKPA, Review of reporting requirements for universities. Background and issues paper, Victoria (PhillipsKPA) 12 September 2012.

Scott, Geoff/Coates, Hamish/Anderson, Michelle, Learning leaders in times of change: Academic leadership capabilities for Australian higher education, Melbourne (ACER) 2008.

Leo Goedegebuure is Director at the LH Martin Institute, being active in the field of higher education policy research and management. Prior to his move to Australia in 2005 (University of New England, Centre for Higher Education Management and Policy), Leo was Executive Director of the Center for Higher Education Policy Studies (CHEPS), at the University of Twente, Netherlands. Leo Goedegebuure's research interests are in the areas of governance and management, both at the systems and institutional level, system dynamics including large scale restructuring policies, university-industry relationships, and institutional mergers. Over his career, he has published some 15 books (both monographs and edited volumes) and over 100 articles, book chapters and papers on higher education policy, mergers, quality assessment, evaluation research, differentiation, system dynamics, engineering education, institutional management and comparative research.

Marian Schoen commenced with the LH Martin Institute as Deputy Director in April 2013. She has had extensive experience in governance and executive management in the public and higher education sectors including roles as General Manager of the Melbourne School of Engineering, as Executive Director of the Melbourne Law School, as the Director, Group of Eight Australia Centre Europe in Germany and as a member and now fellow of the Council of the University of Melbourne. Building on her background in constitutional review and administrative law, she has held executive positions in diverse national organisations such as the National Native Title Tribunal and the Wilderness Society. She is an alumnus of the Institute's Master of Tertiary Education Management and the Graduate Certificate in Quality Assurance programmes.

THE INFLUENCE OF GLOBAL AND LOCAL PRESSURES ON FACULTIES

Malcom Cooper

Tourism Management and Environment Law, Ritsumeikan Asia Pacific University,
Beppu, Japan
cooperm@apu.ac.jp

The business of universities is ideas: the creation of ideas through research and their dissemination through education. But increasingly, business is carried out as much across national borders as within, and as more and more university systems cross borders both physically and virtually there is a need for different mind sets and responses from both faculty and students to those of more localised systems. Pressures also derive from the modern audit society – the need to publish in a competitive environment for funding, a lack of permanent jobs due to the erosion of tenure in favour of cheaper short term contracts, and reductions in finance from government in favour of fee generation and other private sources of funds. In the longer term there are the issues of demographics and maintaining student numbers, and the impact of alternative delivery systems such as Massive Online Courses to consider. All in all, the delivery of higher education appears to be heading for a multi-level crisis, this paper examines some of the factors and issues embodied in this situation.

1. INTRODUCTION

The internationalisation of higher education is not a new concept – scholars and students have been crossing international borders for centuries, and adapting to the situation they then find themselves in. However, during the last several decades global movements have intensified pressures on Faculties in higher education. A core reality that distinguishes the current patterns from those of the past is the scale and scope of what such internationalisation encompasses – changes in the breadth and support requirements of students, status differences and conflicts between international and local academic faculty, changes in the educational outcomes required, and the consequent pressures for the reshaping of many university systems. There is also a growing sense that internationalisation has become an *imperative* in present day higher education, not just a desirable possibility. So while the business of universities has always been the creation of ideas through research and their dissemination through education and implementation, increasingly this is as much across as it is within borders. And it is not just based on the free flow of ideas but is also manifested in the global flow of the students and scholars who generate them.

With easier travel and the Internet providing near instantaneous access throughout the world, more and more university systems now cross borders physically and virtually – with a definite and sometimes deleterious impact on academics, their faculty organisations, and university administrators and management, as well as on the students. One of the paradoxical downsides in this apparent widening of educational opportunities is the increasing personal academic isolation deriving from the fragmentation of local university cultures that is occurring with internationalisation, despite an increasing on-line and 24-hour availability opportunity through the internet that is said to lessen this particular impact.

Pressures on faculty also encompass the trend towards an audit society – the pressure to benchmark the public *value* of education through research and other forms of academic output, as in the requirement to publish in an increasingly competitive environment, to erode tenure in favour of cheaper short term contracts, and to reduce institutional finance from government sources in favour of other sources of income. Longer term there is the looming issue of Massive Online Courses and their potential impact on the governance, finance and involvement of faculty, and the current actual impact of the demographic problems now appearing in developed countries. Then there is the local issues of fees – how to justify the expense of university education at institutional and community levels if it doesn't result in better job chances, but results in massive personal debt on the one hand, and an increasingly difficult funding climate in public education on the other. All in all, the purpose and delivery of higher education is heading for a multi-level crisis, this paper examines some of the factors and issues in this trend.

2. BACKGROUND TO THE CASE STUDY

To provide an introduction to the level and extent of global and local pressures on faculty it is instructive to look at the situation of Japan. The falling birth-rate there in recent times, coupled with the desire of the Government and top Japanese universities to become major international players gave rise to some radical experiments in internationalisation the late 1990s. The large *Sophia, Waseda* and *Ritsumeikan* private university organisations, along with the top national public universities like *Tokyo* and *Kyoto*, all recognised that one possible/desirable response to demographic change could be the attraction of enough students from overseas to offset the expected decline in Japanese students, while also fulfilling the desire for

internationalisation held by these universities and the Ministry of Education.

These pioneering organisations also recognised that the bulk of Japan's potential overseas market for the acquisition of higher education students would lie in East and Southeast Asia in the future despite the historically strong linkages of the country with Europe and America. However, to achieve the desired outcome of maintaining and increasing student enrolments from these sources it was also realised that a large part of the curriculum had to be taught at least in English as well as in Japanese (Eades et al. 2005) in order to be attractive to students and their families, regardless of the actual origin of the students. And, in turn this language requirement necessitated the recruitment of bi-lingual and/or solely English speaking faculty and administrative staff.

While Sophia University has taught in English for many years, but only in its *Faculty of Comparative Culture*, it was only in 1998 that Waseda University established a bilingual graduate programme in Asia Pacific Studies, and a separate small *International College* in 2004. Certain much larger public institutions like the University of Tokyo have also established small additions to their overall teaching portfolios, mainly in the form of international graduate schools. However, to date the only really comprehensive response from the private and public sectors of university education in Japan to the problem of falling student enrolments and the globalisation of education opportunities has been that of the *Ritsumeikan Trust*, which in 2000 opened Ritsumeikan Asia Pacific University in Kyushu, the only fully international large Japanese university in the country (there are the smaller Temple University in Tokyo which is an offshoot of an American University originally and teaches in English, and Akita International University).

The first impact in terms of pressures on Faculties that each of the universities that implemented even limited responses to the globalisation and student number questions being experienced in the late 1990s and early 2000s was that there was an immediate need to create a demand on their Faculties to expand English speaking academic resources within an educational system and a domestic community that did not universally value or support such a change. The next section discusses this situation.

3. COMMUNITY ENGAGEMENT AND HIGHER EDUCATION IN JAPAN

Before discussing this set of impacts it should be understood that there is no lack of energy or ideas on how to deal with globalisation pressures amongst the many individuals within the university sector in Japan, but *Faculty* responses to the question of local and international community engagement have been tightly controlled by both University 'social' obligations and the central government in the past. In relation to the first of these, there is still an undercurrent of opposition in many communities to the idea of globalisation, especially if it involves significant numbers of foreign faculty and students being welcomed to the 'local' and Japanese day-to-day environment. The politics of exclusion still impose limits on the ability of institutions like universities to respond to these pressures in ways that might be more easily adopted by those in other countries.

On top of this, up to 1998 the Japanese Education Ministry's ability to support wider community and international engagement by faculty and staff of universities was circumscribed by its view of the proper relationships between national, city or prefecture and private universities and their stakeholder communities. The concept was that a only a few national universities should meet the needs of the nation in respect of globalisation domestically *and* internationally (e.g. the Universities of Tokyo and Kyoto, and similar national level public institutions), city and prefectural universities should be restricted to only meeting the needs of the *local* community that had established them (e.g. Prefectural and City Universities), and

private universities should be mainly responsive to particular niches that could be identified in the higher education market (Eades 2001, 95; Eades et al. 2005).

It is not surprising therefore that this level of control has given little freedom to individual universities, their academics and their Faculty organisations to work with *all* possible stakeholders (and indeed get students from all possible sources) to create a new response to global pressures. Indeed, it is almost as if the problems were at being defined away for most institutions by their local communities. But perhaps that is being too harsh, and the pattern of avoidance of the situation that they now find themselves in should be seen as merely a continuation of the isolationist/exclusionist policies of Japan in many respects since the end of the Second World War (Cooper et al. 2007). Certainly, local communities receive little value from the research done by Universities in Japan that might provide some impetus and rationale for internationalizing change. Research outputs remain restricted to in-house publications in Japanese, if they are written up at all (this does NOT apply to much scientific work, which does and did in the past reach an international audience, but its origins are limited mainly to the national universities and a few private institutions), so there has been in the past little to attract foreign academic and student interest in the social science and humanities-based universities across the nation.

However, soon after 1998 the pace of reform of the Japanese university system began to accelerate when it was realised that this tri-partite division was not particularly useful if Japan wished to compete in an increasingly international education system especially in East Asia, and to offset falling student demand for places at Japanese universities. The first major new initiative came in 1999 when the government conditionally approved a plan to turn national and prefectural universities into independent administrative institutions (*dokuritsu gyôsei hôjinka*) in order to give them more financial and decision-making autonomy to invest in international education (Eades et al. 2005).

Finally, another strongly held assumption underlying this new Ministry approach was that Asia Pacific communities would need and value Japanese undergraduate and postgraduate courses in science and social science disciplines, including tourism and hospitality, as they developed. This assumption, while being critically important to any resultant funding and recruitment model funded by government, was heavily dependent on *accurate* knowledge of these imputed needs, and the availability of *effective* teaching resources and research facilities at a Faculty and institutional level in Japanese universities. The initially disappointing market reaction to the establishment of international schools and/or Faculties at the few Japanese universities involved also however gave rise to the realisation that Japan as a whole did not have enough quality resources in its desired-to-be competitive disciplinary areas, and this has in turn become another major pressure from the global and local change process for the few universities in this country that have tried internationalisation, and a pressure on Faculties that in many cases they are not equipped to handle.

4. DEMOGRAPHIC CHANGES

The second major influence, that of changing student and community demographics, highlights the fact that within the Japanese market is indeed grim (see for example, Cooper/Eades 2005), but this also raises the possibility that a Faculty and/or institution that could rapidly develop an international profile might well be able to offset the accelerating decline in the number of potential Japanese university students (from 2007 domestic student application numbers have been less than the number of places available each year). In the case of the Ritsumeikan Trust for example the establishment of an international university from the outset was therefore seen as the one advantage that might offset all the negative implications of demographic trends and the need for internationalisation, since it would be a source of new international and domestic research and education strength, attract international students, and thus be of interest to both the diminishing Japanese market and the growing markets in other Asian countries. That this was an advantage that had in truth less substance than originally thought has led to a different set of pressures.

Demographic change is thus creating a buyer's market for university education within Japan and elsewhere while the fluctuating needs of the Asia Pacific region in terms of capacity building add a further dimension of uncertainty for a university sector also dependent to a considerable extent on this market for a viable student intake. The resulting responses of a system that, before now, has operated within the close confines of (1) the traditional Japanese entrance exam system, (2) the centralised Ministry of Education control over curricula, and (3) the job-hunting culture (*Shuishoku Katsudo*) that preoccupies students during their 4th year of undergraduate education, are confused and partial, leading to more pressures on Faculties.

The effect of the first of these is to force the broadening of the teaching base and concentration on vocational rather than academic subjects in order to reach a desirability level (*hensachie*) that will attract parents and students to your institution. From this point of view, the strategy of the Ritsumeikan Trust has been particularly interesting. Even though it does not feature in the *Shanghai Jiaotong* University rankings of excellence for example (Eades et al. 2005), Ritsumeikan University does feature prominently in some Japanese rankings, particularly in those by university presidents, for its vigorous expansion during the last 10-15 years. This has been impressive by any standards, and particularly so given the fall-off in the cohorts of high-school leavers across the country as a whole. Originally the Trust operated Ritsumeikan University itself (with 30,000 students, the second largest in Japan), and three high schools. Since the late 1990s, it has opened a second campus of the original university, Biwako-Kusatsu in Shiga Prefecture, a second university, the

Ritsumeikan Asia Pacific University in Beppu, a law school and main administration office on a new separate campus in Kyoto, and is now building a fourth campus in Osaka. But it is the expansion in places (oriented towards vocational education in the sense of job market influence) that seems to be what has fuelled interest and greater student numbers, not rising academic standards; a fact deplored by certain vocal elements in the Faculty context.

5. GLOBALISATION PRESSURES ON FACULTY AND ADMINISTRATIVE OPERATION

A further complication in the case of globalisation in Japan is the necessity to teach undergraduate and graduate programmes in both English and Japanese in a globalizing world. This is new to Japan (except in certain highly sought after and resourced science-based study areas), and means that universities wishing to internationalise have to recruit people from outside who have not been exposed to the Japanese university system. Even when a fully international and bi-lingual university like APU is developed, only the few internationally recruited faculty know anything about international education and how to engage with international communities, and this puts pressure on them and on domestic faculty to reach some form of balance as to how far they can try to do this without causing major collegial disruptions.

International faculty also create an administrative burden for domestically-oriented administrative staff, as documents have to be translated as well as developed for faculty and university governance meetings and student handbooks, and students and faculty members communicated with directly. Given that many of the bureaucrats are not fluent in English, and usually few of the foreign faculty speak and read Japanese fluently enough, there is considerable tension within the institution from this source

that may not be found in other more open international systems.

Other impacts derive from the effect of the basic vocational-teaching structure of the Japanese university (designed for jobs): the generally high student to permanent-staff ratios in social science and the humanities, the increasingly large number of teachers on short, fixed term contracts, the comparatively heavy teaching loads, the large class sizes in some lecture courses, and the devotion by students of a considerable proportion of the final undergraduate year to actual *job-hunting*. Most crucial of all, many of the teaching staff, and not only in the management courses, are from business and administrative rather than academic backgrounds. This system has developed because there has been until recently an emphasis by university management on teaching at the expense of research, to the point at which the time available during the academic year for actually doing research has been increasingly restricted. The management discourse is of course *publicly* about international excellence in research in many universities, including gaining Center of Excellence status as soon as possible (see section 6), but the vocational-teaching logic of the institutions as a whole means that a coherent programme of externally publishable research has yet to take off in many areas.

In addition, the Ministry of Education reserves the right to monitor University degree programmes and approve them on a fixed and immutable four year cycle, which makes it difficult to change or modify the curriculum to respond to pressures that occur on faster time frames. While each new or revamped university curriculum also has to embody the latest Ministry thinking, it is unable from the start to be flexible enough to cope with some of the problems outlined above because of this level of Ministry control and its duration. Individual faculty and Faculties as a whole have very little input within a newly streamlined administrative structure advocated by the Ministry to support their approach to hierarchical governance that is presided over by an executive president and vice presidents who made most of the decisions following Ministry rules. The earlier 'professors' meetings' model in traditional Japanese universities at least had the virtue that some academic input could make its way into institutional decisions.

6. THE AUDIT CULTURE

There has been an increasing emphasis by the Japanese government on the 'performance' of the university sector in terms of the quality of its research and development activities in the past few years, in line with the audit culture becoming prevalent in the rest of the global academic world. This initiative only dates from 2001 and was first embodied in the *Toyama Plan,* which proposed the establishment of a 'Center of Excellence (COE) Program for the 21st Century' (Shinohara 2002). The Toyama Plan had three main planks: the reorganisation and consolidation of national universities (ominously described as 'scrap and build'); the introduction of private sector management methods to public universities; and the establishment of research 'Centers of Excellence' (COE's) at institutions that could produce work of international quality, and see it through to publication. The budget for the latter programme was substantial and in real terms meant that recipient institutions would receive between 100 and 500 million yen per year for at least five years. This money could be used in a number of ways: to fund international exchanges; to fund Ph.D. research and post-doctoral fellowships; to fund research support and training; to support symposia and workshops for Faculty development; and for the provision of new equipment and space for research (Eades et al. 2005).

As we have seen, a major problem for Japanese universities and their faculty wishing to become more globally oriented is that, in the social sciences especially, research outputs remain restricted to in-house publications, if it is written up at all. While this does not apply to much scientific work, it makes it difficult for non-science based institutions to recruit international faculty

who have necessarily become immersed in the audit culture of their places of origin, as they have no benchmark to evaluate the 'standing' of their proposed employer, and the institutions themselves are unwilling to pay the sort of premiums that some 'high flyers' have come to expect within their home systems. While the COE programme was to some extent designed to offset this, the fact is that most of its funding failed to produce the publication output levels desired, and may therefore be deemed to have failed to assist in the globalisation of Japanese universities (Eades 2005).

The latest pressure on those Faculty wanting and prepared to engage in the audit culture is how to cope in today's crowded, dynamic and dis-intermediated digital scholarly environment, where it is ever more difficult to establish the quality, veracity, authorship and authority of information, and, indeed the quality of the publication and other dissemination outlets now available. Universities and researchers need to come to some agreement on how to assign and calibrate authority and trustworthiness to the scholarly sources and channels they choose to use, cite and publish in in the 21st Century. The proliferation of sources and channels like journals, websites, datasets, and social media, some at least of which appear to be merely profit making enterprises, does not assist in this.

7. ADMINISTRATIONS, ADMINISTRATORS AND EXECUTIVES

Despite the obvious globalisation pressures in today's academia, the administrations of many Japanese institutions do not see internationalisation as integral to their identity or strategy. That few institutions have a deep understanding of and commitment to the needed forms of action to cope with global pressures necessarily follows – particularly in an environment of resource constraints and strong competition for institutional funds, time, and attention in most systems. And, even when internationalisation is universally acknowledged as fundamental to the mission of a particular institution, it is not automatically clear what administrative actions should follow and who should take them. As a result, many of the rhetorical statements made in support of internationalisation by administrations and executives are sound-bites that actually show a lack of understanding of the underlying breadth and depth of resource inputs and changes in approaches to the needs of faculty that are needed to drive strategic action in the new globalisation model.

The importance of good strategic planning is of course recognised throughout higher education. All universities understand the need to clearly identify their mission and objectives, their priorities and targets for improvement, and the action to be taken to achieve them, and good progress has been made over a long period in most systems to improve the rigour of strategic planning. But the challenges and opportunities facing higher education administrations are growing every year. There is a constant need to secure greater value from available resources and to audit the academic side of the business. Also the decisions and choices which institutions have to make are becoming ever more complex as the requirements of students, staff, employers and society change. Thus those responsible for planning now recognise that it is quite likely that an institution's long-term objectives will not be achieved exactly as stated, because unforeseen changes in the internal and external environment are inevitable and may require the objectives to be revised. It is essential therefore for all institutions to retain flexibility to adjust as circumstances change, so that they can exploit unexpected opportunities and respond to unforeseen threats. Consequently, there needs to be frequent review of the overall direction to take account of, and adjust to, actual and potential changes to the organisation or its environment, but this must include input from Faculty and Faculties, by no means a foregone conclusion, especially in the Japanese higher education system given the centralizing and exclusion policies and programmes already outlined in this paper.

As a result, it can be seen that the bilingualism and cultural diversity required to support globalisation that is being hesitantly embraced by Japanese universities comes at a price. If the experience of Ritsumeikan APU is anything to go by a number of the new international faculty will not understand Japanese, and the majority Japanese Faculty and staff will not understand English if this is chosen as the second language, so meetings between them require both simultaneous translation and extensive documentation in both languages. There cannot be easy academic or administrative interaction in such a situation. And given the diversity in backgrounds of both staff and students it is also likely that there will be discrepant expectations about teaching standards, on the necessity of language learning dominating the critical first years of a degree, about the appropriate ways to conduct classes and examinations, and about the amount of work to be expected from students.

Nevertheless, there may also be pleasant surprises, such as the outstanding quality of the best students from *both* domestic and international sources, the relatively low student dropout rate in Japan, and the often very high numbers of foreign and Japanese applicants to places when an international system is in place. Many international students become fluent in spoken Japanese and take jobs in Japan, while the standard of English amongst Japanese students is much higher than in the more traditional universities.

One of the concerns of Japanese administrators is that the recruitment of international students usually has to be heavily subsidised with scholarship money from a variety of sources and that, in the longer term, internationalizing universities will either have to attract more foreign students paying their own way or find permanent sources of scholarship funding. This pressure is also compounded by the likelihood that, if as a result of declining scholarship funds the foreign students disappear, the rationale for many Japanese students coming to such a university will also disappear. There is too the problem of attracting, and keeping, good quality international staff. In a traditionally comparatively isolated and very domestic in orientation university system these are practical issues, as much as those arising from such situations as the common lack of nearby international schools for the children of prospective teaching staff.

Finally, the success of an institution will also depend on its research facilities, both in terms of library resources and IT, and in its attraction and treatment of postgraduate students. Clearly therefore some big decisions are seen to lie ahead for the administrations of internationalizing universities and their faculties, as they attempt to raise themselves to a level where they *can* compete with the best schools internationally. However, impetus is given to this attempt by the thought that if Japan *can* succeed in this transformation, the traditional image of Japanese universities as not being able or willing to engage in the international market could be totally transformed to the benefit of all.

8. CAN A DEAN INFLUENCE ANY OF THIS?

New strategic developments that are identified in organisational plans are often subject to challenge and exploration as part of on-going dialogue between senior managers and administrators, and Departmental Heads (Deans) in any university system. If this can be part of a managed process of innovation the central role of the Dean in such processes means that identification of new developments and opportunities to solve some of these problems can be discussed at the same time with Faculty as are the resource implications that might have to be met to achieve them. Table 1 sets out the basic administrative and academic minima in several important areas that have to be present for this to happen.

The younger generation of Japanese (and foreign) academics is probably a Dean's best hope for influencing those factors outlined in table 1. As they take over from the retiring baby-boomers they are, in many cases, a much more international and cosmopolitan group than their predecessors. Many have been educated abroad, are fluent in English and other foreign languages, and are much more interested in publishing their research internationally. Professional associations and departments with COE research money are taking the lead in establishing new journals and publication outlets in English and other languages – online as well as on paper.

As universities become increasingly concerned with their research profiles, we may also expect the collapse of the age-wage salary structure in Japan as the top scholars begin to bargain for salaries and positions commensurate with their value in the global market place. Those that stay in Japan are also likely to put pressure on their institutions to provide a research infrastructure of international standard and this, in turn, will necessitate the professionalizing of library and IT support staff. While many observers remain sceptical as to whether the transformation of national universities into 'independent administrative institutions' noted above will in general lead to any greater globalisation, what it will certainly do is allow them flexibility in budgetary allocations to support the kinds of changes the Deans require.

Table 1: Resource, Individual and Policy Minima
for Effective Faculty Internationalisation

Enabler	Examples
Attitudes	Positive attitudes to new ideas Incentives provided for people to make contributions Acceptance of the importance of calculated risks is present A willingness to learn from mistakes is present
Aptitudes	Decisiveness Understanding of the effect of change on individuals
Skills required for planning and implementing change	Management and financial accounting skills Understanding and development of effective information systems Effective marketing, whether provided internally or externally Flexible teaching and research personnel Planning and monitoring systems in place Counselling available for faculty and students
Resources necessary to support change	Incentives to cut costs and generate income are appropriate Time to prepare and consult is made available Financing to invest in change is made available Information systems and technology are up-to-date Estate and other physical assets are appropriate A commitment to retraining and staff development is present and implemented
Information for managers	Appropriate data for the analysis of past, present, and future policies and procedures is available Project progress reports are required Monitoring reports on action plans are required Management accounts which identify the true cost of activities are mandatory

9. CONCLUSION

A complete re-vamp of an existing educational system is a monumental task, made even more problematical by the youth and relative international inexperience of the system it is intended to replace (the oldest modern Japanese universities date only from the Meiji restoration period of the 1890s). When lack of international experience at the institutional level is coupled with the difficulties of implementing an internationalizing strategy in universities constrained by the whole country's only lukewarm understanding and acceptance of what this actually means, the outcomes identified in this paper could have been predicted. Take for example conflict over course structures between the various parts of the student body that has occurred in those universities embracing these changes. Japanese students still in the main want the old system of non-specialised education, while international students remain unhappy that they cannot easily prove that they studied courses in Japan of relevance to potential employers. Faculty from the two different basic education traditions of the 'west' and Japan are equally as divided about the merits of a disciplinary-based course system.

It should be noted that, in the case of curriculum change and Japanese students however, there are supportive dynamics in play as well. As Eades (2001) points out, Japanese students (and Deans) are becoming much more aware of their positions as consumers in what is increasingly a buyer's market. In fact, those Japanese students that have up to now appeared to resist learning English and being fully involved with international students, are now expressing much greater confidence in this experience. This in turn is increasing understanding of what it means to be an international university and has created an at times fierce defense of internationalisation in the Japanese system by the very people that had to change most.

In addition Japanese companies now make no secret of the fact that they want graduates with specific internationally realisable skills, and parents see their investment in their children's education as protection for their own futures in an increasingly aged Japan. Moreover, a new generation of high school graduates is appearing who have spent lengthy periods abroad on school exchange programmes. These students have fewer inhibitions about speaking English than their counterparts educated only in Japan, and lower resistance to undergraduate course specialisation, and they therefore constitute a natural market for the kinds of initiatives embodied in, for example, Ritsumeikan Asia Pacific University.

In summary, there have been several bold attempts to set up institutions in response to the pressures from the international market in recent years, including the International University of Japan, Akita International University, and initiatives from both Waseda and Ritsumeikan (Ritsumeikan APU). The scale of these experiments varies, from the very small (IUJ and AIU) to the substantial (APU). They also vary in their approach to the language question, and in the markets they are trying to attract, as well as in the strategies they are using. The Faculties at APU appear to be going down the vocational-teaching route, expanding international undergraduate student numbers, while at the same time trying to maintain an academic-research base, particularly in their graduate schools. How far this strategy will work in the long run is an open question, given that the major universities competing in the international market are generally academic-research based in the first instance. Seeing how these programmes fare in the next few years should make for an interesting study, one which will tell us much about whether the Deans in Japanese universities can gain a foothold in the global mass market for research students as well as for undergraduate students, or whether their futures lie more in an increasingly precarious domestic student market resulting from long-term demographic decline in Japan (Kinmonth 2005).

REFERENCES

Bence, Valerie/Oppenheim, Charles, The role of academic journal publications in the UK Research Assessment Exercise, in: Learned Publishing 17 (1/2004), 53-68.

Cooper, Malcom J./Eades, Jeremy S., Landscape as theme park: Demographic change, tourism, urbanization and the fate of communities in 21st century Japan, in: Tourism Review International, 11 (1/2005), 9-18.

Cutts, Robert L., An empire of schools. Japan's universities and the molding of a national power elite Armonk, NY (M.E. Sharpe) 1997.

Daigaku Rankingu [University Ranking]. Tokyo: Asahi Shimbun, Annual.

Eades, Jeremy S. Reforming Japanese higher education: Bureaucrats, the birthrate, and visions of the 21st century, in: Ritsumeikan Journal of Asia Pacific Studies 8 (2001), 86-101.

Eades, Jeremy S./Goodman, Rodger/Hada, Yumiko, The 'big bang' in Japanese higher education, Sydney (Trans Pacific Press) 2005.

Eades, Jeremy S., The Japanese 21st century center of excellence program: Internationalism in action?, in: *Eades, Jeremy S./Goodman, Rodger/Hada, Yumiko* (eds.), The 'big bang' in Japanese higher education. Melbourne (Trans Pacific Press) 2005, 295-323.

Ebuchi, Kazuhiro, Study on the internationalization of universities, Tokyo (Tamagawa Daigaku Shuppanbu) 1997.

Elton, Lewis, The UK research assessment exercise: Unintended consequences, in: Higher Education Quarterly 54(3/2000): 274-283.

Gwynne, Peter, Multidisciplinary centers take up challenges, in: The Scientist 13 (7/1999), 1.

Hall, Ivan P., Cartels of the mind: Japan's intellectual closed shop. New York (Norton) 1998.

Kerr, Clark, The internationalization of learning and the nationalization of the purposes of higher education: Two laws of motion in conflict?, in: European Journal of Education, 25 (1/1990), 5-22.

Kinmonth, Earl., From selection to seduction: The impact of demographic decline on private higher education. *Eades, Jeremy S./Goodman, Rodger/Hada, Yumiko* (eds.), The 'big bang' in Japanese higher education. Melbourne (Trans Pacific Press) 2005, 106-135.

Kuroda, Kazuo, International student mobility for the formation of an East Asian community, in: Creation of New Contemporary Asian Studies Paper 37, Graduate School of Asia Pacific Studies (Tokyo: Waseda University) 2007.

McNay, Ian, The impact of the 1992 research assessment exercise in english universities, in: Higher Education Review 29 (2/1997): 34-43.

McVeigh, Brian, Japanese higher education as myth. Armonk, NY (M.S. Sharpe) 2002.

Shinohara, Kazuko, Toyama plan: Center of excellence program for the 21st Century, in: National Science Foundation Report (Memorandum No.02-05). Tokyo (Tokyo Regional Office), http://www.nsftokyo.org/index.htm, 2002, accessed 20 May 2009.

Taylor, John, A statistical Analysis of the 1992 research assessment exercise, in: Journal of the Royal Statistical Society, Series A (Statistics in Society), 158 (2/1995), 241-261.

Umakoshi, Toru, Internationalization of Japanese higher education in the 1980's and early 1990's, in: Higher Education 34 (2/1997), 259-273.

Watanabe, Takahiro, The path toward East Asia market integration, Tokyo (Keisoshobo) 2004.

Malcolm Cooper is Professor Emeritus and holds the position of Professor of Tourism Management and Environmental Law at Ritsumeikan Asia Pacific University, Beppu, Japan. He is a specialist in tourism management and development, environmental and water resource management and environmental law, and has published widely in these fields. He has held previous appointments at the Universities of New England, Adelaide and Southern Queensland (Australia), and Waiariki Institute of Technology (New Zealand) and has worked in the environmental planning and tourism policy areas for Federal, State and Local Governments in Australia and as both a private consultant and a consultant to the Governments of China and Vietnam.

STRIKING A BALANCE BETWEEN ACADEMIC EXCELLENCE AND SOCIAL RELEVANCE OF THE UNIVERSITY OF THE PHILIPPINES AND ITS FACULTIES

Christian Joseph R. Cumagun

College of Agriculture, University of the Philippines Los Baños (UPLB), College, Laguna 4031 Philippines
christian_cumagun@yahoo.com

The University of the Philippines (UP) became a national university during its centennial celebration in 2008. As mandated by law, UP has the responsibility to promote academic excellence among its staff and foster social relevance to the society. UP may not compete with the world's greatest universities in terms of academic excellence but its service to society contributes to academic excellence. The UP Ugnayan ng Pahinungod and the Farmer Scientists Training Program (FSTP) are two programmes of UP that attest its relevance to society. Over the years, UP has proven itself worthy in achieving academic excellence and social relevance but balancing the two mandates remains a great challenge.

1. INTRODUCTION

The University of the Philippines (UP), founded on June 18, 1908 through Act No. 1870 of the Philippine Assembly under the American period was to give "advanced instruction in literature, philosophy, the sciences and arts, and to give professional and technical training" to every qualified student regardless of "age, sex, nationality, religious belief and political affiliation".

From being a prime legacy of the Americans to the Filipino people to a centre of Philippine nationalism, UP has become centre of excellence in various academic fields and ranked as the top university in the country (QS World University Rankings 2012). The paper attempts to draw strengths of UP and its faculty in terms of academic excellence and social relevance and strike a balance between the two mandates of the university.

2. BALANCE BETWEEN EXCELLENCE AND RELEVANCE

Great Expectations from a National University

The year 2008 marked the centennial anniversary of the University of the Philippines. It is fitting that during this event, a Republic Act No. 9500 was signed into law by the then Philippine President Gloria Macapagal-Arroyo declaring UP not just a state university but as the national university. Known as the UP Charter, both academic excellence and social relevance are stipulated in the document as its rights and responsibilities. Quoting from section 6 on academic excellence:

"The national university has the responsibility to maintain and enhance its high academic standards in the performance of its function of instruction, research and extension and public service."

And in Section 8 on social relevance, the Charter states:

"The national university is committed to serve the Filipino nation and humanity. While it carries out the obligation to pursue universal principles, it must relate its activities to the needs of the Filipino people and their aspirations for social progress and transformation. The national university must provide venues for students' volunteerism."

So much is expected from students and faculty from a national university. Professor Randolf S. David, UP professor of sociology explained it thus: "We expect our students to top all national examinations and at the same time get involved in the affairs of the nation, to be socially aware and engaged. As UP faculty, we are not only expected to teach well but to serve as the mind, the conscience, and the heart of the nation." Indeed, the public citizenry expect a lot from UP because it is subsidised by their taxes.

Volunteerism Programme at the University of the Philippines

The Oblation is the very symbol of UP. It is a bronze statue of a man facing upward with arms outstretched, symbolizing selfless offering of oneself in the service of the nation. The university staff and students draw much inspiration from this symbol – a reminder of their obligation to the Filipino nation. In 1994, President Emil Q. Javier the then president of the UP institutionalised volunteerism among the university constituents by giving free services to communities in greatest need. The establishment of a university-wide programme known as UP Ugnayan ng Pahinungod, taken from the Tagalog term "Ugnayan" which means linkage among volunteers with the university and with the underserved communities was founded. "Pahinungod" is a Cebuano term which is the closest Filipino translation for Oblation, the UP symbol. UP Ugnayan ng Pahinungod is the country's first university-based formal volunteer service programme. At the University of the Philippines Manila (UPM), the

centre of excellence for medicine, faculty and staff provide direct assistance and sharing of knowledge to alleviate the health conditions of communities that lack medical facilities and expertise.

Universities' Impact to Society as Part of Academic Excellence

I believe every university is founded not only to create and transmit knowledge but to play a vital role in shaping the nation where it belongs. Nowadays the academic community pays very particular attention to ranking of universities using parameters that are geared towards academic excellence rather than its impact to society for which social relevance is measured. For example, the world's top universities are ranked according to the number of Nobel prize winners they produced, number of papers published in ISI journals, their impact factor and author citation index. These figures are remarkable but from the viewpoint of a common citizen in the developing world, they are meaningless. The universities in developing countries may find hard to compete with the world's greatest universities by using these parameters. Nonetheless, as long as universities in developing countries do not neglect to serve their own society, they remain relevant and great in the eyes of their people.

According to the incumbent president of UP, President Alfredo E. Pascual, "academic excellence can only be achieved if the results of research and studies can be effectively applied to solve social problems." If only our role as faculty is to teach and to do research, then we remain to be ivory tower university staff. Indeed ensuring the relevance of research and teaching to development needs remains a major challenge of universities.

Case Study: Putting the Power of Science in the Hands of the Farmers

The Farmer Scientists Training Program (FSTP) of University of the Philippines in

Los Baños (UPLB) is a sterling example as to how to use science and technology to solve human problems. Dr. Romulo G. Davide, a UPLB professor emeritus, established the programme in 1994 in his hometown in Argao, Cebu. Since then it has spread to more than 20 provinces and has trained more than a thousand farmer-scientists. FSTP has been designed to liberate poor farmers from the bondage of poverty and hunger and considers farming as a business enterprise. More than 20,000 FSTP trained farmer scientists in Region 7 alone are now successfully engaged in agri-business. Their annual income has increased to more than 100%. Dr. Davide won the Ramon Magsaysay Award, the Asian version of the Nobel Prize in 2012 for founding and leading this programme.

Warning if Universities Neglect Social Relevance

As a young newly-hired instructor at the then Department of Plant Pathology, College of Agriculture, UPLB in 1993, I reflected on the tri-fold mission of the university namely, instruction, research and extension, a concept which was patterned after the mission of the land grant universities in the US. My task as a teacher was on a full-time basis at that time but I had not yet been granted any research or extension work. During that time, I was drawn to the words of President Nicolas Murray Butler of Columbia University about his views regarding public service and extension work of universities. He warned:

"When the universities in any country cease to be in close touch with the social life and institutions of the people, and fail to yield to the efforts of who would readjust them, their days of influence are numbered."

Reflecting on the statement has strongly convinced me that academic excellence is the not the sole purpose for which any university must aim for. There should be a balance among the three functions of the university. Hence every staff of the university should volunteer as a form of public service. Service and learning should always go to-

gether to live an abundant life in the university.

Developing a New Spirit in Our Universities

The Nobel Laureate in Chemistry Professor Richard R. Ernst of the Swiss Federal Institute of Technology (ETH) has envisioned a new spirit in our universities. Developing a new spirit should have four goals: (1) developing societal responsibility, (2) identifying the real needs of our society, (3) solving the most urgent problems with a multidisciplinary approach and (4) educating society's leaders to implementing these societal goals. Professor Ernst has captured the essence of an ideal university to strive for now and in the future. As university faculty, we are engaged in educating responsible leaders with long-term vision to serve the society. This is most important function of universities. These men and women would later on carve the path to excellence and social responsibility. On the basis of these criteria, UP has so far not deviated from its path to develop this new spirit.

3. CONCLUSION

Since its establishment in 1908, UP has proven itself a leader in academic excellence and an advocate of social change. However, Professor Randolf S. David taught "The quest for world class excellence and pursuit of social relevance, in particular, are two gods we have not always been able to serve with equal fidelity." Balancing academic excellence and social relevance remains a major challenge for UP. This can be compared to the metaphorically on walking on two legs. Walking alone on one leg representing the professional leg (academic excellence) is obviously daunting. It's much easier that one should walk with the other leg representing the compassionate leg (social relevance) to lead and serve. As UP embarks on its next century, its faculties should not serve only as scholars but as agents of change with societal responsibility.

REFERENCES

David, Randolf S., The Burden of Being a National University. Lecture presented during the University System-Wide Conference, Olangapo City, 20-22 May 2009.

Ernst , Richard R., Taking Responsibility for a Better Future. Unpublished.

Pascual, Alfredo E., Making UP a great university. Investiture of Alfredo E. Pascual, 20th President of the University of the Philippines. September 15, 2011.

Rankings 2012.Top Universities. Accessed 19 October 2013.

The University of the Philippines Charter of 2008. An Act to Strengthen the University of the Philippines as the National University.

Christian Joseph R. Cumagun is the Associate Dean of the College of Agriculture and professor of plant pathology at the Crop Protection Cluster, University of the Philippines Los Baños (UPLB). He obtained his B.S. Agriculture and M.S in Plant Pathology from UPLB and his Doctor of Agricultural Sciences (*magna cum laude*) from the University of Hohenheim, Stuttgart, Germany.

Session 5

**Performance Controlling of Faculties
in Higher Education**

BIG DATA IN FACULTY PERFORMANCE MEASUREMENT: THE DEAN'S ROLE IN THE BRAVE NEW (DATA) WORLD

Tobias M. Scholz

Chair for Human Resource Management and Organisational Behaviour, University of Siegen,
Hoelderlinstrasse 3, 57076 Siegen, Germany
tobias.scholz@uni-siegen.de

Typically, performance measurement systems in faculties are dominated by standard parameters of external stakeholders, even though faculties have highly specific contextual factors. Therefore, the faculty's steering requirements are often not met. Furthermore, there is an increasing amount of data available (big data). Deans could use them in order to overcome the limitations of measuring faculty performance based on standard parameters. In this paper, it will be proposed to utilise big data as a source for a more elaborated faculty performance measurement system. Since big data implies an increasing technological dependency, however, the role of the dean has to develop into a supervisor for the big data strategy and usage, also focusing on critical aspects like accuracy, transparency and privacy. Due to the dean's role it will be possible to set the data into a human context, to increase acceptance, and to make an advanced performance measurement more fitting towards the unique setting of a faculty.

1. INTRODUCTION

Faculties are complex systems and due to recent university reforms and the increase in velocity that require changes, it becomes increasingly complicated to monitor the performance within faculties. Furthermore, there are several stakeholders that have varying definitions of performance that interestingly lead to a set of always similar standard measurements criteria such as number of publications or the amount of external funds. Those stakeholders mostly come from outside the faculty, for example the university management or the ministries for higher education. These performance parameters go beyond the disciplinary culture. Such standard performance controlling measurements are inadequately or even not at all capturing the disciplinary characteristics as well as the highly specific steering requirements of a faculty. Even though it seems inadequate to use the same parameters for cross-faculty comparisons, this exactly happens. For example, although third-party funds are consequently higher in engineering than in literature studies, this performance criterion is often used in order to legitimise structural changes at the expense of single faculties within a university. It is, therefore, necessary to consider faculty particularities in the faculty performance measurement systems.

There are several ways to tackle faculty performance controlling: based on self assessment, on key performance indicators, on human capital measurement systems, on strategic faculty management, on economies of scale or on quality management. And there are several more possibilities to measure performance. However, one common denominator in the discussion is that data usage is the crucial challenge. Even though there is an increase in data availability, there is also an increase in data complexity. It is essential for the performance measurement and therefore for the decision making process that there are accurate and relevant data available for establishing a widely accepted faculty performance measurement. Such a process needs a distinct strategy how to deal with the flood of unspecified data, recently coined as 'big data'.

Big data is nowadays the omnipresent buzzword in business and research (Kraska, 2013). Even though there is a hype about the potential of big data, it still looks ambiguous. Supporters promote it as a miraculous solution for modern problems and obstacles, while opponents see it as the sacrifice of any privacy. Since it is not deniable that big data has big potential, applying it still resembles the search for a needle in a haystack. It is therefore essential to plan before implementation (Strohmeier 2007) and start "with questions, not data" (Lavelle et al. 2011, 25).

Especially in the field of higher education big data could be a benefit for modern problems. Subsequently this complex system already generates a vast amount of data that is currently only used for limited purposes. Using this mine of data could help improving a faculty's performance controlling and consequently integrate the faculty's specific circumstances to it. In order to reach this, a big data strategy has to be formulated and executed by a person that has the inside view within the faculty and has the oversight over the data. Therefore, the dean will be the anchor point within a big data strategy of a faculty.

With this paper I want to identify the capabilities of big data to support the performance measurement and controlling within a faculty. Furthermore, I will present the role of the dean within this brave new (data) world and show the chances and risks that have to be mastered in the usage of big data. There are several obstacles until an implementation of big data within a faculty can succeed and obtains a "human face" (Smolan/Erwitt 2013).

2. BIG DATA

"We know our brave new world is being transformed by data" (Hilbert 2008, 8). Re-

searchers state that we are living in a period of big data (Boyd/Crawford 2012, Tene/Polonetsky 2012) and that big data is too big to disregard (Simon, 2013). These days we are surrounded by data and everything as well as everybody is constantly producing data. This sheer amount of data makes it difficult to use classical and out-dated analytical tools to evaluate and finally utilise the data. Big data is moving beyond relational databases (Codd 1970) and is no longer only structured data (Davenport et al. 2012). Interestingly, the definition of big data is not yet clear-cut. Although big data is an emerging and relatively young discipline, the origin of the term is still debated (Diebold, 2012). In addition, big data is also missing a precise definition and is commonly characterised based on dimensions (Schroeck et al. 2012).

Big data is originally categorised in three dimensions: volume, variety and velocity (Laney 2001). Volume states the amount of data that is collected. Big data volumes are currently measured in petabytes (1,000 terabytes), however, the overall amount of data collected is rapidly increasing (McAfee/Brynjolfsson 2012). Variety describes the types and forms of data collection. Data can be collected in structured or unstructured ways and there are myriads of forms, for example numbers, text, audio and video (Aakster/Keur 2012). Velocity is about the pace data is generated and analysed. The speed can be directed to the focus towards data collection and to the challenge to analyse data in real-time (Hendler 2013). Based on recent developments there is a discussion of adding further dimensions to the definition of big data. One recently proposed dimension seems to establish in research, called veracity (Schroeck et al. 2012). This dimension is about the data uncertainty and impreciseness and since the amount of data is large, it could include inconsistencies or incompleteness. There could be errors, redundancies or corruption within big data and such problems lower the veracity of any predictions based on data (Zikopoulos et al. 2012). Researchers are constantly looking for expansions in the dimensions of big data and currently discussing about the inclusion of topics such as privacy and value.

Data is part of the hierarchical view of knowledge (Alavi/Leidner 2001). This view states that data leads to information, information leads to knowledge. As we can see in figure 1, data evolves into knowledge and based on that, decisions can be taken. Data by themselves are informative but do not give insights for decision making or planning. Only by context (Kidwell et al., 2000) and supplied with meaning and by understanding relations (Alavi/Leidner 2001), data becomes information. Information grows to knowledge by combination with experience, cognition, and competence (Zins 2007). Knowledge is, therefore, necessary to deal with given data and information (Kedebe 2010). In analogy to data, big data will as well be essential for any information-based planning process. This hierarchical view underlies the value chain process where data leads to decision (Miller/Mork 2013).

Figure 1: From Data to Knowledge
(Serban/Luan 2002, 9)

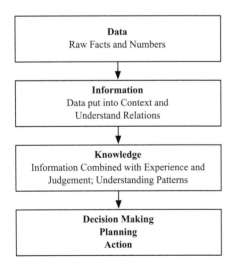

A data value chain (figure 2) is an exemplary process that can be conceptually transferred to the use of big data. Therefore, also big data has to be prepared, organised and finally integrated before it can be analysed.

Figure 2: The Data Value Chain
(Miller/Mork 2013, 58)

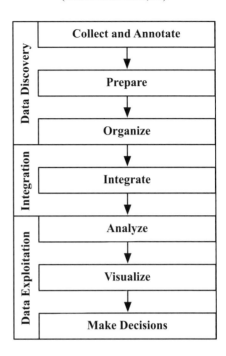

At the beginning, big data has to be collected and often it is the case that this data already exists. After the collection, big data has to be allocated within a database system, providing for specific security and privacy policies. It is evident that access has to be regulated. In addition, any organisation has to record which data are collected. After data preparation, a process of big data organisation gives the collected data a sorted form. This is maybe not important for a finite usage of big data, but all the more important for a permanent usage. Connections and relations within the database can emerge through time. New sources can become available and the database will be enhanced. Subsequently, it becomes evident that data organisation is mandatory in order to sustain a long-time usage of the database. Furthermore, such a widespread organisation can improve the data usage for any department and any purpose within an organisation. Afterwards, big data integration is required before it can be analysed. "Data integration is the problem of combining data residing at different sources, and providing the user with a unified view of these data" (Lenzerini 2002, 233). Such an alignment is necessary to compare, for example, log data and video files. Without such integration process the analysis would be problematic and relations would not be found. At the end of this task, big data will be analysed. There are many technologies that are capable to analyse data; for a detailed discussion it is recommendable to review McKinsey's (2011) list of technologies (e.g. data mining, network analysis et cetera).

In this paper, I will not review technologies, but focus on useful relations and connections of big data that are currently available. Those relations will be researched concerning the purpose of this paper, i.e. faculty performance measurement. Eventually, through this data analysis, in particular a faculty might get a clear picture how the data can be linked towards its specific context.

3. BIG DATA IN FACULTIES

An essential part of the usage of big data is a contextualisation towards its field. Faculties have a unique context based on their discipline, their size within a university, their academic success and, most important, the faculty members. "Big data does not create value, however, until it is put to use to solve important challenges" (Schroeck et al. 2012, 11). Such a challenge is a faculty performance measurement system that intends to measure performance based on the contextualisation of a faculty. This subsequently means that specific context factors of faculties will influence their performance measurement system.

Potentially, there are several forms of data accessible in faculties. Schroeck et al. (2012) specify the following types: transactions, log data, events, e-mails, social media, sensors, external feeds, RFID scans or POS data, free-form text, geospatial data, audio data, images and videos. The question that arises from those forms is: What data can be

collected with those types in context of faculty performance measurement?

I will propose exemplarily some data sources that could be relevant for faculties. First, any kinds of faculty-wide surveys like benchmarkings, employee surveys, balanced scorecards or human capital valuations (Scholz/Stein/Bechtel 2011) can be used to describe the faculty context, for example "hard facts" such as the faculty's competitive position compared to similar faculties as well as "soft facts" such as academic staff commitment and retention. In addition, faculties can collect data (for the later utilisation in an aggregated way) from personnel files, external funds situation, shift schedules, project management, staff assignment, faculty internationalisation status, sickness absence rates, compensations and contract regulations. Other sources will be the common performance indicators in academia such as numbers of publications, graduations, students, funding and evaluations. Such data can be explicitly collected and is described as formal data.

Big data can also generate informal data. Maybe this information becomes useful in a performance measurement purpose, but had once been collected for a different purpose. An example for data with additional value is metadata, which can be described as data about data (NISO 2004). For example, in respect to an e-mail, metadata also records information about the IP address, time zone and several additional data. Other sources are log data, sensors or geospatial data. This data can be used to identify the position of any device and based on the data movements within a building can be tracked (OpenDataCity 2013). Subsequently, movement patterns of people (of course, not of single persons, but of groups in order to uncover process dynamics or informal structures) can be tracked through the data generated by faculty-owned devices. It is, however, important to state that data on its own has no additional value; without its contextualisation it will be impossible to understand the behaviour of the underlying sample (Boyd/Crawford 2012). Faculty members publishing only relatively few journal articles within a year seem to perform poorly, but given a challenging teaching situation with many students, the faculty members might show an acceptable overall performance.

This leads to a crucial part within the data value chain: what to do with this data that are collected and integrated into a form that is usable? We have to keep in mind that the "interpretation is at the center of data analysis. Regardless of the size of data, it is subject to limitation and bias" (Boyd/Crawford 2012, 668).

4. DEAN'S ROLE WITHIN THE BRAVE NEW (DATA) WORLD

If the process of data interpretation is limited and biased in general as well as in a specific faculty, it seems an intelligent strategy to select a person whose bias is based on the contextualisation of the own faculty. Therefore, the dean should have the competencies to lead the big data contextualisation process. The dean's role is in general to deal with conflicting interests within the faculty and to negotiate faculty interests with the outside environment in the context of the academic discipline (Del Favero 2006) what makes a dean capable of overseeing the complete faculty context.

In order to systemise the dean's role as the head of the performance measurement system within the big data strategy, we will follow the value chain stated in figure 2. In the first phase of collection of data it is crucial to establish the basic rules of privacy and data security and furthermore control that privacy and security will be maintained. In the preparation phase the main questions will be: Who will have access to the data and to which degree do those people have access? Some information will have to remain private, others will be irrelevant for certain purposes, and all data is at the end overwhelming for any single user. Here are some rules needed for a collaborative filtering of the big data. Organisation and integration will be also a controlling task. The dean has to check that data will not be changed or removed. However, data discovery and data integration are mostly technical and straightforward.

Data exploitation will be one of the most interesting stages in the big data-based performance measurement. Here, methods like data mining and algorithm-based search for patterns and correlations have to be applied. „Algorithm validation is crucial" (Amaral, 2013). The final dataset is expected to fit for a specific faculty and their faculty members; it is, therefore, essential to keep some scepticism towards the results of that data analysis. How can the results be used for the performance measurement? Do the results fit to the context within the faculty? And how is it possible to use the data to derive improvement recommendations for performance management in the faculty?

The visualisation and decision making parts are the key tasks for the dean. Such data can help to establish performance profiles in real-time and see the performance patterns of faculty substructures to any given time or period. Furthermore it is possible to reveal aspects that have not been discovered before based on correlations. In addition, it will be possible to identify typical behavioural patterns and by that reduce complexity. Perhaps there are several performance-related archetypes within the faculty, each contributing towards the overall faculty performance in a different, but important way. Ideally, it will be possible to establish additional benefits by consequently big data-based decisions (in particular, since most of the data already exist).

Using big data for the performance measurement, such a system has to be implemented in the faculty. Faculty members have to be convinced of the advantages, their resistance has to be overcome (Doppler/Lauterburg 2008), and acceptance has to be generated (Drumm/Scholz 1988). In order to achieve this goal, transparency is a promising way (Richards/King 2013) as well as clear and precise privacy rules (Ohm 2013) are. Furthermore, the dean should realise that the performance measurement is temporary and should be dynamic and changeable. Even though the advanced big data-based system might be better than the previous one, it should continually be questioned and improved. Another important factor to minimise resistance is, that decisions are data-driven but not decisions made by the algorithm (Chien/Chen 2008) or based on predictive analytics (Siegel 2013). In the end, the dean acts as a systemic and holistic supervisor of the big data process, ensuring to "place data in a human context" (Thorp 2011).

5. CONCLUSION

In this paper, big data was conceptualised to improve performance measurement within a faculty and align its parameters to the specific situation of a faculty. It becomes obvious that a context-related faculty performance measurement is possible from the technical perspective and could have a beneficial value towards the faculty. But without the "human context" (Thorp 2011), this will feel like any other unspecified external and number-oriented approach. It is therefore essential that the system is connected and supervised within the faculty. Furthermore, the system should be tuned to the faculty's context and retrofitted in case of changes. The emotional connection becomes even more relevant due to the increasing attention to the topics of transparency and privacy as well as ethical usage of big data. The dean can inherit such a leading role and help optimising the system's fit. If a human face can be signalised, big data bears the opportunity to improve the faculty's performance and help "finding hidden value that no one else is going after and capturing it for yourself" (Lay 2012).

REFERENCES

Aakster, Laurens/Keur, Ron, Big data: Too big to ignore. What organizations can learn from the American presidential elections, in: Compact (2/2012), 1-8.

Alavi, Maryam/Leidner, Dorothy E., Knowledge management and knowledge management sys-

tems: Conceptual foundations and research issues, in: MIS Quarterly 25 (1/2001), 107-136.

Boyd, Danah/Crawford, Kate, Critical questions for big data. Provocations for a cultural, technological, and scholarly phenomenon, in: Information, Communication & Society 15 (5/2012), 662-679.

Chien, Chen-Fu/Chen, Li-Fei, Data mining to improve personnel selection and enhance human capital: A case study in high-technology industry, in: Expert System with Applications, 34 (1/2008), 280-290.

Codd, Edgar F., A relational model of data for large shared data banks, in: Communications of the ACM 13 (6/1970), 377-387.

Davenport, Thomas H./Barth, Paul/Bean, Randy, How 'big data' is different, in: MIT Sloan Management Review 54 (1/2012), 22-24.

Del Favero, Marietta, An examination of the relationship between academic discipline and cognitive complexity in academic deans' administrative behavior, in: Research in Higher Education 47 (2006), 281-315.

Doppler, Klaus/Lauterburg, Christoph, Change Management. Den Unternehmenswandel gestalten, Frankfurt/Main (Campus), 12. ed. 2008.

Drumm, Hans J./Scholz, Christian, Personalplanung. Planungsmethoden und Methodenakzeptanz, Bern – Stuttgart (Haupt), 2. ed. 1988.

Hendler, Jim, Broad data: exploring the emerging web of data, in: Big Data 1 (1/2013), 18-20.

Hilbert, Martin, How much information is there in the "Information Society"?, in: significance 9 (4/2012), 8-12.

Kebede, Gashaw, Knowledge management: An information science perspective, in: International Journal of Information Management 30 (5/2010), 416-424.

Kidwell, Jillinda/Vander Linde, Karen M./Johnson, Sandra L., Applying corporate knowledge management practices in higher education, in EDUCAUSE Quarterly 4 (2000), 28-33.

Kraska, Tim, Finding the needle in the big data systems haystack in: IEEE Internet Computing 17 (1/2013), 84-86.

Laney, Doug, 3D data management: Controlling data volume, velocity, and variety, in: META Group Application Delivery Strategies (2001), 1-3.

Lavelle, Steve/Lesser, Eric/Shockley, Rebecca/Hopkins, Michael S./Kruschwitz, Nina, Big data, analytics and the path from insights to value, in: MIT Sloan Management Review, 52 (2/2011), 21-31.

Lay, Dwane, Why the WSJ is dead wrong nbout Moneyball, in: http://leanhrblog.com/why-the-wsj-is-dead-wrong-about-moneyball/, 17.04.2012, retrieved on 16.09.2013.

Lenzerini, Maurizio, Data integration: A theoretical perspective, in: Proceedings of the 21st ACM SIGMOD-SIGACT-SIGART Symposium on Principles of Database Systems (2002), 233-246.

McAfee, Andrew/Brynjolfsson, Erik, Big data: The management revolution, in: Harvard Business Review 90 (10/2012), 61-68.

Miller, H. Gilbert/Mork, Peter, From data to decisions: A value chain for big data, in: IT Professional 15 (1/2013), 57-59.

National Information Standards Organization, Understanding metadata, Bethesda (NISO Press) 2004.

Ohm, Paul, Branding privacy, in: Minnesota Law Review, 97 (2013), 907-989.

OpenDataCity, re:log – Besucherstromanalyse per re:publica W-Lan, in: http://apps.opendatacity.de/relog, 2013, accessed on 28.08.2013.

Richards, Neil, M./King, Jonathan H., Three paradoxes of big data, in: Stanford Law Review Online, 66 (2013), 41-46.

Scholz, Christian/Stein, Volker/Bechtel, Roman, Human Capital Management, München (Luchterhand) 3. ed., 2011.

Schroeck, Michael/Shockley, Rebecca/Smart, Janet/Romero-Morales Dolores/Tufano, Peter, Analytics: The real-world use of big data – How innovative enterprises extract value from uncertain data, in: IBM Global Business Services (2012), 1-20.

Serban, Andreea M./Luan, Jing, Overview of knowledge management, in: New Directions for Institutional Research 2002 (113/2002), 5-16.

Siegel, Eric, Predictive Analytics: The power to predict who will click, buy, lie, or die. Hoboken (Wiley) 2013.

Simon, Phil, Too big to ignore – The business case for big data, Hoboken (Wiley) 2013.

Smolan, Rick/Erwitt, Jennifer, The human face of big data. New York (Sterling) 2013.

Strohmeier, Stefan, Research in e-HRM: Review and implications, in: Human Resource Management Review, 17 (1/2007), 19-37.

Tene, Omer/Polonestsky, Jules, Privacy in the age of big data, in: Stanford Law Review Online 64 (63/2012), 63-69.

Thorp, Jer, Make data more human, http://www.ted.com/talks/jer_thorp_make_data_more_human.html, 09.2011, acccessed on 16.09.2011.

Zikopoulos, Paul/Deroos, Dirk/Parasuraman, Krishnan/Deutsch, Thomas/Corrigan, David/Giles, James, Harness the power of big data – The IBM big data platform, New York (McGraw Hill) 2013.

Zins, Chaim, Conceptions of information science, in: Journal of the American Society for Information Science and Technology 58 (3/2007), 335-350.

Tobias M. Scholz studied Business Administration at the TU Kaiserslautern, Goethe University Frankfurt and UCLA Anderson. After his diploma, in 2010 he started his Ph.D. at the Chair for Human Resource Management and Organisational Behaviour at the University of Siegen in Germany. He is primarily interested in the field of big data and the influence data can and will have on Human Resources and organisations – a field where a critical discussion is essential to reveal potential and risks. Other interests are concerning the increase in complexity and dynamics in modern Human Resources and organisations. He co-publishes the bi-annual eSports Yearbook, which is a collected edition about stories and research in the competitive gaming scene. He also published in the Thunderbird International Business Review and the Journal of Virtual Worlds Research.

KPI-BASED STAFF AND FACULTY EVALUATION IN THE COLLEGE OF ENGINEERING TECHNOLOGY, CANTHO UNIVERSITY, VIETNAM

Chi-Ngon Nguyen

CanTho University, 3/2 Street, CanTho City, Vietnam
ncngon@ctu.edu.vn

This paper presents some first results on trial running a KPI-based staff and faculty evaluation tool in the College of Engineering Technology (CoET), at the Can Tho University, Vietnam. In the old evaluation progress, at the end of a school year, top 30% "excellent" staff and faculties were voted by an emulation committee. The polling result of "excellent" rank always comes to people who are the managers of the organisation or the leaders from the communist party such as heads of departments, dean board and general secretary of the party. Young faculties have less chance to achieve the excellent rank. Therefore, there is a lack of motivation for them to dedicate themselves to the college. After the development of a KPI-based evaluation tool and applying it in the school year 2012-2013, the results indicated those faculties who have involved in research and publication getting more chance to be ranked as excellent persons. And the number of people who hold high positions in the organisation with teaching only, and without doing research is decreased up to 40% in total of excellent rank of the college comparing to the data of the last 2 years.

1. INTRODUCTION

Staff and faculty evaluation can serve to improve a higher education institution, and it can help to make decisions for retention, promotion, tenure and salary increases (Cashin 1996). However, for a long time, this activity has not been effectively implemented in many universities in Vietnam, especially in the College of Engineering Technology (CoET), Can Tho University (CTU). In this paper, we present a case study of using key performance indicators (KPI) for staff and faculty evaluation in the CoET.

Background and Context

Founded in 1996, CTU is a multidisciplinary university in Vietnam. CTU's main missions are training, conducting scientific research, and transferring technology to serve the regional and national socio-economic development. With 2,038 staff and faculties, CTU offers 89 undergraduate programmes and 40 postgraduate programmes for over 50,000 students (CTU 2012). CTU is organised by 15 schools and colleges. At one of biggest colleges in CTU, CoET was established in 1977. It offers 15 bachelor programmes and 10 master joint-programmes for over 6,000 students in engineering (CoET 2012). CoET has 169 faculty and 39 staff being organised in 7 departments, 3 service centres, 1 mechanical workshop and 44 laboratories. At beginning of the new dean tenure, the CoET's dean board made a SWOT analysis and identified some weaknesses of CoET including:

Income of the faculty is low, especially young faculty and those who are purely administrative. This leads to the liability for the work psychologically affected, "foot in, foot out" alike. It does not reassuring for staff and faculty work, therefore the efficiency is not high. Internal potentials have not been used, especially the collaboration within the college in the fields of scientific research, technology transfer, and goods production. The quality of higher education has not fully been verified, and postgraduate training has not been well organised. The administrative work consumes a lot of time for too many meetings while the information flow is not really smooth and efficient. The number of students per class is high. Scientific prestige of the faculty is low; scientific publications are weak; tasks involved in scientific research of the faculty are not required so that many staff members just purely teach; facilities still have not met the needs of scientific research, especially basic studies. This may affect the search efficiency for projects, especially projects with foreign elements and scientific research contents. The potential contributions from alumni, companies and enterprises are not fully exploited for the development of the college.

One of most important reasons causing these weaknesses is a lack of effective tools for staff and faculty evaluation although this activity has been done in the college. Indeed, every school year, staff and faculty are rated into four ranks of "excellent", "good", "fair" and "poor" (MoET 2012). A person who has an "excellent" rank will receive many benefits on getting higher priority in increasing salary and rewards (Vietnamese Congress 2003). Due to the regulation of the Ministry of Education and Training (MoET), only 30 percent of total staff and faculties in the college can be ranked as "excellent" persons (MoET 2012). For a long time, the progress of staff and faculty ranking needs several rounds from department level to college level based on voting impulsively by an emulation committee. Finally, the "excellent" rank always comes to people who are the managers of the organisation or the leaders from the party such as heads of departments, dean board and general secretary of the communist party, etc. Young faculties have very little chance to achieve the excellent rank. Therefore, there is a lack of motivation themselves to them to dedicate for the college. That is a problem in the CoET.

Changing in the CoET

At the new dean tenure for 2012 to 2017, the CoET's managers have strengthened the college strategic plan. In this strategy, by 2017 the college has to achieve six basic goals, including:

Personnel who are involved in the common activities of the college will receive additional income at least equal to his/her base salary. At least 05 training programmes will be certified with the quality assurance in undergraduate education with AUN standard, while the remaining programmes will be completed with quality self-assessment. At least 01 training programme will be linked to international training system. Offer the master training for at least 04 majors and work towards doctoral training. Sufficient competitive capacity to acquire funding for scientific research, and international cooperation projects, reaching VND 10 billion/year. Consolidate and build a modern working and teaching-learning environment.

Pursuing above goals, a KPI-based staff and faculty evaluation tool is developed and applied for the school year 2012-2013. Some first results will be presented in the following sections.

2. KPI – BASED EVALUTION TOOL DEVELOPMENT

In Vietnam, employee evaluation procedure is stipulated by the Ministry of the Interior with eight criteria that all public organisations have to follow up, including:

- Criteria 1: Execution of policies and laws of the State
- Criteria 2: Working results
- Criteria 3: The spirit of discipline
- Criteria 4: The spirit of collaboration in the work
- Criteria 5: Honesty in the work
- Criteria 6: Lifestyle and ethics
- Criteria 7: The spirit of learning to improve professional capacity
- Criteria 8: The spirit and attitude at

work

At the end of each year, based on these criteria, each organisation has their own process to evaluate employees. For a long time CoET did not develop its quantitative evaluation tool that was causing a problem for promoting staff and faculties while there exist many comprehensive systems for the evaluation of staff faculties in HEIs (Paulsen 2002). Researchers suggested assigning credits for all activities of staff and faculties (Rikakis 2009). Using KPIs for that purpose is a good way for performance measurement (Fitz-Gibbon 1990, Reh 2013).

Since 2012, CoET has developed a KPI-based evaluation tool that the proportion of each criterion is presented in table 1. The working results of staff (i.e. non-academic staff) and faculties (i.e. academic staff) are most important appropriating 50% of total credits. The KPIs have been defined differently for staff and faculty in the college. However, within this section, we only present the KPIs for faculty evaluation.

Applying this KPI-based evaluation tool, each faculty needs to clarify and provide proofs for his/her successes. For getting an excellent rank, the faculty has to meet the minimum requirement for all criteria above, indicated by minimum value of points. And top 30 percent of staff and faculties who have highest marks will be ranked as excellent persons.

In this evaluating process, after getting the self-assessment data from each faculty, it is assessed at department level and then at the college level. The ranking of staff and faculty ranking decision will be submitted to the university council for getting approval. Results of the first trial run in the academic year 2012-2013 are presented in the next section.

3. RESULTS AND DISCUSSION

The KPI-based evaluation tool was applied at CoET for the school year 2012-2013, just finished on May 2013. In comparison to the voting evaluation process before, the results

are encouraging to continue to improve and apply for the future. Indeed, figure 1 and figure 2 present the excellent ranking results for three school years from 2010-2011 to 2012-2013.

In figure 1, the top 30% of staff and faculties who were ranked as excellent persons are divided by groups of age. Before applying KPIs, the excellent rank was voted to the old persons with the age from 46 to 60. After using KPIs, the excellent rank focuses on the young ones with the age from 36 to 40. Concretely, the number of persons who were ranked as excellent ones with the age in group of [36-40] increased from 4% to 33% of total excellent persons, and the age in group of [51-55] and [56-60] decreased from 57% to 9%.

Figure 1: Number of excellent persons for three years divided by groups of age

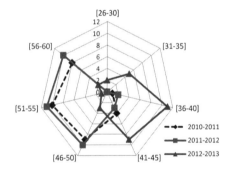

Figure 2: Number of excellent persons for three years divided by groups of position

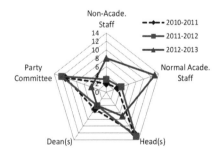

Similarly, when divided by groups of positions in the college, from figure 2, we can see the excellent rank for normal academic

staff those are not holding high positions increased from 10% to 36% of total excellent persons, and the excellent rank for the managers and leaders decreased from 70% to 30%.

The results show that applying KPIs is totally different from voting process for staff and faculty evaluation. Faculty members who are involved in research and publication will get more chance to be ranked as excellent persons. And, people who are holding high positions in the organisation, but only focusing on teaching without doing research and publication, will have less chances to be ranked.

4. CONCLUSION

This paper presented the first results on using a KPI-based staff and faculty evaluation tool in the CoET. The KIPs were developed to measure performance of staff and faculties in the college. When getting a successful activity, people can earn corresponding credits and when getting failure or violation they will be fined some credits from their account. The KPIs were applied one year in the CoET and compared with data of the last 2 years. The results indicate that using KPIs is totally different from voting process for staff and faculty evaluation. And they are really encouraging to continue to improve the KPIs tool and apply them for the future.

Table 1: Key Performance Indicators

Criteria 1: Execution of policies and laws of the State (minimum: 5 points)			
KPI	**Mark (point)**	**Proof**	**Sum**
Good execution	+5p		
Being disciplined by reprimand or more	-5p		
Administratively sanctioned	-5p		
Violation of traffic laws	-5p		
No complete academic records, training...	-3p/time		
Other violations pool formal criticism (registered in the minutes of the meeting)	-1p/time		
Criteria 2: Working results (minimum: 40 points)			
Academic activities (min: 35 points)			
KPI for teaching activities (minimum: 20 points)	**Mark (point)**	**Proof**	**Sum**
Complete teaching duties assigned by unit	+15p		
Not finished teaching duties assigned by the unit, such as teaching, assessment of learning, teaching history, exam, etc.	-1p/time		
Registration of book writing	+1p/author/book		
Book publication	+3p/author/book		
No complete book writing contract	-2p/author/book		
Joining the programme quality self-assessment team	+2p/curri./year		
Other contributions in teaching activities	+2p/time		
KPI for research activities (minimum: 10 points)	**Mark (point)**	**Proof**	**Sum**
Research proposal writing	+1p/proposal		

Member of research project Univ./Ministry level	+3p/+5p/year		
Leader of research project	+7p/+10p/year		
Publish paper in proceedings of national conference	+6p/paper/author		
Publish paper in proceedings of international conference	+10p/paper/author		
Present in internal conference/workshop	+4p/presentation		
Present in College seminar	+2p/presentation		
Being delayed research project	-2p/time		
Supervise student's research project	+2p/project		
Do not finish student's research project	-1p/project		
Other contributions in research activities	+1d/time		
KPI for international relations, projects and technical transfers (minimum: 5 points)	**Mark (point)**	**Proof**	**Sum**
Member of project proposal and concept note writing	+3p/proposal		
Leader of project proposal and concept note writing	+5p/proposal		
Member of international project execution	+2p/project		
Leader of international project execution	+5p/proposal		
Participating in technical transfers, training/workshop organizing…	+3p/year		
Other contributions in international relations, project & technical transfer	+1p/time		

Other activities (minimum: 5 points)

KPI for having initiative, improvements or perform other works	**Mark (point)**	**Proof**	**Sum**
Having initiative/product/scientific research result applied in reality	+3p/time		
Construction processes, solutions and strategies for the college: members/leader	+2p/+1p/time		
Having initiative/improvement for Lab development	+1p/time		
Joining curriculum design/redesign team	+2p/mem./curri.		
News posting/providing contents for college's website (except posting announcements or quoting other posts)	+1p/news		
Other contributions	+1p/time		
KPI for doing tasks assigned by the party or unions	**Mark (point)**	**Proof**	**Sum**
Participated/cheered the sporting activities organised by university/college labour-unions	+2p/+1p/year		
Received certificates of merit at university level	+2p/certificate		
Verify resume and complete profile for new party members admitted	+1p/profile		
Do not complete the task assigned by the party or unions, and criticism from reprimand	-1p/time		
Other contributions/other violations	+1p/-1p/time		
KPI for assessing leaders and managers (Party, Administration, Unions)	**Mark (point)**	**Proof**	**Sum**
Complete missions and not censure from reprimand level	+1p/year		

Leading and managing the units getting certificates of merit at university level or higher	+2p/year		
Leading and managing the units that employees were disciplined by reprimand or higher	-1p/time		
Leader/manager who did not complete his/her tasks and was disciplined by reprimand or higher	-2p/time		
Other contributions/other violations	+1p/-1p/time		

Criteria 3: The spirit of discipline (minimum: 5 points)

KPI	Mark (point)	Proof	Sum
Having good discipline	+5p/year		
Violation of activities related to the: finance, exam, etc. that was disciplined by reprimand or higher	-3p/time		
Failing to comply with the directive assigned by leaders/managers	-1p/time		
Unexcused absence of conferences, meetings convened by the department/college	-1p/time		
Other violations	-1p/time		

Criteria 4: The spirit of collaboration in the work (minimum: 5 points)

KPI	Mark (point)	Proof	Sum
Organizing workshop, conference, seminar, training, other events…: leader/member	+3p/+2p/time		
Finding and getting scholarships for students	+5p/donor		
Finding and getting donors for investing equipment	+5p/ donor		
Finding and getting scholarships for staff/faculty	+5p/scholarship		
No spirit of cooperation, lack of job responsibilities that was disciplined by reprimand or higher	-2p/time		
Other contributions	+1p/time		

Criteria 5: Honesty in the work (minimum: 5 points)

KPI	Mark (point)	Proof	Sum
Full report and honesty with superiors	+5p		
Hide, conceal mistakes that was discovered/criticised	-5p		
Other violations	-1p/time		

Criteria 6: Lifestyle and Ethics (minimum: 5 points)

KPI	Mark (point)	Proof	Sum
Good execution	+5p		
Being complaints and disciplinary committee concluded from the reprimand or higher	-2p/time		
Slander, distort, denounce exceeding supply, causing disunity, internal sow divisions ... be disciplined by reprimand or more	-2p/time		
3rd child and other offenses affecting the overall performance of the organisation, was disciplined by reprimand or higher	-5p		
Participate in blood donation	+2p/time		
Being local residence praise and reward	+3p/time		

Other violations relating to Lifestyle and Ethics	-1p/time		

Criteria 7: The spirit of learning to improve professional capacity (minimum: 5 points)

KPI	Mark (point)	Proof	Sum
Achieving higher certification in foreign language skills	+5p/certification		
Attending short-term training courses, conferences, seminars, exchanges, summer schools ...: scholarship/ self /funding of college	+5p/+5p/+1p/time		
Getting a scholarship to study M.Sc. / Ph.D.	+5p		
Getting M.Sc./Ph.D. certificates	+5p		
Fully participating the training courses on party resolutions, political, professional skills, etc.	+3p/year		
Unexcused absence of the training courses on party resolutions, political, professional skills, etc.	-2p/year		
Other contributions	+1p/time		

Criteria 8: The spirit and attitude at work (minimum: 10 points)

KIP for overall assessment (minimum: 5 points)	Mark (point)	Proof	Sum
The spirit and good work attitude	+5p		
Overdue tasks assigned by leaders/managers without suitable reason	-2p/time		
Do not teaching in classes without reason	-2p/time		
Participating in meetings not on time	-1p/time		
Having unaffable attitude, harassment, causing troublesome difficulty for students, colleagues, customers while performing the tasks	-2p/time		
Having indifference, neglect that was affecting work progress	-2p/time		
Other violations	-1p/time		
KPI for leaders/managers assessment (maximum: 5 points)	**Mark (point)**	**Proof**	**Sum**
Emulation council assesses dean			
Dean assesses vice deans, head of departments, directors and head of administrative office			
Head of departments/directors/ head of administrative office assess each member in his/her unit			

REFERENCES

Cashin, William E., Developing an effective faculty evaluation system, in: IDEA Paper 33 (1996), 1-6.

CoET, Annual Report, CanTho University, 2012.

CTU, Annual Report, CanTho University, 2012.

Fitz-Gibbon, Carol T., Performance indicators, in: BERA Dialogues 2 (1990).

Paulsen, Michael B., Evaluating teaching performance, in: New Directions for Institutional Research, 114 (2002), 5-17.

Reh, F. John, Key Performance Indicators (KPI) – How an organization defines and measures progress toward its goals, http://management.about.com/cs/generalmanagement/a/keyperfindic.htm, 2013, accessed June 2013.

Rikakis, Thanassis, Innovative faculty evaluation criteria for incentivizing high-impact interdisciplinary collaboration, 39th ASEE/IEEE Frontiers in Education Conference, 2009.

Vietnamese Congress, Law on emulation and reward, No. 15/2003/QH11, 2003.

Vietnamese Ministry of Education and Training, Circular on guiding the emulation and reward activities in the education sector, No.: 12/2012/TT-BGDĐT, 2012.

Acknowledgement: The author would like to thank the DAAD for sponsoring him participating the International Dean's Course – South East Asia 2012-2013 – because during that training course he had strengthened the CoET's strategic plan and developed the KPI-based evaluation tool for the organisation.

Chi-Ngon Nguyen is a senior lecturer in control engineering and the dean of the College of Engineering Technology at the Can Tho University, Vietnam. His research interests are including intelligent control, medical automation, speech recognition, Vietnamese text to sign language translation system, and HEIs management.

STRATEGIC MANAGEMENT AND HUMAN CAPITAL MANAGEMENT AT THE UNIVERSITY. WOULD IT BE BENEFICIAL TO THE PONTIFICAL CATHOLIC UNIVERSITY OF PERU IF DEANS ADOPT IT?

Monica Bonifaz

Academic Department of Management Sciences, Pontifical Catholic University of Peru,
Av. Universitaria 1801, San Miguel, Lima 32, Peru
mpbonifaz@gmail.com

At the present time, universities are confronted with adverse environmental conditions that exceed the capabilities of traditional government and managerial systems. In an uncertain and hostile environment, limited resources, social demand for wider access to the system, accountability, efficiency and effectiveness, university main authorities urge universities to develop new management skills that enable them to cope successfully with the future. This report outlines the general background and analytical framework of strategic management in universities and then focuses on the analysis of deans' roles at Pontifical Catholic University in Peru. It describes the formal roles of deans and the benefits to incorporate strategic management practices as part of their governance and administrative roles in their faculties in order to deal with complexity and uncertainty. Besides, it underlines the relevance of human capital management in faculties, inherent in a leadership position within the strategic framework.

1. BACKGROUND INFORMATION

Modern universities act in a constantly changing environment, resulting from the advent of the knowledge society, globalisation, the fast development of ICT, and revolutionary educational models, among others trends. Additional stressful conditions for the development of the university are resource scarcity (a consequence of global economic crises), increasing demand for access to higher education (leading to system overcrowding) and increasing social and political demand for poorly understood institutional autonomy.

Given those environmental conditions, universities must face the fact that good old days are gone and may never return. In a different world, new institutional capabilities are required, far different from those traditionally employed. Research reports on current challenges faced by universities usually call for institutional reforms and leading authorities action in order to face that future successfully (Eastman 2003; Tavernier 2005; Torn/Soo 2006; Goedegebuure 2007; Harman/Treadgold 2007; Henkel 2007; Morris et al. 2007; de Boer/Goedegebuure 2009; Elena-Perez et al. 2011; Gershberg et al. 2011; Decramer et al. 2012).

The inability of governments to take the total bill required by the higher education system appears among the main factors impacting the traditional university governance. It is too costly to support organisations requiring a huge amount of resources to perform research, training, and knowledge production and transfer. In the near future tuition fees or treasury funds will hardly cover the costs of such organisations.

In the context of knowledge society, universities are responsible for attracting and developing human capital that is able to innovate, design and deliver products and services highly valued by society and market because of the benefits they supply. If universities have talented human capital to make use of these benefits it is reasonable to assume that they can afford part of the invoice. In major developing countries, even in those with a traditional system, universities are hybrid organisations: semi-public and semi-private. In the same context, the knowledge explosion involves rapid technological development and major changes in teaching methods. The traditional model of university cathedra will not guarantee sufficient learning compared to the vast amount of available knowledge; education systems will tend to move toward individual learning and curricular reforms will be required. The traditional objectives of knowledge accumulation will be replaced by objectives oriented to the development of search and information management skills. This situation consequently implies changes in professors' careers management and the institutional expectations of teachers' and researchers' contributions.

Finally, given the vast amount of knowledge and complexity of the environment, it is reasonable to doubt that a single university will be able to reach its goals alone. Carrying out major academic projects, undertaking large investments in infrastructure for scientific development and providing excellent training systems will need cooperation and strategic alliances with up to then unthinkable partners, and will require organisational systems that are able to support and facilitate cooperative work and networking (Tavernier 2005; Goedegebuure 2012).

2. ANALYTICAL FRAMEWORK OF STRATEGIC MANAGEMENT

Why Strategic Management in Universities?

University main stakeholders (society, government, enterprises and the university community) highly value education and knowledge and have great expectations on its power to create better opportunities for development and welfare. Stakeholders critically observe the effectiveness and efficiency of the university as a service institution. They not only demand transparency on how and where resources are allocated, but also claim for university accountability on excellence and quality in research and education, especially in regard to the relevance and social contribution of their achievements (Torn/Soo 2006; Altbach/Salmi 2011; Ferreira et al. 2013).

Changes in higher education funding systems, the debate about institutional autonomy, demand increase and social claiming for accountability have intensified the discussion on how universities should be governed and managed. In the current competitive context (regarding economic resources and human talent) an entrepreneurial attitude is expected; university contribution to social welfare must come together with the fulfilment of quality, efficiency and effectiveness criteria.

Therefore, efficient government systems and leadership with managerial skills become strategically important for universities since in the context of autonomy and collegial representation it will lead to greater flexibility and the will to adapt to the changing environment, adequate decisional processes and systems that respond to environmental conditions, a goal-oriented attitude and visionary capacity to face the challenges of the future (Harman/Treadgold 2007; Goedegebuure 2007; Elena-Perez et al. 2011).

Strategic Management Concepts and Approaches

Strategic management can be defined as a form of management suitable for complex and uncertain environments, which prepares people to envision themselves into the future, emphasizing on organisational learning and development. Strategic management teaches how to run organisations under efficiency criteria focused on their mission, how to respond to demand, and thereby achieving above-normal outcomes and results (Eastman 2003).

The rapid adoption and popularity of strategic management is due mainly to its common sense and straightforward approach in the process of decision making to address competitive contexts. It starts with three basic questions: Where am I? Where do I want to go? And how do intend to get there? To answer them systematically means to analyse its environment from the perspective of threats and opportunities, and to perform an internal audit of the organisation in both their strengths and weaknesses (Tavernier 2005).

Strategic management has been enriched from different approaches or schools that respond to the experiences and learning of different types of organisations in which it is applied. In fact, an industrial organisation of mass production will require a different strategic approach to that of a university. The approach depends on the size, structure, complexity and the regulatory framework, as well as the values and culture of the organisation. Mintzberg (1998) studied various schools of which two are applicable to the university institution, considered as a professional bureaucracy: the school of planning and the learning school.

The planning school is geared consistently towards formalizing the processes and activities necessary to achieve strategic objectives, which should be measurable through specific data and should allow constructing indicators for analysis and performance assessment. Organisations implementing strategic management through the planning school perspective require a team of highly qualified experts accountable to higher authorities. This perspective has been widely welcomed by big private corporations and has been adopted by public entities in the form of the New Public Management. From another perspective, the learning school understands that the world is too complex to delegate the strategic planning to a well-informed group of planners. In this school, the permanent search of the organisation to play its roles differently or to assume different roles appropriate to the environmental conditions is stressed. It is strongly associated with four learning skills in its human capital: ability to absorb knowledge and to disseminate it and the ability to produce new knowledge and to exploit it. For the learning school human capital is essential and expertise to manage and mobilise it towards creativity and productivity is crucial. There is a wide consensus that this school is the most suitable to face complex and turbulent environments.

Is Strategic Management Beneficial for the University Today?

Universities, considered as professional bureaucracies, have natural resistance to incorporate the strategic management framework since this is associated with *business thinking*. Scholars tend to reject this model as they assume hierarchies and corporate decision-making systems are risky to their freedom within the institution. Universities, by their own systems of government (democratic collegiate tradition) and organisational structures (assemblies, senates, councils, vice chancellors, deans and academic departments) tend to be multi-mission organisations, with a predominant culture of collegial governance based on the egalitarian distribution and control of resources. Their systems of government prioritise academic prestige, rather than the recognition of managerial skills related to education provision, financial and operational affairs and, above all, human capital management (Elena-Perez et al. 2011).

Despite what is stated above, case studies on successful implementation of strategic management in universities in Anglo-American countries (Tavernier 2005) allow to systematise and identify the benefits of applying strategic management in universities in general and especially in their fundamental academic units, the faculties. Among them we can identify the following:

- *Alignment and cooperation:* Having an explicit institutional mission, operating as the declaration of "the constitution", allows the community to know where they are going and how they intend to reach the destination set. The institutional mission is a precondition to decentralise the decision-making processes in different instances and levels of the organisation. If this is clear and shared then it will contribute to the alignment of efforts and cooperation even from different disciplinary perspectives. The institutional mission, from the learning approach, enables to work on broad goals rather than imposing specific goals and instructions from above, the control systems will be *ex-post* and *ex-ante* allowing the organisation to learn through periodic self-assessment processes. Performance evaluation of the organisation and its human capital is a critical component of the strategic management framework, because it allows feedback of decision making process and learning in relation to the achievements and failures.

- *Effectiveness by direction towards institutional priorities (core business):* The definition of the mission and its consequent institutional priorities, combined with the ability to delegate the decision making process at different levels of the institution facilitates the achieve-ment of expected results, distinctive of competitive modern organisations. The definition of institutional priorities may collide with the expectations of academic autonomy and freedom, this will require preserving academic freedom to mobi-

lise individual creativity and explore new areas of research.

- *Productivity through the delegation of managerial decision-making process:* Universities are, from the point of view of organisational theory, "professional bureaucracies" in which the experience and knowledge is diluted in government bodies and in classrooms, laboratories and research centres. The strategic management framework (based on objectives, indicators and assessment) creates the decentralised conditions for decision makers to boost knowledge production and transfer.

- *Strategic alliances and networking:* Although the traditional universities tend to develop from within and for themselves, it is logical to think that in the current context any college will be too small to start alone the challenge of producing new relevant knowledge. Partnerships and networks are strategic mechanisms that allow sharing with others access to more resources (money or infrastructure), to share the risks in exploring new areas, but they also help to preserve and share talent and human capital and thus contribute to institutional goals.

- *Human capital management and organisation sustainability:* In a the current context of knowledge society, universities are the organisations responsible for attracting and developing human capital capable of producing and transferring knowledge required by society, governments and businesses. Universities are specialised organisations in the function of knowledge production, and this function is in the hands of their academics. The ability to identify, motivate and encourage human talent is a *conditio sine qua non* to boost innovation capacity and academic and scientific productivity.

3. PONTIFICAL CATHOLIC UNIVERSITY OF PERU: DEANSHIP IN A COMPLEX AND TURBULENT ENVIRONMENT

The Pontifical Catholic University of Peru (PUCP), founded in 1917, is the oldest private university in the country. It has legal status as a non-for profit organisation dedicated to higher education. The university community consists of 4,700 employees, as well as nearly 20,000 undergraduate and graduate students and about 57,000 students in continuous education programmes. The university funds its operations with private income sources from training services revenue and from services, research funding, property assets and financial incomes.

The university is ruled under the University Act of Peru (Law 23733) and the University Bylaws, approved by the University Assembly. Under this legal framework, the University Assembly is the highest governing body of the university and the University Council is the governing body responsible of the promotion, planning and execution of the university. The Faculties, according to the University Law and PUCP Bylaws, are the fundamental units of the organisation and are responsible for academic and professional education. The Dean is the individual who represents its Faculty before the governing bodies of the university and is responsible for directing and coordinating the activities of the Faculty and taking all steps required for its proper functioning.

A Changed University Environment in Peru

Peru has been considered as one of the "new tigers of Latin America" because of its remarkable economic growth based on the efficient exploitation of its natural resources allowing an average annual growth rate of GDP was 6% for the last ten years and a GDP PPP per capita of ca. US$ 11,000, which is among the five highest in the region. Peru has a population of 30 million inhabitants of which 25% are aged for higher education but only 700,000 are in college.

In Peru, as in the Latin American region, higher education is highly valued by society and parents allocate a significant percentage of their income on their childrens' education. Research presented by Yamada (2012) and Diaz (2006), being in line with several studies of the World Bank, reported that access to university education significantly reduces the probability of falling into poverty and that a quality higher education increases employability and contributes to upward social mobility.

In the last 40 years, the demand for access to higher education in Peru has increased significantly. Whereas in 1970 around 70,000 students applied to 31 universities, in 2010 applicants passed 550,000 and the overall number of universities reached 120 (Diaz 2006; ANR 2012). Despite the increase in enrolment, there are still many unmet demands. Peru, as most of the countries in the region, has responded to the growing demand for university education by diversifying and deregulating its provision. From the 1990s, in most parts of the region the state (with little ability to respond to the pressure of the demand and to manage the public university system) has encouraged the private sector to provide it in for-profit way. In this context the Peruvian State decreed in 1996 the Law 882 on Investment Promotion in Education, authorizing the creation of private for-profit universities, operating as business. Since then an average of 3.5 private universities were established each year. Now private for-profit universities have developed dynamically and have become a powerful player in Peruvian higher education system.

In a context of growing demand, high expectations and a poor quality university education, we are debating the reform of our legal framework. The project of a new University Act seeks to order and solve the huge problem of university education in Peru. Among the major reforms being discussed the principle that all universities are public service organisations, without discrimination of its public or private origin emerges as critical. It establishes the mandatory conditions of transparency and accountability of resource management, research and accreditation and certification to improve the quality of education processes and outcomes. The project establishes also greater demands on teachers and lays grounds for sanctions and dismissal for bad behaviour and poor performance (not established in the previous law).

Challenges for Deanship at PUCP

Despite university type (public or private, non for-profit or for-profit), the Faculty is always regarded as the fundamental unit in the university. Embracing one or more study programmes, Faculties are the university basic unit of service to society. The Faculty Dean is the individual authority responsible for leading and organizing education and research activities, as well as executing all the academic, administrative and financial duties of the school.

Although the social image of Deans as prestigious scholars remains, in the last twenty years it incorporated also that of a business man: politics aware and sharply skilled for finance and managing tasks, the current dean's profile resembles a smart executive. Accordingly, the changing nature of deanship (tasks, roles, and challenges) in a context of meeting demands from different stakeholders has become a research subject (Wolverton/Wolverton/Gmelch 1999; Montez/Wolverton/Gmelch 2002; Johnsrud/Rosser 2003; Jackson 2004; de Boer/Goedegebuure 2009; Scholz/Stein/Fraune 2012).

In the following sections, formal responsibilities and current roles of PUCP deans are described and analysed; afterwards a strategic framework is used to analyse and propose a redefinition of Deanship, with roles and functions designed to properly meet new internal and external demands and expectations.

What Deans Do: Is It What Stakeholders Expect Them to Do?

According to the legal framework in force (Law) and the university Bylaws PUCP (PUCP 2012), the Dean's individual authority comprises three main types of duties: representation among peers and with the authority; academic liability for the provision of university-level education; and direct administrative responsibility on personnel, financial and operative issues.

- *In the representation role,* the Dean is formally responsible to stand for its faculty at internal and external spheres, to express opinion and vote acting on behalf of the school. He "runs the show" but he is not the boss, acting as a persuader and negotiator, balancing group interests and serving constituencies who claim for equity.

- *In the academic role,* Faculties are devoted to the provision of academic education services where students and faculty members participate. The Faculties become service units where professors are key actors for providing knowledge and contents to the syllabus. Deans are expected to build consensus on educational goals and motivate peers to participate on them which are both core components of a Faculty study programme's "prestige".

- *The administrative role,* at internal level, concentrates the greatest amount of responsibilities and duties for Deans and may require the support of specialised teams depending on demand size and diversity. As administrators, Deans require clear and foreseeable processes enabling fluid relationships between students, professors and study programmes. Although many Deans are not directly involved with course schedules and enrolment or infrastructure and technology deployment neither certification and graduation systems, they are formally responsible for the results of all these activities.

Therefore, Dean roles and tasks currently performed at PUCP are formal, traditional and focused on responding to internal demands of authorities and other university constituents. Present conditions described previously (growing demand for higher education, political pressure to over-regulate the institution, aggressive competition and a thriving business sector requiring qualified professionals to contribute to innovation and productivity) are deliberately and explicitly not considered. Tasks and responsibilities related to transparency and accountability of resource allocation and outcomes, academic productivity and impact, quality and pertinence of research and curricula are not yet incorporated.

Could Deanship Meet Better the Internal and External Demands by Applying the Strategic Management Framework?

So far the question is what does it really take to get the job at faculties well done under the described environmental conditions and the answer seems to be that Deans should emulate the strategic business thinking. Academic governance system, formal structure, culture and values that preserve the collegiate and egalitarian participation differ very much from business thinking. Despite these differences universities recognise the need for internal changes and new evolving roles that allow them to be better prepared to respond to the demands and pressures (Surface 1971; Montez et al. 2002; Goedegeebure 2007; Scholz/Stein/Fraune 2012).

Strategic management approach: It is rooted in business practice but not exclusively applicable to business organisations. Tools provided by strategic management (like strategic planning) allow the faculty to define objectives, linked to an institutional mission, and indicators that enables better decision-making process. The strategic framework is based on participation, cooperation and alignment, improves transparency on resource allocation and outcomes in order to meet the institutional mission and thus contributing to public accountability at internal and external level.

Mission and purpose for good governance: Deans, beyond representation, shall perform a political role to clarify the purpose of its governance, and achieve agreements allowing the sustainability of its academic mission at the institutional (internal), social and market (external) levels. The role of good-governance requires that the Dean develops the political capacity to aligning and not only balancing the interests of constituents. It will require the ability to create participation and cooperation with clearly defined objectives that allow joining efforts and reducing opportunistic behaviours, as well as agency problems given the associative nature of university. Collegial mission statement is a powerful way to meet different demands and maintain Faculty equilibrium.

Strategic priorities for academic and administrative effectiveness: Knowledge and learning of quality are the consequence of research of quality and adequate teaching processes respectively. Academic excellence refers firstly to outcomes (strategic objectives and results), and then efficiency refers to its required support processes (necessary but not enough). If the Dean sets collegially Faculty priorities in relation to knowledge production and learning to be assured, then Faculty and administration will have clarity about the goals to be achieved. This is a requirement for productivity with effectiveness that can prove to stakeholders, internal and external, the positive impacts and contributions of the deanery.

Decentralised decision making to foster productivity: Deans are part of a professional bureaucracy. If mission has been established by the Faculty and is clearly stated, then the Faculty should define the objectives that contribute to it. In addition to formally established governance structures (by law and statutes), working groups, research groups, project teams, and other formal and informal teams must be encouraged to boost knowledge productivity and transfer, and the decision making process delegated to them. Autonomy and sense of freedom to decide, under a collegial mission, will enforce people commitment and productivity.

Strategic alliances to achieve major breakthroughs: Cooperation between universities and Faculty for research is natural in the academic world; networking has the power of convening and join forces in pursuit of a common goal. Promoting cooperation on a larger scale, not at a research project but joint creation of a new discipline or investing in a large laboratory for research, with partners before unimagined allows not only more resources but also to share risks. Although alliances also raise the risks of choosing new members, they are key mechanisms that will allow the dean to better manage the expectations and demands of the environment.

Guidelines and criteria provided by the strategic framework take into account internal and external factors that deanship must consider for properly managing and governing the Faculty. Even though strategic framework proposes prioritisation criteria and results orientation that seem to collide with the values of equality and balance, proper of university tradition, the strategic framework is based on participation, cooperation and commitment to fulfil of institutional purpose. The strategic framework has a broad and comprehensive view of internal and external conditions that contribute to a more informed university management and provide tools to make decisions and be accountable for the results achieved. Responsibilities related to accountability of resource allocation and outcomes, academic productivity and impact, quality and pertinence of research and curricula could be better-faced applying strategic framework and instruments.

Human Capital Management: Do Deans Have to Deal With It?

Given current conditions of the Peruvian labour market, the growth of economic activity and the emergence of many universities, it stands to reason that the universities' demand for talented people is growing. We should also note that wage conditions in the education sector are not necessarily attractive compared with other sectors of the economy. Under this situation, Deans have to ensure for their faculties human capital capable of producing and transferring the knowledge needed for the success of their academic programmes.

In order to strengthen this responsibility of Deans as human capital managers little has been investigated yet. Research is mainly concentrated on the difficulties encountered in universities to rejoining the human resource management as an academic function to ensure adequate human capital, superior academic performance and achievements of institutional goals (Morris et al. 2007; Ulferts 2009; Khasawneh 2011; Elena-Perez et al. 2011; Hobeanu 2011; Decramer et al. 2012).

In practice Deans cannot avoid their responsibility for people management. They have a natural role dealing daily with their Faculty with the following restrictions: first, the timing and nature of his position, second the availability of the right people and third the professional ability and willingness to manage human capital.

The first is related to tradition. Deans at PUCP govern and manage a professional bureaucracy, characterised by a sense of *inter pares* relationship where they are temporarily the *primus*. Peers expect that the Dean plays the role of facilitator, provider and negotiator, and they elect the dean to represent their academic interests sometimes of higher priority than those of the institution.

The second is related with the struggle to have the right Faculty. Deans have to deal with human capital scarcity because the stock of human capital formed for higher education in Peru is very low, with few qualified professionals, let alone with master's degrees and almost lack of professionals with doctorates. Given the scarcity of professionals in the market and the low wages in the education sector, Deans have to develop human capital from their own source of young players and have to design creative mechanisms to find and attract qualified practitioners, with high opportunity costs in the market, to pursue partially current academic teaching needs.

And finally, there is the big challenge of wanting and being able to manage human capital. Deans are not obliged to perform this duty of managing their peers, it is risky for their stability as *primus inter pares*. Deans are willing to convene and motivate their academic peers but they do not feel confortable with assessing or controlling their performance. However, motivation is needed as well as performance to boost academic excellence and to be accountable for it. Deans should incorporate human capital management practices because they guarantee people with the required skills for the current and future needs, meritocratic career development and institutional performance improvements.

4. CONCLUSION

Under the current environmental conditions in Peru is necessary to rethink the traditional role of the Deans and Faculties in the university. The formal roles established in the regulations for the Faculties and Deans are primarily for administrative responsibilities and concentrate on deanery representative functions but not on their responsibility in fulfilling the mission of the institution and their results. If Faculties are the fundamental units of the universities, they and their authorities should be accountable for their outcomes and impacts.

The strategic management framework does contribute significantly to respond to internal and external demands relating to accountability, achievement of goals and social impact. The collegiate definition of an institutional mission and the respective objectives are powerful mechanisms to guide the university community towards achieving results. If such a strategic framework is implemented under a participatory logic this should not pose a risk to collegialism, autonomy and academic freedom. Besides, within the strategic framework, the responsibility to human capital management that contributes to achieving the goals of the faculty emerges as a new element in the evolving role of the Dean.

While theoretically it is positive and feasible to adopt the strategic framework in Faculties, additional studies should be conducted to determine the willingness of current and future Deans at PUCP to practice and implement the strategic framework in their units. And if Deans are willing to perform as strategic managers it would be required to define new the institutional conditions and management skills development programmes.

REFERENCES

Altbach, Philip G./Salmi, Jamil (eds.), The road to academic excellence, the making of world-class research universities, Washington D.C. (The World Bank) 2011.

Asamblea Nacional de Rectores (ANR), Datos Estadísticos Universitarios, Lima (Asamblea Nacional de Rectores) 2012.

de Boer, Harry/Goedegebuure, Leo, The changing nature of the academic deanship, in: Leadership 5 (3/2009), 347-364.

de Boer, Harry/Goedegebuure, Leo, On limitations and consequences of change: Dutch university governance in transition, in: Tertiary Education and Management 7 (2/2001), 163-180.

Decramer, Adelien/Smolders, Carine/Vanderstraeten, Alex/Christiaens, Johan/Desmidt, Sebastian, External pressures affecting the adoption of employee performance management in higher education institutions, in: Personnel Review 41 (6/2012), 686-704.

Díaz, Juan J., Educación Superior en el Perú: Tendencias de la Demanda y la Oferta, in: Análisis de Programas, Procesos y Resultados Educativos en el Perú: Contribuciones Empíricas para el Debate, Lima (GRADE) 2008.

Eastman, Julia, Strategic management of universities, in: Canadian Society for the Study of Higher Education, Professional File 24 (2003), 1-56.

Elena-Pérez, Susanna/Saritas, Ozcan/Pook, Katja/Warden, Campbell, Ready for the future? Universities' capabilities to strategically manage their intellectual capital, in: Foresight 13 (2/2011), 31-48.

Ferreira, Francisco G./Messina, Julia/Rigolini, Jamele/López-Calva, Luis F./Vakis, Renos, Panorámica General: La Movilidad Económica y el Crecimiento de la Clase Media en América Latina. Washington, DC: Banco Mundial (2013).

Gershberg, Alec I./Gonzales, Pablo/Meade, Ben, Understanding and improving accountability in education: A conceptual framework and guideposts from three decentralization reform Eexperiences in Latin America, in: World Development 40 (5/2012), 1024-1041.

Goedegebuure, Leo, Mergers and more: The changing tertiary education landscape in the 21st century, in: HEIK Working Paper Series 1 (2012), 1-18.

Goedegebuure, Leo/Hayden, Martin, Overview: Governance in higher education – concepts and issues, in: Higher Education Reasearch & Development 26 (1/2007), 1-11.

Harman, Kay/Treadgold, Elaine, Changing patterns of governance from Australian universities, in: Higher Education Research & Development 26 (1/2007), 13-29.

Henkel, Mary, Can academic autonomy survive in the knowledge society? A perspective from Britain, in: Higher Education Research & Development 26 (1/2007), 87-99.

Hobeanu, Loredana V., The human resources and evaluation management in the academic environment, in: Journal of Advance Research in Management 2 (1/2011), 28-45.

Jackson, Jerlando F. L., Toward a business model of executive behavior: An exploration of the workdays of four college of education deans at large research universities, in: Review of Higher Education 27 (3/2004), 409-427.

Khasawneh, Samer, Human capital planning in higher education institutions: A strategic human resource development initiative in Jordan, in: International Journal of Educational Management 25 (6/2010), 534-544.

Mintzberg, Henry/Ahlstrand, Bruce/Lampel, Joseph, Strategy safari: A guided tour through the wilds of strategic management, New York (The Free Press) 1998.

Montez, Joni M./Wolverton, Mimi/Gmelch, Walter H., The Roles and Challenges of Deans, in: The Review of Higher Education 26 (2/2002), 241-266.

Morris, Leanne/Stanton, Pauline/Young, Suzanne H., Performance management in higher education – development versus control, in: New Zealand Journal of Employment Relations 32 (2/2007), 17-31.

Pontificia Universidad Católica del Perú, Estatuto Texto Vigente, Lima (PUCP) 2012.

Rosser, Vicki J./Johnsrud, Linda K./Heck, Ronald H., Academic deans and directors: Assessing their effectiveness from individual and institutional perspectives, in: The Journal of Higher Education 74 (1/2003), 1-25.

Shattock, Michael, Managing good governance in higher education perspectives: Policy and practice, in: Higher Education 12 (3/2008), 85-89.

Scholz, Christian/Stein,Volker/Fraune, Cornelia, Evolving structures of higher education institutions: The dean's role, in: Bergan, Sjur/Egron-Polak, Eva/Kohler, Jürgen/Purser, Lewis/Vukasović, Martina (eds.), Leadership and governance in higher education. Handbook for decision-makers and administrators, Vol. 2, Berlin (Raabe) 2012, 1-24.

Surface, James R., Universities aren't corporations: Why corporate management won't work, in: Business Horizons 14 (3/1971), 75-80.

Tavernier, Karel, Relevance of strategic management for universities, in: Tijdschrift voor Economie en Management 50 (5/2005), 769-785.

Thorn, Kristian/Soo, Maarja, Latin American universities and the third mission, in: Trends, Challenges and Policy Options, World Bank Publications 4002 (2006).

Turk, James L., Anatomy of Corporate Takeover, in: The Unesco Courier 54 (11/2001), 18-20.

Ulferts, Gregory, Wirtz, Patrick/Peterson, Evan, Strategic human resource planning in academia, in: American Journal of Business Education 2 (7/2009), 1-9.

Wolverton, Mimi/Wolverton, Marvin L./Gmelch, Walter, H., The impact of role conflict and ambiguity on academic deans, in: The Journal of Higher Education 70 (1/1999), 80-106.

Yamada, Gustavo/Castro, Juan F./Rivera, Mario, Educación Superior en el Perú: Retos para el Aseguramiento de la Calidad, Lima (Sistema Nacional de Evaluación, Acreditación y Certificación de la Calidad Educativa) 2012.

Strategic Management and Human Capital Management at the University

Monica Bonifaz has a M.Sc. in Information Management at University of Sheffield (UK). She is Associate Professor of the Academic Department of Management Sciences and currently Chairman of the Government Commission of the Faculty of Management at the Pontifical Catholic University in Peru. Monica Bonifaz has over 15 years of executive experience in the private and public sector. Her topics of interest are Strategic Management of Higher Education Institutions, Human Resource Management, Organisation Theory and Corporate Social Responsibility.

ECONOMIES OF SCALE AT FACULTIES

Matthias Klumpp

University of Duisburg-Essen & FOM University of Applied Sciences, Essen, Germany
matthias.klumpp@pim.uni-due.de

Today, universities and faculties have become used to being analysed with performance or productivity measurement instruments. Methods have broadened and integrate qualitative and quantitative approaches. This research gives an overview regarding approaches to efficiency analysis in higher education. It asks how far efficiency is already a question for faculty management, includes a case study regarding faculty-based efficiency measurement for an example of 25 German economics and business administration schools and derives implications for higher education research and in particular for faculty management.

1. INTRODUCTION

Higher education efficiency has been traditionally an important research question, especially in relation to research productivity (Bottomley/Dunworth 1974; Barth/Vertinsky 1975; Banker, 1986; Ahn et al. 1988; Cohn et al. 1989; Johnes/Johnes 1993; Ramsden 1994; Beasley 1995; Dundar/Lewis 1995; Hashimoto/Cohn 1997; Glass et al. 1998; Stahl et al. 1998). But during the last 15 years, this small and usually qualitative field of analysis within universities and faculties has been broadened in terms of methods and comparative international views as well as implications for the practice of higher education management in many countries (Madden et al. 1997; Ng/Li 2000; Jongbloed/Vossensteyn 2001; Korhonen et al. 2001; Feng et al. 2004; Johnes 2006; Kocher et al. 2006; Kao/Hung 2008; Sarrico, 2010; Zangoueinezhad/Moshabaki 2011; Klumpp/Zelewski 2012).

Tight budgets impel public stakeholders as well as university leadership persons to ask for instruments for accountability – which are often interpreted as performance or productivity measurement instruments. This research gives an overview regarding approaches to efficiency analysis in higher education (sections 2 and 3), including a case study regarding faculty-based efficiency measurement for an example of 25 German economics and business administration schools (section 4). It reports on some distinguished international findings and outlines the implications for higher education research and management.

2. EFFICIENCY AS A QUESTION FOR FACULTY MANAGEMENT

The efficiency or productivity of university and faculty operations has been a discussed and reported management question (Scholz/Stein 2013) and is *complex* due to the very special nature of the university (and the faculties) as an organisational *type* and due also to the complexity of university and faculty *outputs*. Since the objective functions in higher education in the three areas of research, teaching and 'third mission' (often termed 'transfer', 'outreach', 'community services', see Zomer/Benneworth 2011, 82) contain of a multitude of output indicators, possible productivity measurements are by definition manifold.

Nevertheless, there are specific expectations regarding the output of universities, which can be expressed through equally specific efficiency questions. Those questions are essential for university management as many decisions taken within universities address resource allocation and are therefore directly connected to production settings. Examples of such management questions linked to higher education decisions are depicted in table 1.

Table 1: Management Questions and Management Decisions Regarding Efficiency

	Management Question (*Example*)	Management Decision (*Example*)
Re-search	How efficient are specific research groups, institutes, faculties (compared to all groups, institutes, faculties)?	Should specific research groups and faculties receive more funding? Should specific groups receive more management support?
Teach-ing	How efficient are specific teaching/study programmes (compared to other programmes)?	Should specific programmes be supported by advertising efforts or other forms of central resources? Should specific programmes be closed?
Third Mission	How efficient are specific university co-operations within the region?	Should specific university or faculty co-operations be prolonged or ended?

The *comparative* view regarding several universities (or more seldom: faculties) has been established by research publications, e.g. Beasley (1995); Dundar/Lewis (1995); Glass et al. (1998); Ng/Li (2000); Korhonen et al. (2001); Kocher et al. (2006); Kao/Hung (2008) and Sarrico (2010). One of the latest *data collection endeavours* supporting a comparative international is the EUMIDA project supported by the European Commission, collecting for example staff, student and graduate data (Bonaccorsi et al. 2010).

3. EFFICIENCY ANALYSIS WITH THE DATA ENVELOPMENT ANALYSIS (DEA)

Methodologies used in measuring the efficiency of higher education operations have been manifold – and have interestingly many similarities to ranking endeavours in the output field. Table 2 provides a structuring overview regarding the basic categories (A to D) for performance and productivity measurement.

Table 2: Comparison of Performance and Productivity Measurement Schemes

	One-dimensional Output Measurement	Multi-dimensional Output Measurement
Simple Output Indicators (*Performance* Measurement)	(A) Simple Output Metrics, e.g. ▪ Number of graduates per university per year ▪ Number of reviewed publications per university per year ▪ Number of patents registered per university per year	(B) Complex (Combined) Output Measurement Systems, e.g. ▪ Ranking systems as e.g. AR-WU, Leiden or Times Higher Education World Universities Ranking ▪ Performance-based funding systems with several indicators
Input and Output Indicator *Relation* (*Productivity* Measurement)	(C) Simple Productivity Metrics, e.g. ▪ Total teaching cost *per* graduate at one university ▪ Number of reviewed publications or citations in reviewed journals *per* Faculty head (three years) ▪ Amount of third party/industry income per Faculty head ▪ Total number of registered patents per 1 Mio. Euro (currency) university budget	(D) Complex Productivity Calculations, e.g. ▪ Stochastic frontier analysis for number of Faculty members and number of graduates and amount of third party/industry income ▪ Data envelopment analysis for university budget (input) and number of graduates, number of publications as well as number of patents (output)

The four depicted categories and their examples according to table 2 can be outlined in detail as follows:

(A) Simple one-dimensional outputs as *performance measurements* with just *one* output indicator are quite often used in higher education management and policies, e.g. for comparing universities (or departments thereof) regarding their number of graduates per year; or universities, faculties and even research groups regarding the number of publications, patent registrations or citations per year. For third mission activities, indicators such as number or turnover of spin-offs or the total number of their employees are used to measure performance on a university or faculty level.

(B) Usually, most university and even faculty ratings use a number of *output indicators* combined in relation to the specific objective of the ranking (see for example Van Vught/Ziegele 2012). For a ranking of teaching quality a combination of teacher-student-ratio, student satisfaction, international orientation and expert reputation might be used. For a research ranking a combination of industry income (third party funding), publications, citations and peer reputation might be used. The most commonly used method to calculate the overall score for such combined indicator rankings is weighted scoring systems, allocating each indicator a share out of a total of 100 per cent weighted distribution. All individual scores (with the same span of possible values e.g. from 0 to 100) are multiplied with this weighting and then added up for the total score.

(C) Simple *productivity* metrics usually operate with a relation between one output indicator (e.g. number of publications) and one input indicator (e.g. one researcher per one million Euro [currency] budget). Essential for the distinction between performance and productivity measurement (efficiency) is the inclusion of an input indicator, commonly addressed as the 'size question' (as usually performance indicators favour larger institutions or units which more easily reach higher output numbers for example in terms of graduates or publication numbers). Though the division of output numbers by input numbers is used most often, theoretically also the division of inputs by outputs is feasible and may also yield interesting insights: For example the question of what budget has been spent on average to recruit one student or graduate or achieve one publication.

(D) For the inclusion of multiple input and multiple output indicators, a number of methods are available in order to calculate a measurement result; the two most commonly used ones are *stochastic frontier analysis* (SFA) and *data envelopment analysis* (DEA):

(i) SFA: The *stochastic frontier analysis* uses a given production function in order to calculate productivity measures from the input and output data (Aigner et al. 1977; Kumbhakar/Lovell 2000). If such a production function is known this is a very feasible method, as it indicates clearly the improvement potential for all non-efficient units (Jacobs 2001; Cullinane et al. 2006; for universities see for example: Stevens 2005). But if there is no known production function for all relevant inputs and outputs this is less valuable though assumptions may be made (Coelli 1995).

(ii) DEA: The *data envelopment analysis* was proposed in 1978 and developed further as a non-parametric multi-criteria efficiency measurement method (cf. Charnes et al. 1978; Charnes et al. 1991; Seiford 1996; Pedraja-Chaparro et al. 1997; Cooper et al. 2000; Kleine 2004; Zhu/Cook 2007; Thannasoulis et al. 2008). It is commonly used in multi-dimensional output industries such as service industries (health care: Butler/Li 2005, ecological

analysis: Dyckhoff/Allen 2001) and also *higher education* (i.e. McMillan/Datta 1998; Taylor/Harris 2004; McMillan/Chan 2006).

Existing *criticism* regarding the different fields of measurement usually addresses the following areas: It is acknowledged that *single* output indicators naturally cannot depict the complex task of a university, especially since they do not take into account the distinction between the objective areas of research, teaching and third mission, neglecting the *Humboldt Principle* of an assumed or desired unity of these areas within universities as a founding principle. Additionally with just one output measurement the size of the higher education institution is crucial: larger universities have a comparative advantage in this perspective (*Matthew Effect*). From these typical critical arguments it is obvious that in developing adequate measurement and comparison systems in higher education the tendency should be directed towards systems in Category D with simultaneous multiple input and multiple output measurements. The methodology options in this last field are outlined further in the next section in the form of a small case study of faculty efficiency.

4. FACULTY EFFICIENCY CASE STUDY

In order to connect a current and relevant efficiency example regarding faculty efficiency, data for 25 German faculties for economics and business administration are analysed. A data envelopment analysis (DEA) studies different Decision Making Units (DMUs), the definition of which is rather open in order to guarantee flexibility in the term's application. In order to ensure relative comparisons, different DMUs are evaluated and compared with each other, each DMU showing a specific level of managerial effort and decision-making success. Based on the latest Handelsblatt Ranking 2013 in Germany (number of professors as input and publication points for journal publications as output; Handelsblatt 2013) and the research funding data from the German DFG (competitive research funding grants from DFG as output; DFG 2013) an efficiency analysis is carried out (see table 3 below). For the seven universities in Austria and Switzerland incorporated in the Handelsblatt ranking but without data from DFG (only German – public – universities are eligible for funding) an efficiency calculation was *not* possible.

Table 3: Case Study Data Regarding Faculty Efficiency (Output-oriented, BCC Model DEA)

University	Prof.	DFG 2008-2010 in Mio. €	Publication Points 2012	Efficiency Score
Aachen RWTH	12	353.812,55 €	42	99,20%
Augsburg Uni	14	445.889,07 €	30	60,40%
Berlin ESMT	10	0,00 €	35	100,00%
Berlin FU	17	2.701.107,21 €	30	70,50%
Berlin TU	11	875.591,94 €	30	80,20%
Bonn Uni	31	5.033.319,83 €	25	82,10%
Darmstadt TU	9	59.266,42 €	30	97,80%
Duisburg-Essen Uni	28	850.289,71 €	36	43,20%
EBS Uni	26	0,00 €	42	49,40%
Frankfurt/Main Uni	27	1.486.697,92 €	70	83,70%
Frankfurt School of Finance and Man.	28	0,00 €	44	51,80%
Giessen Uni	6	124.494,41 €	15	100,00%
Graz Uni	*15*	*0,00 €*	34	-
Hamburg Uni	32	278.261,45 €	68	80,00%
Hannover Uni	11	843.168,76 €	26	69,80%
Innsbruck Uni	*15*	*0,00 €*	46	-
Jena Uni	10	1.430.750,02 €	33	100,00%
Kiel Uni	8	875.238,69 €	14	100,00%
Koblenz/Vallendar WHU	25	0,00 €	55	64,70%
Köln Uni	25	1.625.446,88 €	68	81,60%
Kühne Logistics Uni	6	0,00 €	18	100,00%
Magdeburg Uni	12	247.446,60 €	24	56,80%
Mannheim Uni	24	6.129.920,61 €	78	100,00%
München LMU	22	4.622.675,13 €	69	94,80%
München TU	23	746.163,98 €	85	100,00%
Münster Uni	18	756.286,40 €	33	51,50%
St.Gallen Uni	*44*	*0,00 €*	118	-
Wien Uni	*16*	*0,00 €*	91	-
Wien WU	*45*	*0,00 €*	87	-
Würzburg Uni	10	154.300,00 €	18	52,00%
Zürich ETH	*12*	*0,00 €*	63	-
Zürich Uni	*27*	*0,00 €*	89	-

5. CONCLUSION

It has to be emphasised that for management implications and decisions, *further analysis* of all efficiency measurements is needed in order to understand the complex connections regarding productivity in university operations. Detailed analytical approaches should address the interaction of research and teaching as well as other success factors for university operations such as location and regional networks, gender issues, leadership and organisational matters. From the outlined case study as well as previous research regarding university efficiency the following *implication* areas and hypotheses may be derived:

- No empirical evidence for economies of scale can be found (hypothesis not falsified but increasing probability for a diseconomies of scale hypothesis).
- Possible reasons and influences may be coordination efforts, increasing "mission diversity" and "mission creep" with institutional size.
- A positive view may see that benchmarking reveals efficiency potential in most settings and analyses – for *all* subgroups (large/small, private/public).
- The efficiency view may be a complementary and necessary (new) perspective.

For the practical *faculty management* context, some implications can be named as additional hypotheses:

- Faculties shall cease from "size matters" strategies – or use this only in very cautious applications, i.e. only with "checks and balances".
- Faculties shall rethink objectives, strategies and excellence concepts – in combination with "quality profiling", because otherwise efficiency measurement has no real meaning.
- Faculties shall make "excess costs of excellence and size" internally visible in institutions (and also provide "fair" cost allocation).

- Faculties shall make the efficiency view a *complementary* standard KPI / management question in major decisions (e.g. see research results for long-term efficiency costs of mergers, cp. Klumpp/Zelewski 2012).

According to the presented results it has become obvious that *university efficiency* is a major question that has to be addressed in research as well as in higher education university leadership concepts in order to create the modern and successful institutions that all university stakeholder are striving for.

REFERENCES

Ahn, Taesik/Charnes, Abraham/Cooper, William W., Some statistical and DEA evaluations of relative efficiencies of public and private institutions of higher learning, in: Socio-Economic Planning Sciences 22 (6/1988), 259-269.

Aigner, Dennis/Lovell, C. A. Knox/Schmidt, Peter, Formulation and estimation of stochastic frontier production function models, in: Journal of Econometrics 6 (1/1977), 21-37.

Banker, Rajiv D./Charnes, A./Cooper, W .W., Some models for estimating technical and scale inefficiencies in data envelopment analysis, in: Management Science 30 (9/1984), 1078-1092.

Banker, Rajiv D./Conrad, Robert F./Strauss, Robert P., A comparative application of data envelopment analysis and translog methods: An illustrative study of hospital production, in: Management Science 32 (1/1986), 30-44.

Barth, Richard T./Vertinsky, Ilan, The effect of goal orientation and information environment on research performance: A field study, in: Organizational Behavior and Human Performance 13 (1975), 110-132.

Beasley, John E., Determining teaching and research efficiencies, in: Journal of the Operational Research Society 46 (1995), 441-452.

Bonaccorsi, Andrea/Brandt, Tasso/De Filippo, aniela/Lepori, Benedetto/Molinari, Francesco/Niederl, Andreas/Schmoch, Ulrich/Schubert, Torben/Slipersaeter, Stig, Feasibility study for creating a European university data collection, Brussels (EU Commission Documents) 2010.

Bottomley, Anthony/Dunworth, John, Rate of return analysis and economies of scale in higher education, in: Socio-Economic Planning Sciences 8 (1974), 273-280.

Butler, Timothy W./Li, Ling, The utility of returns to scale in DEA programming: An analysis of Michigan rural hospitals, in: European Journal of Operations Research 161 (2/2005), 469-477.

Charnes, Abraham/Cooper, William W./Rhodes, Eduardo, Measuring the efficiency of decision making units, in: European Journal of Operational Research 2 (1978), 429-444.

Charnes, Abraham/Cooper, William W./Thrall, Robert M., A structure for classifying and characterizing efficiency and inefficiency in data envelopment analysis, in: Journal of Productivity Analysis 2 (3/1991), 197-237.

Chu Ng, Ying/Li, Sung K., Measuring the research performance of Chinese higher education institutions: An application of data envelopment Analysis, in: Education Economics 8 (2000), 139-156.

Coelli, Tim, Estimators and hypothesis tests for a stochastic frontier function: A Monte Carlo analysis, in: Journal of Productivity Analysis 6 (1995), 247-268.

Cohn, Elchanan/Rhine, Sherie L. W./Santos, Maria C., Institutions of higher education as multi-product firms: Economies of scale and scope, in: Review of Economics and Statistics 71 (1989), 284-290.

Cooper, William W./Seiford, Lawrence M./Tone, Kaoru, Data envelopment analysis – A comprehensive text with models, applications, references and DEA-Solver software, New York (McGraw-Hill) 2007.

Cullinane, Kevin/Wang, Teng-Fei/Song, Dong-Wook/Ji, Ping, The technical efficiency of container ports: Comparing data envelopment analysis and stochastic frontier analysis, in: Transportation Research Part A: Policy and Practice, 40 (4/2006), 354-374.

DFG, Förderatlas 2012 – Kennzahlen zur öffentlich finanzierten Forschung in Deutschland, Bonn (DFG) 2012.

Dundar, Halil/Lewis, Darrell R., Departmental productivity in American universities: Economies of scale and scope, in: Economics of Education Review 14 (1995), 199-244.

Dyckhoff, Harald/Allen, Karin, Measuring ecological efficiency with data envelopment analysis (DEA), in: European Journal of Operational Research 132 (2/2001), 312-325.

Feng, Y. J./Lu, H./Bi, K., An AHP/DEA method for measurement of the efficiency of R&D management activities in universities, in: International Transactions in Operational Research 11 (2004), 181-191.

Glass, J. Colin/McKillop, Donal G./O'Rourke, Gary, A cost indirect evaluation of productivity change in UK universities, in: Journal of Productivity Analysis 10 (1998), 153-175.

Handelsblatt, Ranking der BWL-Fakultäten 2013, http://tool.handelsblatt.com/tabelle/index.php?id=118&so=1a&pc=100&po=0, 2013, accessed 24 June 2013.

Hashimoto, Keiji./Cohn, Elchanan, Economies of scale and scope in Japanese private universities, in: Education Economics 5 (1997), 107-116.

Hollnagel, Erik, Dependability of joint human-computer systems, in: Computer Safety, Reliability and Security, Lecture Notes in Computer Science, 2434 (2002), 4-9.

Hollnagel, Erik, The ETTO Principle – efficiency-thoroughness trade-off: why things that go right sometimes go wrong, Farnham, Burlington (Ashgate) 2009.

Jacobs, Rowena, Alternative methods to examine hospital efficiency: Data envelopment analysis and stochastic frontier analysis, in: Health Care Management Science 4 (2/2001), 103-115.

Johnes, Geraint/Johnes, Jill, Measuring the research performance of UK economics departments: An application of data envelopment analysis', Oxford Economic Papers 45 (1993), 332-347.

Johnes, Jill, Measuring efficiency: A comparison of multilevel modelling and data envelopment analysis in the context of higher education, in: Bulletin of Economic Research 58 (2/2006), 75-104.

Jongbloed, Bill./Vossensteyn, Hans, Keeping up performances: An international survey of performance-based funding in higher education, in: Journal of Higher Education Policy and Management 23 (2/2001), 127-145.

Kao, Chiang/Hung, Hsi-Tai, Efficiency analysis of university departments: An empirical study, in: Omega 36 (4/2008), 653-664.

Kleine, Andreas, A general model framework for DEA, in: *Omega* 32 (2004), 17-23.

Klumpp, Matthias/Zelewski, Stephan, Economies of scale in Hochschulen - Das Beispiel der Hochschulfusion Duisburg-Essen, in: Hochschulmanagement 7 (2/2012), 47-52.

Kocher, Martin G./Luptácik, Mikulás/Sutter, Matthias, Measuring productivity of research in economics: A cross-country study using DEA, in: Socio-Economic Planning Sciences 40 (2006), 314-332.

Korhonen, Pekka/Tainio, Risto/Wallenius, Jyrki, Value efficiency analysis of academic research, in: European Journal of Operational Research 130 (2001), 121-132.

Kumbhakar, Subal C./Lovell, C. A. Knox, Stochastic frontier analysis, Cambridge (Cambridge University Press) 2000.

Li, Mingshu/Boehm, Barry W./Osterweil, Leon J., Unifying the software process spectrum, in: International Software Process Workshop, SPW 2005, Berlin, Heidelberg (Springer) 2005.

Madden, Garry/Savage, Scott/Kemp, Steven, Measuring public sector efficiency: A study of economics departments at Australian universities, in: Education Economics 5 (2/1997), 153-168.

Maleki, Golnaz/Klumpp, Matthias/Cuypers, Marc, Higher education poductivity and quality modelling with data envelopment analysis methods, in: *Klumpp, Matthias* (ed.), The 2012 European Simulation and Modelling Conference Proceedings, Essen, 2012, 231-233.

McMillan, Melville L./Chan, Wing H., University efficiency: A comparison and consolidation of results from stochastic and non-stochastic methods, in: Education Economics 14 (1/2006), 1-30.

McMillan, Melville L./Datta, Debasish, The relative efficiencies of Canadian universities: A DEA perspective, in: *Canadian Public Policy* 24 (4/1998), 485-511.

Pedraja-Chaparro, Francisco/Salinas-Jimenez, Javier/Smith, Peter, On the role of weight restrictions in data envelopment analysis, in: Journal of Productivity Analysis 8 (2/1997), 215-230.

Ramsden, Paul, Describing and explaining research productivity, in: Higher Education 28 (2/1994), 207-226.

Sarrico, Cláudia S., On performance in higher education – Towards performance government, in: Tertiary Education and Management 16 (2/2010), 145-158.

Sarrico, Cláudia S./Teixeira, Pedro/Rosa, Maria J./Cardoso, Margarida F., Subject mix and productivity in Portugese universities, in: European Journal of Operational Research 197 (2/2009), 287-295.

Scholz, Christian/Stein, Volker, The dean in the university of the future, in: Working Paper 112, Chair for Organisation, Human Resource Management and Information Management, University of Saarland, Saarbrücken, 2013.

Schwarz, Jürgen, Messung und Steuerung der Kommunikations-Effizienz. Eine theoretische und empirische Analyse durch den Einsatz der Data Envelopment Analysis, Dissertation, Basel (Universität Basel) 2013.

Seiford, Lawrence. M., Data envelopment analysis: The evolution of the state of the art (1978-1995), in: The Journal of Productivity Analysis 7 (1996), 99-137.

Stahl, Michael J./Leap, Terry L./Wei, Zhu Z., Publication in leading management journals as a measure of institutional research productivity, in: Academy of Management Journal 31 (3/1998), 707-720.

Stevens, Philip. A., Stochastic frontier analysis of English and Welsh universities, in: Education Economics 13 (4/2005), 355-374.

Taylor, Brian/Harris, Geoff., Relative efficiency among South African universities: A data envelopment analysis, in: Higher Education 47 (1/2004), 73-89.

Thanassoulis, Emmanuel, Introduction to the theory and application of data envelopment analysis: A foundation text with integrated software, Dordrecht (Springer) 2001.

Thannasoulis, Emmanuel/Portela, Maria C. S./Despic, Ozren, Data envelopment analysis: The mathematical programming approach to efficiency analysis, in: *Fried, Harold O./Lovell, C. A. Knox/Schmidt, Shelton S.* (eds.), The measurement of productive efficiency and productivity growth, Oxford, New York (Oxford University Press) 2008, 251-419.

Van Vught, Frans A./Ziegele, Frank, Multidimensional rankings – The design and development of U-Multirank, Dordrecht (Springer) 2012.

Westrum, Ron, A typology of resilience situations, in: *Hollnagel, Erik/Nemeth, Christopher P./Dekker, Sidney* (eds.), Resilience engineering perspectives: Remaining sensitive to the possibility of failure, Aldershot, Hampshire, Burlington (Ashgate) 2008, 55-65.

Woods, David D., How to design a safety organisation: Test case for resilience engineering, in: *Hollnagel, Erik/Woods, David D./Leveson, Nancy* (eds.), Resilience engineering: Concepts and precepts, Aldershot, Hampshire, Burlington (Ashgate) 2006, 315-325.

Wreathall, John, Properties of resilient organizations: An initial view in: *Hollnagel, Erik/Woods, David D./Leveson, Nancy* (eds.), Resilience engineering: Concepts and pre-

cepts, Aldershot, Hampshire, Burlington (Ashgate) 2006, 275-285.

Zangoueinezhad, Abouzar/Moshabaki, Ashgar, Measuring university performance using a knowledge-based balanced scorecard, in: Iran International Journal of Productivity and Performance Management 60 (8/2011), 824-843.

Zhu, Joe/Cook, WWade D. (eds.), Modeling data irregularities and structural complexities in data envelopment analysis – A problem-solving handbook, New York (Springer) 2007.

Zomer, Arend, Benneworth, Paul, The rise of the university's third mission, in: *Enders, Jürgen/de Boer, Harry F./Westerheijden, Don F.* (eds.), Reform of higher education in Europe, Rotterdam (Sense) 2011, 81-102.

Acknowledgement: This chapter presents results connected to the research project HELENA, supported by the German Ministry for Education and Research (BMBF), administrated by DLR with the ID No. 01PW11007. The author is grateful for this support.

Matthias Klumpp studied economics and business administration at the Universities of Leipzig and Strasbourg as well as education at Humboldt University Berlin and University of Kassel (INCHER). Since the Ph.D. at University of Leipzig in 2007 he is professor for business administration at FOM University of Applied Sciences, Essen, Germany. Since 2011 he also leads the BMBF research group HELENA at University of Duisburg-Essen. His research addresses efficiency questions in higher education as well as higher education management, Bologna, EQF and ESCO implementation.

DEAN'S ROLE ON THE POLICY IMPLEMENTATION: SOME LESSONS FROM THE IMPLEMENTATION OF BOLOGNA PROCESS IN SPAIN

Marina Elias

Education and Employment Research Group, Department of Sociology , Autonomous University of Barcelona, Campus Mundet. Passeig de la Vall d'Hebron 171. 08035. Barcelona. Spain
marina.elias@uab.cat

This paper presents conclusions of analysed results from researches on higher education institutions in Spain done by our research group over the last fifteen years (Grup de Recerca en Investigació i Treball – Education and Employment Research Group of the Department of Sociology at the Autonomous University of Barcelona (GRET-UAB)). The latest two major research works carried out by the research group and founded by the Spanish Ministry of Education are based on the implementation of Bologna Process in Spain. First one during 2005-2007 period focus on the impacts of implementation of Bologna Process on academics (BSO2003-06395/CPSO) and the second research carried out from 2009-2011 focuses on the impacts of implementation of Bologna Process on students (CSO2008-02812).

1. INTRODUCTION

Faculty deans provide academic and strategic leadership within their Faculty. They play a pivotal role in the overall academic and strategic development of the institution. The deans[1], as leaders and as managers, have to be aware of the redesign of the mission, vision and values underpinning their institution are a response to the demands of a new economic climate, shifting ideological stances and changing organisational priorities affecting higher education the world over.

Academic literature and research works about implementation of different institutional reforms, as Bologna process, have concluded that taking into account that one of the most negative consequences that may result from collegial model is the inefficiency of the government system to adapt to rapid changes and the excessive weight of the corporate interests of academics in decision-making at different levels (Mora y Vidal 2003). Then, "the challenge remains the establishment by the leadership of high level management, balanced with space for bottom-up initiatives within departments and faculties" (EUA 2005).

A good strategy to implement a reform is that the management team avoids the obstacles that may hinder it (Lewin 1956; Senge 2002) and, also, analyse past experiences if they worked well or not (Martin 1999). For instance, avoid applying a unique recipe for every degree because there are different traditions and paradigms (Becher 1989). The hardest thing in the implementation of a reform is to generalise and maintain it, and then persistent efforts are needed over time (Lewin 1956). For this reason "it is required intense intra-institutional communication and government teams' stiff but open to dialogue" (EUA 2005).

---

[1] In this paper, the term "dean" is used. It could be changed for any middle manager in a higher education institution, as heads of departments, vice deans etc.

2. CONTEXT OF SPANISH HIGHER EDUCATION

Historically, the Spanish higher education system has been governed according to the principles of the bureaucratic model of French tradition governed by administrative law and public patterns of government. This model sharpened its characteristics due to centralisation and lack of democracy in the last period authoritarian Franco's dictatorship (1939-1975).

The first higher education law in current democratic period, the University Reform Act of 1983, profoundly changed the management of the university pulling the collegiate model, developing university autonomy and the internal democratisation of the university.

Successive state and regional laws have been outlined throughout this process, bringing even more Spanish universities to the managerialist model, changing the election office systems, restricting participation in collegiate bodies, expanding the presence of civil society in the highest organ of institutional governance (Governing Council), decreasing the weight of civil servants and imposing a more centralised access to permanent jobs. At the same time, it normalises the incorporation of universities to the European Higher Education Area. Still, it is a weak model of managerialism compared to other countries with higher-level managers of the organisation, since in Spain such managers are elected among academics of the university.

In brief, the general trend of the Spanish university has been the shift from a bureaucratic model to a collegiate model, with the permanence of some aspects of the bureaucratic model and incorporating more recently, some other aspects from business or managerialist model.

This leadership model places deans in a difficult position of balancing values, norms and expectations of their fellow teachers and managers higher up in the organisation who are also also academics. It is, therefore, not surprising to find many of these deans in contradictory situations with responsibility but without power or urging other to make decisions even positioning themselves against such measures (Deem 1998; Santiago et al. 2006).

3. RESEARCH METHODOLOGY

The first piece of research was carried out in ten degree programmes in one university; six of them are integrated into an experimental plan in order to incorporate the European Credit Transfer System (ECTS). The main focus of the research was to answer the question how the deans of the experimental degrees follow up different strategies of management, generation of consensus and communication, in order to carry out the implementation of the ECTS. The academics responses – in terms of management evaluation, attitudes around the reform and perceived information degree – were as well examined. The analysis lets identify some opportunities and constrictions, which the deans have to take into account.

The data collection techniques include in-depth interviews to three or more institutional managers (leaders) of each degree programme (at least the Dean, Head of Department and Coordinator of degree). Also we surveyed the faculty involved in the degree (full or a minimum of 50 questionnaires) and we analysed many types of documentation (evaluations, presentation handouts of degrees, minutes of meetings, websites, etc.).

The second piece of research mentioned was about the impacts of Bologna Process implementation on students. In any case, it should be pointed out that the data have been triangulated, interviews have been carried out with people holding positions at the university (deans and coordinators) and the secondary data have been analysed. All the results point mainly in the same direction as students' perceptions.

The data was collected through four public universities in Barcelona Metropolitan Area, with 857 student questionnaires collected. Ten degree programmes using the criterion of the hard-soft division (Health, Engineering and Sciences as hard and Social sciences and Arts as soft) were chosen. In each area, it was selected one degree with a more defined professional profile and one with a less defined one, along the same lines of applied rather than non-applied criteria used by Becher (2001). Degree programmes analysed were Architecture, Telecommunications Engineering, Chemistry, Biology, Social Education, Business Studies, Pharmacy, Nursing, Translation and Interpretation, and Humanities.

Implementation of the Bologna Process in Spanish higher education system could be used as an example of the process of implementation of a law and the role developed by faculty deans. Analyzing the impacts on academics, staff and students depending on the managerial decisions of deans involved in the process.

Departing from these research, works and other theoretical and empirical knowledge accumulate through the research group over fifteen years, a list of main conclusions regarding management at higher education institutions, specifically on dean role, is presented below.

4. RESEARCH CONCLUSIONS OF THE DEANS' ROLE

Policy Development

The mostly present collegiate model in Spanish higher education institutions rejects any reform project that in the process of definition is considered that it violates legitimate rules of the institution. In this model, down directives should be an opportunity for upward reforms, in this sense, top-down policies should gather bottom-up ones. Accordingly, firstly, fit factors between top and bottom level policies are needed and secondly, there must be a connection between the proposed project with past higher education reforms to avoid starting from zero to each reform.

Regarding Leadership

It may be obvious, but nevertheless it is important to mention that the assumption of responsibility and leadership from the dean's is inescapable. A member of the corporate leadership team should take responsibility for the process, developing a proactive leadership. This leadership at all levels requires genuine dialogue capacity while proposing global lines, especially early in the process.

To carry out properly the dean's role, he/she must have clear congruence between practices and discourses. In this sense, in the best situation we found in our analysed data, deans have much capacity to act on the definition of the reform project and the process to implement it, and they are faced with the possibility of legitimizing and make the project acceptable for the rest of the staff.

There are some clue points to develop in order to legitimate the dean's authority, for instance, whether a successful reform is planned, the management team who drive the change must consider the causes of discontent among teachers and students and take steps to find solutions.

However, bearing in mind that university power is widely distributed and the academic profession is complex, we found that it is almost impossible to pull out a reform without the positive collaboration of those actors most directly involved. In this sense, in some institutions, student unions and other leaders must facilitate the implementation tasks.

Another essential clue point is that the dean recontextualises the general policy which means looking at the needs of its faculty and applying the change by adapting to the context, assessing what has been done so far and following top directions (rector/president). The case analysed in our research reinforces the idea of the need for recontextualisation processes in line with the traditions of scientific disciplines and Faculties avoiding homogenizing processes piloted exclusively from the central authorities (Troiano et al. 2010).

In order to develop the recontextualisation of the general law, guidelines and official laws are undergoing this process in the sense that the different authorities and agents involved in them are undergoing a process of adapting official texts. Following this idea, a way of action that increases the chance of success is to create a project for the institution, which is able to combine internal idiosyncracies trends and the requirements that come from the outside. As pointed out above, this project will need to undergo an intense recontextualisation when own tradition clash with external requirements, however, may be more easily adjustable when both "philosophies" are in the same line (Troiano et al. 2011).

Finally, it is also necessary to analyse deeply possible effects, those expected and unexpected.

Communication and Coordination

Regarding this topic, the analysed data suggest that there should be a proper balance between regulation and coordination of national and institutional autonomy. Furthermore, a massive dissemination of information will be necessary: by many different channels and repeated in time to arrive for all academics.

Related to groups of academics, there is the need of a coordination group at the faculty level in which the dean or a vice dean plays a coordinating role. Dialogue should be extended throughout the academic community. Specifically, to implement teaching changes is convenient to create teamwork among teachers (Troiano 2000).

Recourses and Results

State financial support is essential to implement properly any reform. This might be obvious but it has not occurred in the Bologna Process implementation in Spain. The development was conducted with no money involved.

Furthermore, with pressure to devote more time to teaching duties without providing those necessary resources to the departments, faculties run the risk of producing an erosion of their research goals, which then leads to new cost of recovering. A good

balance among teaching, research and other duties is needed. Also, the existence of incentives (material or not) is important in some points (Masjuan/Troiano 2009). It requires a good assessment of all decisions and that the effort investment is clearly rewarded by the results.

At the same time, if this process does not take into account inequalities among discipline areas, institutions and faculties it will be difficult to compare efficiencies, and probably over time the inequalities will increase (Masjuan/Troiano/Elias 2007).

Finally, data shows how trying to implement too much changes in a short period of time or quick changes entail confusion, scepticism and counter reactions.

5. CONCLUSION

There are some aspects to learn from the Spanish experience of Bologna Process implementation. Sometimes, concrete policies that are successful in one context (for instance, one country) are applied in another context without a complete analysis of the context, such as the implementation needs or possible consequences related with the implementation. Major risks are related with that, e.g. important reforms without sufficient resources could mean less changes at the end, and burn-out of actors who have been devoting effort to carry out the reforms. In this sense, when there is not enough time to assimilate the overall reform, there is the risk of placing a part of the academics against the deans.

Regarding autonomy, distance and autonomy of the collegiate model, it could entail more freedom but there is a risk at the end in the current competitive world and within the evaluation system. This process has pushed universities to find alternative financing funds, being subject to increasingly exhaustive processes of accountability.

In this overall situation, the dean's role becomes even more complicated. Deans have to struggle with laws, academics, budgets, ideas, reforms and results.

REFERENCES

Becher, Tony, Academic tribes and territories. Buckingham (Open University Press) 1989.

Deem, Rosemary, New "managerialism" and higher education: The management of performances and cultures in universities, in: International Studies in the Sociology of Education, 8 (1/1998) 47-70.

Elias, Marina, Recontextualisation of the Bologna process: Impacts on students. Jubilee Press visiting scholars' papers. Nottingham (Nottingham Jubilee Press) 2012.

EUA, European University Association, Tendències IV: Les universitats europees implementen Bolonya, Barcelona (Generalitat de Catalunya, DURSI) 2005.

Lewin, Kurt, La teoría del campo en la ciencia social, Barcelona (Paidós) 1956

Martin, Elaine, Changing academic work. Developing the learning university, Buckingham (Open University) 1999.

Masjuan, Josep M./Troiano, Helena, Incorporación de España al espacio europeo de educación superior: el caso de una universidad catalana, in: Calidad en la Educación 31 (2009) 123-142.

Masjuan, Josep M./Troiano, Helena/Elias, Marina, Los factores de éxito de las universidades europeas en el proceso de incorporación al espacio europeo de educación superior y la experiencia de una universidad catalana, in: Educar 40 (2007) 49-67.

Mora, José-Ginus/Vidal, Javier, Two decades of changes in Spanish Universities. Learning the hard way. Cher 16th Annual Conference, Porto, 4th-6th September 2003.

Santiago, Riu/Carvalho, Teresa/Amaral, Alberto/Meek, V. Lynn, Changing patterns in the middle management of higher education institutions: The case of Portugal, in: Higher Education, 52 (2006) 215-250.

Senge, Peter M., La quinta disciplina. El arte y la práctica de la organización abierta al aprendizaje. Barcelona (Granica) 2002.

Troiano, Helena, Estrategias para el cambio de las prácticas docentes en la universidad, in: Educar 27 (2000) 137-149.

Troiano, Helena/Masjuan, Josep M./Elias, Marina, La recontextualización de las políticas de incorporación al Espacio Europeo de Educación Superior: Un estudio de caso, in: Revista de Educación 351 (2010).

Troiano, Helena/Masjuan, Josep M./Elias, Marina, Estrategias de gestión y comunicación de los líderes intermedios en la aplicación de los ECTS, in: Papers. Revista de Sociologia 96/4 (2011), 1235-1255.

Acknowledgments: This piece of research is part of the "National Plan for scientific research, technological development and research" (CSO2008-02812) funded by the Spanish Ministry of Science and Innovation, which is entitled "The students in front of new university reform'. And other research from the same National Program with the reference BSO2003-06395/CPSO, entitled "Academics in front of institutional changes". The authors are part of the GRET, the Education and Employment Research Group at the Universitat Autònoma de Barcelona. The written version of this article has been re-drafted and discussed with the rest of the GRET members taking part in this research: Helena Troiano, Lidia Daza, Albert Sanchez-Gelabert and Josep Maria Masjuan.

Marina Elias is lecturer teacher at Sociological Theory Department in Barcelona University. Member of Fondation des régions européennes pour la recherche en éducation et formation (FREREF) Network. Research interests in higher education students, drop-outs, social inequalities, social justice.

PART III

CONFERENCE OUTCOME

UNIVERSITY GOVERNANCE: A RESEARCH AGENDA

Christian Scholz[1], Volker Stein[2], Stefanie Müller[3] and Tobias M. Scholz[4]

[1,3]Chair for Organisational Behaviour, Human Resource Management and Information Systems,
Universität des Saarlandes, Campus A5 4, 66123 Saarbrücken, Germany
[2,4]Chair for Human Resource Management and Organisational Behaviour, University of Siegen,
Hoelderlinstrasse 3, 57076 Siegen, Germany
[1]scholz@orga.uni-sb.de, [2]volker.stein@uni-siegen.de, [3]sm@orga.uni-sb.de, [4]tobias.scholz@uni-siegen.de

Universities are complex institutions with inherent interest conflicts between the top university management and the productive units such as faculties. University governance becomes increasingly important. Still, however, research on university governance lacks a systematic approach. Therefore, the objective of the paper is to conceptualise a research agenda on university governance, consisting of situation, configuration and effectiveness components. The resulting framework serves to map the theoretical conceptions of university governance, helps identify blind spots in university governance research and points to university governance risks. The discussion of international university governance systems exemplifies the benefits of applying the research agenda. This paper ends up with implications for higher education management and policy.

1. INTRODUCTION

Current State of Universities

Within the past decade, higher education has gone through major reforms in many countries of the world (e.g. De Boer/Jongbloed/ Enders/File 2010). In order to make higher education more efficient and effective, structures have been transformed, processes were changed, and financial resources were shifted. Universities, however, still face high external and internal pressure that makes it difficult to consolidate the changes.

External pressure. Applying the paradigm of "New Public Management" (e.g. Aucoin 1990; Hood 1991) to higher education, political reforms were initiated in order to increase university performance through the implementation of competitive and managerial elements (e.g. Bogumil/Heinze 2009; Fumasoli/Lepori 2011; Santiago/Carvalho 2008; Schimank 2005). Redefinitions of goals for universities and new legitimacy demands (e.g. Hüther 2010) affected self-conception, mission, strategies and the overall image of universities. Universities had to develop new competencies in order to adequately cope with new claims of internal and external stakeholders and the conditions of an increasingly international, technological competition in the field of higher education (e.g. von Trotha 2002). The traditional Humboldtian model of universities, still being prevalent in some countries such as Japan, Germany and Canada, is in danger of being completely replaced by the paradigm-shifting "corporate" model of universities which follows the rationale of (more or less modern) corporations.

Internal pressure. Regarding their organisational configuration, universities are torn between two opposing principles (e.g. Carnegie/Tuck 2010; Christensen 2011; Delbecq/Bryson/Van de Ven 2013; Scholz/ Stein 2011b). One principle is the centralised model of universities with strong control of the university president at the expense of the faculties. Based on central hierarchical planning, the president can decide on the whole range of university and faculty matters, including overall strategy, election of deans, appointment of professors, budget allocation and additional pay. The faculties mainly execute the decisions of the president. The other principle is the collegial approach, reviving subsidiarity, decentralisation and participative bottom-up management. This democratic structure tries to strengthen the academic freedom. Faculties provide services for professors, while the university president is in charge of attracting funds and endowments for the university and concentrates on external representation.

This pressure leads to continuous adaptations but covers that one far more fundamental question is still open: Which of the discussed directions will be able to contribute to the long-term viability and success of universities? Which underlying logic of university governance will be able to retain the desired social and economic functions of universities for different countries in their respective situations?

The Power of Words

The constructivist perspective (e.g. Berger/Luckmann 1966; Chia 1996, 15-16) tells us that the wording of phenomena shapes reality. It matters *that* people phrase what they are concerned with and it matters *how* people name it. The fact that they phrase it means that they make the phenomenon apparent and share it with others. The way how they name it means that they give it a specific notion and contribute to the disclosure of hidden sense.

Naming the future challenges of university governance is only at the first glance an abstract political issue. At the second glance, it is also a very personal issue for everyone being involved in the university system. It enables people to clarify the legitimacy of their actions and to determine for which decisions and behaviours they are willing to take responsibility.

Therefore, it will be important to talk about the university governance phenome-

non in a way that starting positions, alternative actions and expected outcomes become clear and the university system's future can be shaped in the light of transparent opportunities and risks. Hence, as a matter of intense discussion not only in the academic sphere but also in the political sphere both within and around the university (e.g. Scholz/Stein 2009), the concretisation of university governance lacks a systematic approach.

Objective of the Paper

The objective of our paper is to conceptualise a research agenda on university governance in order to clarify the basis of academic and political discussion. The research agenda serves to define the field and map existing research as well as research gaps.

Based on the research background of university governance, we will develop the research agenda by integrating situation, configuration and effectiveness of university governance in one framework. Then we will discuss general conditions for the international application of this research agenda as well as its expected benefits. We will end up with implications for higher education management and policy.

2. RESEARCH BACKGROUND

Governance Issues in Universities

A university is a complex type of organisation. It is headed by a university president (or, depending on the situational terminology, by a rector or vice-chancellor or CEO) and a board of trustees. The university top management assumes roles such as providing the funding of the university, defining the university-wide strategy and offering an attractive selection of academic disciplines. The substructures of a university such as faculties, departments, institutes and schools play the most important role for the university's service provision. Consisting of academic staff (such as professors, associate professors, assistant professors, research assistants, lecturers) and administrative staff, university divisions are responsible for academic research and teaching. Administrative units of the university provide the bureaucratic and technological infrastructure.

Inherent tensions and conflicts occur between the interests of the university management on the one hand and the interests of the faculties and their academic staff on the other hand (e.g Carnegie/Tuck 2010, 434). The crucial question is: who governs whom? In the sense of an "autocratic leadership" in the centralised model, the university management would claim the lead in all issues of university policy, including organisation and content definition of research and teaching. In the collegial model, almost in the sense of a "servant leadership" (Greenleaf 1977), the university management would serve the interests of the university divisions and grant a high degree of strategic, academic and administrative autonomy.

These tensions and conflicts become apparent when the opposing interests collide. Both parties try, in times of decreasing public funding, to gain control over scarce financial resources for their own activities. Both parties might have different views on the relevance of university stakeholders such as companies and on their influence on research and teaching contents. In order to win the competition for students and academic staff, both parties have different ideas on which processes to standardise and which to flexibilise. Taken together, the inherent tensions and conflicts within universities are a question of centralisation–decentralisation and depend on the extent of academic and organisational autonomy.

Since a university can be called a "professional bureaucracy" (Mintzberg 1983, 189), university management requires an increased awareness of how this kind of organisation works. This occurs at three levels. At the macro-level, the main subject of management is the relationship between the political sphere, represented by the ministerial bureaucracy, and the academic sphere, represented by the president of a university in combination with different kinds of university boards. The prevalent question at the macro-level is the allocation of predominantly public and state funds (e.g. Paradeise/Reale/Goastellec 2009, 198). The meso-level focuses the mechanisms of the internal coordination of diverse interests of university management and faculties. The micro-level deals with the decisions of individual actors such as professors (e.g. Wilkesmann 2011, 307).

How governance issues on the meso-level are coordinated in universities is strongly influenced by the academic sphere as the university's source of standardisation and regulation: "[T]he standards of the Professional Bureaucracy originate largely outside its own structure, in the self-governing associations its operators join with their colleagues from other Professional Bureaucracies. (...) the Professional Bureaucracy emphasises authority of a professional nature – the power of expertise" (Mintzberg 1983, 191-192). University governance regulations can, therefore, be seen as the result of a complex bargaining process, dominated by some internal key players, ignored by the majority of affected academic staff, and with stakeholders such as politicians, professional associations, and companies interfering in it. "In fact, not only do the professionals control their own work, but they also seek collective control of the administrative decisions that affect them – decisions, for example, to hire colleagues, to promote them, and to distribute resources. Controlling these decisions requires control of the middle line of organisation, which professionals do by ensuring that it is staffed with 'their own'. Some of the administrative work the operating professionals do themselves. (...) Moreover, full-time administrators who wish to have any power at all in these structures must be certified members of the profession and preferably be elected by the professional operators or at least appointed with their blessing. What emerges therefore, is a rather democratic administrative structure" (Mintzberg 1983, 197).

In universities, this idealistic democratic picture is again and again challenged by reality. From time to time, academics point out "that university governance is sick" (Yoder 1962, 222). Since the early 1960s, the question of balancing the interests between university management and academic staff, between administration and faculties, is repeatedly raised (chronologically e.g. Corson 1960; Yoder 1962; Barrett 1963; Larsen, Maassen/Stensaker 2009; Kretek/Dragšić/Kehm 2013; Shattock 2013; Taylor 2013). They all agree implicitly or explicitly on the need for university governance regulations but usually have different opinions about the content. And once the intentions of university governance are negotiated, the consecutive problem is compliant behaviour. University governance regulations can be easily violated because effective control of their compliance is extremely difficult. However, the extent of observing university governance influences the subsequent extent of conflicts that bear the risk of limiting university operations.

Corporate Governance as Blueprint

One general solution to moderate tensions within organisations is governance (e.g. Clarke/Branson 2012; Kooiman 2003; Monks/Minow 2011; Williamson 1996). Management science has all along formulated corporate governance principles for a correct and orderly management of corporations. Leadership in accordance with these regulations should ensure the sustainability of the organisation.

There are four types of corporate governance regulations: first, the self-created, experientially-based company rules, for example management guidelines and internal control regulations (e.g. Picou/Rubach 2006); second, customs and usances with a claim for universality, for example principles of orderly accounting (e.g. Moxter 2003); third, voluntarily chosen certification standards, for example ISO norms or quality models like the EFQM (e.g. Hakes 2007) and the OECD Principles of Corporate Governance (OECD 2004); fourth, binding laws, for example the Sarbanes-Oxley-Act from

2002. Taken together, all of these types reflect the current maturity level of management knowledge as well as the predominant ethical viewpoint in management.

Those principles exist due to the insight that meeting a minimum amount of regulations by the top management and supervisory bodies is essential in order to secure long-term and sustainable success (e.g. Monks/Minow 2011, xxii). Corporate governance regulations help avoid rudimentary management mistakes and promote mutual gains (e.g. Williamson 1996). For this reason they include regulations for the effectiveness of management and supervision structures, for the inclusion of the interests of stakeholders such as investors, customers and employees and, overall, for the provision of informational transparency.

Characterizing these principles by initiator and by obligation, we can again identify several forms (e.g. OECD 2004, 12). For single companies it is possible that the company owners declare regulations as binding for the executive managers and all employees, backed by an internal control of the compliance. Within an industry, several companies can join forces in order to voluntarily set a binding framework for corporate governance which will later be controlled by an industry association. Regarding a whole country, its legislative body is able to codify corporate governance and compliance regulations which are subject to legal supervision. Even supranational governance regulations exist for the companies of all respective member countries, also covered by legal supervision.

The context-related entirety of management and supervision principles is called governance. This term is used in a descriptive sense as a generic term for corporate regulatory systems, serving to reveal systematic and sometimes unperceived management risks. Moreover, it is used in a normative way as an imperative that has to be obeyed. This "good governance" (e.g. Aguilera/Cuervo-Cazurra 2009; Fauver/Fuerst 2006; OECD 2004, 3) implies from the beginning a differentiation in "good" and "bad". The underlying idea is that the efficacy of alternative modes of governance can be assessed and optimised (e.g. Williamson 1996, 11).

Governance regulations are predominant in companies (e.g. Monks/Minow 2011; Shleifer/Vishney 1997) but also cover politics (e.g. Chaturvedi 2005) and economics (e.g. Bell 2002; Tabb 2004). Besides the primary field of private enterprises, governance regulations exist for example for public administrations (e.g. Osborne 2010), cooperatives (e.g. Eckart 2009), in the health care system (e.g. Youde 2012), for utility services (e.g. Guy et al. 2011) and for educational institutions such as schools (e.g. Altrichter/Brüsemeister/Wissinger 2007).

University Governance as Specification

Although the number of academic contributions to the topic of university governance is compared to corporate governance not very large, university governance is more than a side issue in higher education management and policy. Two main streams of research can be identified.

The first research stream is based on new institutional economics (e.g. Jensen/Meckling 1976; Williamson 1975), dealing with aspects such as organisational arrangements for effective individual and collective behaviour and modes of governance in hierarchical structures. For example, the issue of distributed governance in universities among management, faculties and professors can be based on the analysis of property rights (e.g. McCormick/Meiners 1988). The impact of governance on performance output is surveyed empirically (e.g. Brown Jr. 2001) and principal–agent structures in universities are analyzed (e.g. Cunningham 2009; Scholz/Stein 2010). This research stream results in the description of alternative governance modes in universities.

The second research stream is an explorative one, looking to the existing diversity in the field of university governance. Coined as higher education governance, it covers the search for general differences in university governance, taking into account different cultural settings throughout the world, different traditions, different reforms and different ownership structures. Detailed cross-national analyses are provided for example by the OECD (e.g. OECD 2003; 2012). Based on this, there is a search for comprehensive patterns of university governance.

3. RESEARCH AGENDA

In order to sketch out the research agenda for university governance, we will integrate the different research streams into one framework. This framework will consist of a situation component, a configuration component and an effectiveness component.

Situation: Evolutionary Stages

Assessing university governance from country to country or from university to university needs to consider the specific structural conditions. Situational analysis is based on the insight that effective outcomes can best be reached if actions are adapted to the specificities of the respective system, for example its environment, its maturity and its competencies. Therefore, in the context of university governance a description of the situation is needed that allows determining the situational starting point.

We propose a differentiation by evolutionary stages of university governance structures that describe settings of tensions and conflicts being inherent to the structure consisting of university top management (here named as university president) and the research and teaching units (here named as faculties). Structural change leads to different stages of university governance and, therefore, to different types of interaction between university president and faculties. These stages are widely country-independent, since they describe a sequential pattern derived from the fundamental organisation theory on the dynamics of intrasystem change like, for example, Greiner (1972) has developed. Of course, the effectiveness of national systems of higher education is country-dependent, but the stages are not. The evolutionary stage model using here

(Scholz/Stein 2010; 2011a; 2011b) describes six archetypical developmental stages of university governance:

Faculty Silos depicts the situation where faculties as the core organisational units of the traditional university are divided along professional boundaries. Independently providing research and teaching, they fulfil their tasks according to the standards developed by their respective scientific community. The president of a university as an academic person plays a rather weak role; his managerial tasks are more or less restricted to representation. Centralised service units provide services to the faculties. The relationship between faculties and university top management is based on partnership and not on formal top-down authority. Professors have relatively high academic autonomy, which is supposed to bring about creativity and open up an appropriate scope of action to succeed within the competition for scientific reputation (e.g. Kern 2000, 29; Reichwald 1997, 7).

Academic Kindergarten is the structural degeneration of "Faculty Silos", sketching the relationship of the university with individual professors who are opportunistic, with opportunism defined as self-interest-oriented individual behaviour without taking third-party implications into account (Williamson 1975). Some professors, left to themselves and not being compelled into loyalty, begin to seek their own advantages, in particular financial resources, more staff for their research team and prestige. They still have free access to a broad range of university services, a situation that favours free-rider behaviour of single university professors at the expense of others who contribute stronger to the overall university's interests (e.g. Wilkesmann 2011, 305-306). This works because the individual professors' accountability is not claimed.

Presidential Feudalism reflects the corporatisation model of universities. The university president is the key player, who decides on everything which affects the future of the university. His completely centralised structure helps him interfere in the remotest corners of the university. He counteracts individual optimisation strategies of individ-

ual professors by increasing his own decision-making power, to the disadvantage of the autonomy of faculties and professors who in this stage have only a minor voice in the university.

Individual Negotiation Jungle is the structural degeneration of "Presidential Feudalism". Professors who have been revoked a great amount of individual as well as faculty autonomy, start to adapt to their new role and increase their negotiation capacity focused on extrinsic motivation. Since the university president is the only negotiation partner left for the professors, they will access him with all their problems. They will ask for moral support, more research money, higher salaries, new target agreements, bonuses, incentives, etc. The logical consequence is that the president's negotiation capacity will be exceeded. Increasing system complexity will lead to a system overload with the danger of a collapsing university management. Moreover, the president's formal authority decreases because he faces hundreds of well-trained negotiation partners on eye level. The role of faculties is reduced to a minimum, since each professor negotiates his working conditions opportunistically, even at the expense of the faculty's and the colleagues' interests. University effectiveness and efficiency become a zero-sum game among all university members.

University Collegialism reflects that tasks and problems within a university are carried out by groups of professors in a cooperative way. This democratic structure resembles "Faculty Silos" but, in order to resolve its negative results, introduces new elements. Collegialism follows a normative principle shaped by academic freedom and competition. On the one hand, professors regain full autonomy. They make decisions according to the principle of collegiality regarding the services portfolio provided by their university. On the other, professors are held accountable for their decisions. They are responsible for meeting the demands of stakeholders and, therefore, undertake the risk of failure. The accountability of professors is supposed to lead to their participation in working groups in order to deliver excellent research and teaching. Faculties are strengthened as service providers for the professors, with deans being responsible for the implementation of the academic staff's decisions. The influence of the university president, however, is reduced to external representation and fundraising.

Dean Steering is the structural degeneration of "University Collegialism". In this stage, deans turn out to behave opportunistically, taking advantage of the withdrawn role of the university president as well of the professors who were sidetracked by coordination efforts. They develop their own agenda, pleading the faculty's interests, and behave within the faculty in as feudalistic a manner as the university president in the stage of "Presidential Feudalism".

Taking these six stages, the structural contingencies of university governance can be determined. In its situation, power is specifically distributed, the inherent tensions and conflicts can be mapped, and the extent of effectiveness and efficiency can be explained.

Configuration: Norm – Codex – Index

In order to assess situationally how university governance works in practice, we have to identify the configurations being used for balancing power and solving conflicts in different evolutionary stages. Our conceptualisation, making recourse to corporate governance, consists of three configuration components in the sense of institutional arrangements. The university governance norm, deduced from university ethics, is the basis consensus of reasonable principles for university governance. The university governance codex specifies the principles for university governance based on the university governance norm. The university governance index measures the degree of fulfilment of those governance principles specified in the university governance codex. Taken together, these three configuration components translate governance intentions into evidence of governance-compliant behaviour.

University Governance Norm. For companies, explicit corporate governance has been developed in the 1990s, however, implicitly it existed long before (e.g. Daily/Dalton/Cennella Jr. 2003). For example it was common consensus what an "honourable merchant" is in business life and which business conduct can be expected. With the increasing strategic and technological complexity of corporate systems and due to the observation that the boundaries of those implicit rules were increasingly checked out, a formalisation of that implicitness was required.

Meanwhile, regulation of former implicitness reaches universities. In this regard, implicit traditions are no longer automatically the guidelines of action. It rather seems that everything is permitted that is not explicitly prohibited. However, to uphold governance flexibility for the people in power, it is reasonable to establish normative guidelines, contrary to the alternative of an extensive catalogue of prohibitions.

At first sight, a university governance norm seems difficult to deduce, in particular due to the divergent starting positions of the advocates of centralised and of decentralised governance. It is evident that there are different opinions concerning the formulation of a university governance norm. The respective actors, who feel in danger to be limited in their room of manoeuvre, are likely to oppose such a norm. However, the given social system in which politics, economy and education takes place sets a collective-ethical framework that prefers certain behaviour and excludes other behaviour. This ethical framework is constantly and dynamically evolving and stringently affects all areas of social relations.

In regard to corporate governance, it was possible to find such a normative basis. Companies focused on superordinated principles such as sustainability and transparency, where, despite all situational differences, non-compliance will increase the risk of failure and management collapse. Examples such as the Enron and Arthur Andersen case (e.g. Branson 2003; Dossani/Jo 2010) substantiate this assertion. In contrast to that, there are no obvious cases where deficits in university governance led to an extensive collapse of universities. This is because the government always has the option to intervene directly and directly revise the undesirable development.

Consequently, "good university governance" normatively refers to superordinated principles resembling those of "good corporate governance". They base upon the same understanding of a democratic, open, mutually committed society. In addition to that, "good university governance" has to consider the institutional particularities of universities.

First, superordinated principles for university governance derive from the university's democratic constitution. No single actor can claim the exclusive governance power. Sharing it leads to partial equilibriums of influence. In a fragile system of checks and balances, a democratic balance of power will emerge, being achievable through democratic elections of decision makers and through separation of powers among legislation (decision makers), the executive (management functions) and the judiciary (controller). Accountability for compliant behaviour is demanded in public organisations of higher education (e.g. Paradeise et al. 2009, 199-200).

Second, superordinated principles for university governance derive from the basis nature of a university as a loosely coupled system (e.g. Weick 1976), i.e. an interrelated community of lecturers and learners with own identities concerning teaching and research. This leads to the norm of joint governance across university subgroups, integrating committees with substantial collegiality (e.g. Orton/Weick 1976) and respecting different socialisations based on tradition and sustainability.

Therefore, the university governance norm is based on distributed influence among the actors in a university, participation rights, transparency of decisions and minimisation of sustainability risks.

University Governance Codex. The university governance codex, being deduced from the university governance norm, is the overall system of guidelines for the embodiment of sustainable and reasonable universi-

ty governance. There are several types of guidelines:

- Basic guidelines: The university governance codex defines regulations which are compulsory and regulations which are recommended for voluntary application.

- Structural guidelines: The university governance codex lays down the object areas and the principles of university governance assessment and measurement.

- Process guidelines: The university governance codex prescribes how universities report on their compliance of university governance norms and how they establish transparency on whether, where and how far they diverge from the norms.

- Sanction guidelines: The university governance codex specifies the sanction modalities that apply if university governance norms are violated.

The sense of defining those guidelines is to protect the university actors' interests against unilateral discrimination. Therefore, all four types of guidelines have to be monitored concerning their compliance.

University Governance Index. Usually, governance is operationalised by indicator systems and combined in an index. One step further, rankings can make the status of the governance system and the position in cross-organisational comparison transparent. Davis et al. (2012) show the enormous role that such indicator systems already play and analyze effectiveness, reliability and impacts on policy making. It becomes obvious that the design of indicator systems has a significant influence on the effectiveness of governance regulations.

In university governance, there is the analog need for indicators and derived rankings. A university governance index will exceed the general comparison of higher education systems and the autonomy of university from politics. More precisely, it has to show the implementation of regulations of the university governance codex and report the status of the realisation of single aspects. This can be linked to the four above types of guidelines.

In regard to the basic guidelines, it has for example to be systematically determined under which university law and university foundation act a university is governed and which university governance norms these laws and acts fulfil. For example, a score-card for political university autonomy in Europe exists (Estermann/Nokkala/Steinel 2011), distinguishing the autonomy of universities concerning organisation, funding, staff recruiting, and profile formation and resulting in a performance ranking of European countries in those four dimensions. Similar to that it would be possible to establish a university governance index that is able to identify the balance of centralised and decentralised, collegial control in university regulations.

In the field of structural guidelines, catalogues of items can already be found that capture the extent of decentralised university governance and its realisation in universities. Ramo (1998) scans seven key indicators for distributed university governance: governance climate, institutional communication, the role of university supervising bodies, the role of the university president, the role of faculties, collective decision-making and the steering mechanisms of structural governance regulations. Scholz/Stein/Fraune (2012) develop a criteria catalogue for the assessment of decentralised university governance on the faculty level with aspects such as development of a faculty strategy, funding of the faculty, incorporation of the faculty in administrative structures and faculty information systems.

Concerning the process guidelines, the central question is the intensity of efforts to maintain the compliant execution and supervision of the university governance codex. The effectiveness of university governance over time has to be measured: How is transparency established regarding the process of decision-making? How are existing incentive schemes, for example salaries of the university management or supervisory bodies, monitored in respect to their effects and, if necessary, modified? Which key performance indicators, classifications and rank-ings are used for university governance? Does an evaluation of the university governance exist and how independent is it from the people involved in university governance?

As to the sanction guidelines, they assess the consequences in case that university governance violates the basic norms. Furthermore it is essential that an independent and neutral reporting system on governance norm violation and the sanctioning exists.

The resulting points system tells us the maturity of university governance in a specific university. The university governance index serves as operationalisation and quantification of governance issues. It will be interesting to determine single indices such as

- an index for the collegiality and participation fit of university laws;
- an index for the transparency of the election of university presidents;
- an index for the transparency of incentive and bonus systems for people with a university leadership role;
- an index for the extent of mandatory and voluntary compliance of guidelines university governance codex guidelines;
- an index for the quality of university governance reporting;
- an index for the dynamic development of the university governance codex.

Those single indices can be merged to one overall index. A university governance index brings along a complexity reduction as long as the aggregation rule for transforming various subindices into one substantial index is transparent.

Effectiveness: Object-Level and Meta-Level

One fundamental idea of governance is to reach mutual gains for example in situations of bilateral dependencies (e.g. Williamson 1996). Therefore, governance-inherent issues of conflict resolution and quality assurance in a broader sense as well as their effectiveness become crucial. But this is only one facet of university governance effectiveness related to the object-level, since there are criteria on a meta-level: how effective the monitoring of governance effectiveness is, and how effective the continuous improvement of university governance is.

Conflict Resolution Effectiveness. The prevalent function of a governance system is to balance inherent tensions and conflicts among decision makers and stakeholders (e.g. Boivard 2005). University governance is effective if it contributes to a university system which is not distracted from its genuine functions. Moreover, university governance has to find a mode of conflict resolution which is minimal in respect to transaction costs (e.g. Williamson 1996, 13).

Quality Assurance Effectiveness. However, university governance contributes to the overall appearance of a university. Stakeholders perceive the output quality in teaching and research. Therefore, successful university governance strengthens the overall competitiveness of the university in the market for higher education. Another important aspect of quality is the overall identity of the university, leading to a shared value system among the university's staff. Thinking this further, university governance contributes to social sustainability for academic professions (e.g. Hammond/Churchman 2007).

Monitoring Effectiveness. Once the university governance is defined in a university, it will be essential to repeatedly survey appropriate data und make them available for tracing. Monitoring over time helps increasing compliance towards the norms. The monitoring results allow conclusions on the common consciousness of university governance. Effectiveness can be increased if, similar to corporate governance, monitoring will be based on the definition and application of indices as part of an overall audit system (Cohen/Krishnamoorthy/Wright 2002) and if it will be connected with other parts of the university's governance system such as financial accounting. Monitoring effectiveness is evaluated not only internally but also from the outside. The "market" in the sense of specialist media issue rankings for universities, and researchers in higher education might specialise on single subindices.

Continuous Improvement Effectiveness. A long-term aspect of effectiveness focuses the capability of university governance to adapt to new realities. There must be a competence for constant review and change of the most important scopes such as the way of assigning the university president, the decision-making power of the university management and the faculties and the overall transparency of the decision-making system (e.g. Armour/Hansmann/Kraakman 2009). Furthermore it is necessary to regularly assess the effectiveness of the sanctioning system in case of violation of university governance.

Composing the Framework

Binding together the components of the framework leads to figure 1. It shows the six situational stages of structural university development. In each stage it will be possible to specify the prevalent university governance norm, a university governance codex, and main areas of the university governance index. In the end, the effectiveness of every situational configuration in respect to university governance can be assessed along the four effectiveness criteria on the object-level and the meta-level.

Figure 1: Research Framework for University Governance

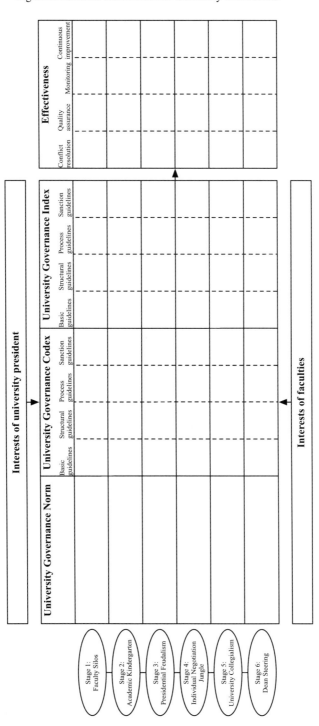

The meaning of "research agenda" is that this framework can be used according to both streams of research of university governance. Taking the first research stream that is based on new institutional economics, the cells are to be filled with theoretically based concretisations of sense-making and efficient organisational arrangements for effective individual and collective behaviour of university presidents and faculties. The result will be the stage-dependent picture of changing modes of governance in hierarchical university structures. Taking the second stream of research that is explorative, the cells are to be filled with empirical results on university governance in different evolutionary stages, looking for patterns of effective configurations and of "best university governance" and comparing university governance internationally. Taking evidence of different national university governance systems together, they represent a benchmark for university effectiveness.

4. DISCUSSION

Which benefit does the proposed research agenda on university governance have? First, it serves to map the theoretical conceptions, second, it helps identify blind spots in university governance research, and third, it points to governance risks and long-term threads to the sustainability of the university system.

Applying the research agenda to comparisons of international university governance, it is obvious that on a worldwide scale, systems of higher education differ very much (e.g. Paradeise et al. 2009). University systems of different countries can be located in different situational stages. There are many indications that the Japanese (e.g. Yamamoto 2004) and Latin American as well as African (e.g. Waswa/Swaleh 2012) university system are still in stage 1 (faculty silos) or 2 (academic kindergarten), while German universities have moved to stage 3 (presidential feudalism) (e.g. Scholz/Stein 2010). The Australian (e.g. Goedegebuure/Hayden/Meek 2009; Withers 2008), New Zealand,

Malaysian and Singapore (e.g. Mok 2008) and US universities are far ahead in the application of New Public Management reforms (e.g. Christensen 2011, 503) that are supposed to reflect "modern management principles" and, therefore, can be located in stage 4 (individual negation jungle), while Dutch universities follow their own culture that resembles stage 5 (university collegialism).

In particular in the US, university governance is under close observation. The *American Association of University Professors* argues the case for decentralised university governance. Since the middle of the 1990s, the AAUP progressively addresses collegial university governance (e.g. Euben 2003) and its evaluation (e.g. Ramo 1998), provides checklists for university president search committees (e.g. Poston n.y.) and indicator systems for good university governance (e.g. Ramo n.y.). Still, current university governance is moving towards the centralised model (e.g. Kamola/Meyerhoff 2009).

Comparing that with the German situation, the relevance of university governance rises as well, albeit with a big time lag to the corporate governance debate. Prevailing are the statements of proponents of centralistic university governance, like the German Rectors' Conference (e.g. Hochschulrektorenkonferenz 2011) or the Centre for Higher Education (e.g. Müller-Böling 2000). However, more collegial university governance concepts are discussed and assessed for their effectiveness (e.g. Bogumil/Heinze 2009) and their governance-compliant implications for the relationship between universities and companies (e.g. Scholz/Stein 2012a; 2012b).

The condition of faculties can serve as a useful indicator for the maturation level of a national university system. It is fascinating to compare faculties around the globe which are run in different ways (e.g. Amrhein/Baron 2013; Meek et al. 2010). It is an empirical task to relate university governance, for example university governance norms on faculty autonomy, university governance guidelines in the sense of a codex, and university governance indices and measurement systems of the different systems, to their performance, their effectiveness and their overall competitiveness.

Reflecting the international differences in university governance, a very important discussion starts, focusing international system transfer. It leads us to a critical view on international convergence and assimilation of university governance. The so-called "Americanisation" of university systems pushing university systems internationally in the same direction of centralistic governance (e.g. Kamola/Meyerhoff 2009) might not be reasonable. While situational factors differ from country to country, competitive advantages can only be achieved if different systems – and not equalised systems – compete (e.g. Page 2007).

Another discussion is put on the research agenda: How can modes of university governance be described in detail? Interestingly, the underlying concept of the centralistic model is the corporation of the 1980s, the centralised, departmental, regulated company with strong top-down management, rather than the modern, decentralised company of the 2010s which is the template for university governance in the sense of the collegial model. The related problem of the centralistic model is complexity: the more complex the university system becomes and the more stakeholders are linked to it, the less appropriate is centralistic leadership (e.g. Birnbaum, 1988: 198-199). Higher education management and policy should reflect that situational university governance is multifaceted and affects the whole range of system properties.

5. CONCLUSION

Like corporate governance diffuses into corporate culture and corporate behaviour, university governance has to find its way into university culture and then into behaviour of the actors in universities. The more conscious the modes of university governance are, the more it will be possible to instrumentalise it for university effectiveness and competitiveness in the international competition in higher education. Even if it currently seems that in many national discourses university governance is perceived to be the problem, it might turn out that university governance in the end will be the solution to create an identity of the university system and strengthen a sustainable and competitive position. Applying the above research agenda on university governance is an important step of enhancing this discussion.

From this point of view, university governance is more than something theoretical and something abstract. It is of utmost relevance for the practical motivation and retention of qualified academic staff in the university system. The substantial human capital of universities ultimately depends on the university governance system. Therefore, human resource development and training of decision makers in universities (e.g. Scholkmann 2008) has to be adjusted to university governance. For instance, university presidents and faculty deans should be trained in respect to modern, situationally effective university governance.

Finally, university governance develops a symbolic momentum of its own by the power of words. The way a university talks about its governance influences collective identity construction as well as individual motivation and commitment. Again, it matters *that* people phrase what they are concerned with and it matters *how* people name it. The fact that they phrase university governance means that they make it apparent and share with others how they want to shape their own future. The way how they name university governance means that they give it a specific notion and contribute to the disclosure of the hidden sense, i.e. the extent of centralised or decentralised autonomy.

REFERENCES

Aguilera, Ruth V./Cuervor-Cazurra, Alvaro, Codes of good governance, in: Corporate Governance: An International Review 17 (3/2009), 376-387.

Altrichter, Herber/Brüsemeister, Thomas/Wissinger, Jochen (eds.), Educational governance. Handlungskoordination und Steuerung im Bildungssystem, Wiesbaden (Verlag für Sozialwissenschaften) 2007.

Amrhein, Carl G./Baron, Britta (eds.), Building success in a global university: Government and academia – redefine worldwide in the relationship, Bonn – Berlin (Lemmens) 2013.

Armour, John/Hansmann, Henry/Kraakman, Reinier, Ageny problems and legal strategies, in: *Kraakman, Reinier/Armour, John/Davies, Paul/Enriques, Luca/Hansmann, Henry/Hertig, Gerard/Hopt, Klaus/Kanda, Hideki/Rock, Edward* (eds.), The anatomy of corporate law. A comparative and functional approach. Oxford (Oxford University Press) 2. ed., 2009, 35-54.

Aucoin, Peter, Administrative reform in public management: Paradigms, principles, paradoxes and pendulums. Governance, in: An International Journal of Policy and Administration 3 (2/1990), 115-137.

Barrett, Arnold L., University governance: Some omitted aspects, in: Academy of Management Journal 6 (2/1963), 170-172.

Bell, Stephen, Economic governance and institutional dynamics, Melbourne – New York (Oxford University Press) 2002.

Berger, Peter L./Luckmann, Thomas, The social construction of reality, New York (Doubleday) 1966.

Birnbaum, Robert, How colleges work. The cybernetics of academic organization and leadership, San Francicso – London (Jossey-Bass) 1988.

Boivard, Tony, Public governance: Balancing stakeholder power in a network society, in: International Review of Administrative Sciences 71 (2/2005), 217-228.

Bogumil, Jörg/Heinze, Rolf G. (eds.), Neue Steuerung von Hochschulen. Eine Zwischenbilanz, Berlin (edition sigma) 2009.

Branson, Douglas M., Enron – When all systems fail: Creative destruction or roadmap to corporate governance reform?, in: Villanova Law Review 48 (4/2003), 989-1021.

Brown Jr., William O., Faculty participation in university governance and the effects on university performance, in: Journal of Economic Behavior & Organization 44 (2/2001), 129-143.

Carnegie, Garry D./Tuck, Jacqueline, Understanding the ABC of university governance, in: The Australian Journal of Public Administration 69 (4/2010), 431-441.

Chaturvedi, J. C. (ed.), Political governance, New Delhi (Isha) 2005.

Chia, Robert K. G., Organizational analysis as deconstructive practice, Berlin – New York (de Gruyter) 1996.

Christensen, Tom, University governance reforms: potential problems of more autonomy?, in: Higher Education 62 (4/2011), 503-517.

Clarke, Thomas/Branson, Douglas, The SAGE handbook of corporate governance, Thousands Oaks (SAGE) 2012.

Cohen, Jeff/Krishnamoorthy, Ganesh/Wright, Arnold M., Corporate governance and the audit process, in: Contemporary Accounting Research 19 (4/2002), 573-594.

Corson, John J., Governance in colleges and universities, New York (McGraw-Hill) 1960.

Cunningham, Brendan M., Faculty: The administrator's keeper? Some evidence, in: Economics of Education Review 28 (4/2009), 444-453.

Daily, Catherine M./Dalton, Dan R./Cennella Jr., Albert A., Corporate governance: Decades of dialogue and data, in: Academy of Management Review 28 (3/2003), 371-382.

Davis, Kevin E./Fisher, Angelina/Kingsbury, Benedict/ Merry, Sally E. (eds.), Governance by indicators. Global power through classification and rankings, Oxford (Oxford University Press) 2012.

De Boer, Harry/Jongbloed, Ben/Enders, Jürgen/File, Jon, Progress in higher education reform across Europe: Governance reform, Brussels (European Commission) 2010.

Delbecq, André L./Bryson, John M./Van de Ven, Andrew H., University governance: Lessons from an innovative design for collaboration, in: Journal of Management Inquiry 22 (4/2013), 382-392.

Dossani, Asad/Jo, Hoje, Corporate governance and the fall of Enron, in: Review of Business Research 10 (3/2010), 13-24.

Eckart, Mischa, Cooperative governance. A third way towards competitive advantage, Saarbrücken (Südwestdeutscher Verlag für Hochschulschriften) 2009.

Estermann, Thomas/Nokkala, Terhi/Steinel, Monika, University autonomy in Europe II. The scorecard, Brüssel (European University Association) 2011.

Euben, Donna R., Some legal aspects of collegial governance. Paper presented at AAUP 2003 Governance Conference: Making Teamwork Work, Indianapolis, Indiana (10 November 2003), http://www.aaup.org/AAUP/issues/governanc e/legal-govern.htm, accessed on 11 February 2012.

Fauver, Larry/Fuerst, Michael E., Does good corporate governance include employee representation? Evidence from German corporate boards, in: Journal of Financial Economics 82 (3/2006), 673-710.

Fumasoli, Tatiana/Lepori, Benedetto, Patterns of strategies in Swiss higher education institutions, in: Higher Education 61 (2/2011), 157-178.

Goedegebuure, Leo/Hayden, Martin/ Meek, V. Lynn, Good governance and Australian higher education: An analysis of a neo-liberal decade, in: *Huisman, Jeroen* (ed.), International perspectives on the governance of higher education, New York – London (Routledge) 2009, 145-159.

Greiner, Larry E., Evolution and revolution as organizations grow, in: Harvard Business Review 50 (4/1972), 37-46.

Greenleaf, Robert K., Servant leadership: A journey into the nature of legitimate power and greatness, New York (Paulist) 1977.

Guy, Simon/Marvin, Simon/Medd, Will/ Moss, Timothy (eds.), Shaping urban infrastructures. Intermediaries and the governance of socio-technical networks, London – Washington, DC (Earthscan) 2011.

Hakes, Chris, The EFQM excellence model to assess organizational performance – A management guide, Zaltbommel (Van Haren) 2007.

Hammond, Cathryn/Churchman, Deborah, Sustaining academic life. A case for applying principles of social sustainability to academic profession, in: International Journal of Sustainability in Higher Education 9 (3/2007), 235-245.

Hochschulrektorenkonferenz, Entschließung „Zur Hochschulautonomie". Entschließung der 10. Mitgliederversammlung am 05 March 2011, http://www.hrk.de/positionen/gesamtliste-bes-chluesse/position/?tx_szconvention_pi1[decisi on]=8&cHash=e502fe8b7d4f8b

f05965491284427b81, accessed on 11 March 2012.

Hood, Christopher, A public management for all seasons?, in: Public Administration 69 (1/1991), 3-19.

Hüther, Otto, Von der Kollegialität zur Hierarchie. Eine Analyse des New Managerialism in den Landeshochschulgesetzen, Wiesbaden (Verlag für Sozialwissenschaften) 2010.

Jensen, Michael C./Meckling, William H., Theory of the firm: Managerial behavior, agency costs, and ownership structure, in: Journal of Financial Economics 3 (4/1976), 305-360.

Kamola, Isaac/Meyerhoff, Eli, Creating commons: Divided governance, participatory management, and struggles against enclosure in the university, in: Polygraph 21 (2009), 5-27.

Kern, Horst, Rückgekoppelte Autonomie. Steuerungselemente in lose gekoppelten Systemen, in: *Hanft, Anke* (ed.), Hochschule managen? Zur Reformierbarkeit der Hochschulen nach Managementprinzipien, Neuwied (Luchterhand) 2000, 25-38.

Kooiman, Jan, Governing as governance, Thousand Oaks (SAGE) 2003.

Kretek, Peter M./Dragšić, Žarko/Kehm, Barbara M., Transformation of university governance: on the role of university board members, in: Higher Education 65 (1/2013), 39-58.

Larsen, Ingvild M./Maassen, Peter/Stensaker, Bjørn, Four basic dilemmas in university governance reform, in: Higher Education Management and Policy 21 (3/2009), 1-18.

McCormick, Robert E./Meiners, Roger E., University governance: A property rights perspective, in: Journal of Law and Economics 31 (2/1988), 423-442.

Meek, V. Lynn/Goedegebuure, Leo/Santiago, Rui/ Carvalho, Teresa (eds.), The changing dynamics of higher education middle management, Dordrecht (Springer) 2010.

Mintzberg, Henry, Structure in fives: Designing effective organizations, New Jersey (Prentice Hall) 1983.

Mok, Ka H., Positioning as regional hub of higher education: Changing governance and regulatory reforms in Singapore and Malaysia, in: International Journal of Educational Reform 17 (3/2008), 230-250.

Monks, Robert A. G./Minow, Nell, Corporate governance, Chichester (Wiley) 5. ed., 2011.

Moxter, Adolf, Grundsätze ordnungsgemäßer Rechnungslegung, Düsseldorf (IDW) 2003.

Müller-Böling, Detlev, Die entfesselte Hochschule, Gütersloh (Bertelsmann Stiftung) 2000.

OECD, Changing patterns of governance in higher education, in: *OECD* (ed.), Education policy analysis 2003 edition, Paris (OECD) 59-78, 2003, http://www.oecd.org/education/highereducatio nandadultlearning/35747684.pdf, accessed on 11 March 2012.

OECD, OECD Principles of Corporate Governance, Paris (OECD) 2004.

OECD, Education at a glance 2012. OECD indicators, Paris (OECD) 2012.

Orton, J. Douglas/Weick, Karl E., Loosely coupled systems: A reconceptualization, in: Academy of Management Review 15 (2/1990), 202-223.

Osborne, Stephen P. (ed.), The new public governance? Emerging perspectives on the theory and practice of public governance, Milton Park – New York (Routledge) 2010.

Page, Scott E., The difference: How the power of diversity creates better groups, firms, schools and societies, Princeton (Princeton University Press) 2007.

Paradeise, Catherine/Reale, Emanuela/ Goastellec, Gaële, A comparative approach to higher education reforms in Western European countries, in: *Paradeise, Catherine/Reale, Emanuela/Bleiklie, Ivar/Ferlie,* Ewan (eds.), University governance. Western European comparative perspectives, Dordrecht (Springer) 2009, 197-225.

Picou, Armand/Rubach, Michael, Does good governance matter to institutional investors? Evidence from the enactment of corporate governance guidelines, in: Journal of Business Ethics 65 (1/2006), 55-67.

Poston, Muriel E., Presidential search committee checklist. Washington, DC: American Association of University Professors (n.y), http://www.aaup.org/AAUP/issues/governanc e/postart.htm, accessed on 03 November 2012.

Ramo, Keetjie, Assessing the faculty's role in shared governance: Implications of AAUP standards, Washington, DC (American Association of University Professors) 1998.

Ramo, Keetjie, Introduction to „Indicators of sound governance". Washington, DC: Ameri-

can Association of University Professors (n.y.), http://www.aaup.org/AAUP/issues/governanc e/ramintro.htm, accessed on 11 March 2012.

Reichwald, Ralf, Universitätsstrukturen und Führungsmechanismen für die Universität der Zukunft. Arbeitsbericht Nr. 13 des Lehrstuhls für Allgemeine und Industrielle Betriebswirtschaftslehre der Technischen Universität München, Munich (February 1997), http://www.aib.wiso.tumuenchen.de/neu/eng/ content/publikationen/arbeitsberichte_pdf /TUMAIB%20WP%20013%20Reichwald%2 0Universitaetsstrukturen.pdf, accessed 18 June 2013.

Santiago, Rui/Carvalho, Teresa, Academics in a new work environment: The impact of New Public Management on work conditions, in: Higher Education Quarterly 62 (3/2008), 204-223.

Schimank, Uwe, 'New Public Management' and the academic profession: Reflections on the German situation, in: Minerva 43 (4/2005), 361-376.

Scholkmann, Antonia, Dekaninnen und Dekane als „universitäre Führungskräfte": Herausforderungen im Arbeitsalltag – Ansatzpunkte für die Personalentwicklung, in: *Scholkmann, Antonia/Roters, Bianca/Ricken, Judith/Höcker, Marc* (eds.), Hochschulforschung und Hochschulmanagement im Dialog. Zur Praxisrelevanz empirischer Forschung über die Hochschule, Münster (Waxmann) 2008, 71-82.

Scholz, Christian/Stein, Volker (eds.), Bologna-Schwarzbuch, Bonn (Deutscher Hochschulverband) 2009.

Scholz, Christian/Stein, Volker, Bilder von Universitäten – Ein transaktionsanalytisch-agenturtheoretischer Ansatz, in: Betriebswirtschaftliche Forschung und Praxis 62 (2/2010), 129-149.

Scholz, Christian/Stein, Volker, Überlebenskritische Fragen zur Struktur von Universitäten, in: Forschung & Lehre 18 (1/2011a), 26-28.

Scholz, Christian/Stein, Volker, Les universités allemandes en mutation et les leçons à tirer par les administrations publiques pour leur gestion axée sur les connaissances, in: Télescope 17 (3/2011b), 31-53.

Scholz, Christian/Stein, Volker, Unternehmerisches Co-Produzententum von Bildung als Passungsautomatik: ein systemischer Irrtum, in: SEM Radar. Zeitschrift für Systemdenken und Entscheidungsfindung im Management 11 (1/2012a), 77-95.

Scholz, Christian/Stein, Volker, Wo sich Wirtschaft und Universitäten treffen: fünf Gestaltungsmodelle und eine eindeutige Antwort, in: *Tomaschek, Nino/Hammer, Edith* (eds.), University meets industry. Perspektiven des gelebten Wissenstransfers offener Universitäten, Münster (Waxmann) 2012b, 69-83.

Scholz, Christian/Stein, Volker/Fraune, Cornelia, Evolving structures of higher education institutions: The dean's role, in: *Bergan, Sjur/Egron-Polak, Eva/Kohler, Jürgen/Purser, Lewis/Vukasović, Martina* (eds.), Leadership and governance in higher education. Handbook for decision-makers and administrators, vol. 2, Berlin (Raabe) 2012, 1-24.

Shattock, Michael, University governance, leadership and management in a decade of diversification and uncertainty, in: Higher Education Quarterly 67 (3/2013), 217-233.

Shleifer, Andrei/Vishny, Robert W., A survey of corporate governance, in: Journal of Finance 52 (2/1997), 737-783.

Tabb, William K., Economic governance in the age of globalization, New York (Columbia University Press) 2004.

Taylor, Mark, Shared governance in the modern university, in: Higher Education Quarterly 67 (1/2013), 80-94.

von Trotha, Klaus, Internationalisierung als Gegenstand der Aus- und Weiterbildung an deutschen Hochschulen, in: *Krystek, Ulrich/Zur, Eberhard* (eds.), Handbuch Internationalisierung. Globalisierung – eine Herausforderung für die Unternehmensfüh-rung, Berlin – Heidelberg – New York (Springer) 2. ed., 2002, 231-248.

Waswa, Fuchaka/Swaleh, Sauda, Faculty opinions on emerging corporatization in public universities in Kenya, in: Education and General Studies 1 (1/2012), 9-15.

Weick, Karl E., Educational organizations as loosely coupled systems, in: Administrative Science Quarterly 21 (1/1976), 1-19.

Wilkesmann, Uwe, Governance von Hochschulen. Wie lässt sich ein Politikfeld steuern?, in: *Bandelow, Nils C./Hegelich, Simon* (eds.), Pluralismus – Strategien – Entscheidungen. Wiesbaden (Verlag für Sozialwissenschaften) 2011, 305-323.

Williamson, Oliver E., Markets and hierarchies, analysis and antitrust implications: A study in the economics of internal organization, New York (Free Press) 1975.

Williamson, Oliver E., The mechanisms of governance, New York – Oxford (Oxford University Press) 1996.

Withers, Glenn, Letter to the universities of Australia concerning „Inquiry into the desirability of a national higher education accreditation body" (03 April 2008), http://www.universitiesaustralia.edu.au/resources/605/1077, accessed on 11 March 2012.

Yamamoto, Kiyoshi, Corporatization of national universities in Japan: Revolution for governance or rhetoric for downsizing?, in: Financial Accountability & Management 20 (2/2004), 153-181.

Yoder, Dale, The faculty role in university governance. A faculty member's perception. The diagnosis and treatment of organizational pip, in: Academy of Management Journal 5 (3/1962), 222-229.

Youde, Jeremy, Global health governance, Cambridge – Malden (Polity Press) 2012.

Christian Scholz holds the Chair of Business Administration, especially Organisational Behaviour, Human Resource Management and Information Management. He is founding Director of the MBA School as part of the Europa-Institut at the Universität des Saarlandes. From 2010 until 2012 he was the Dean of the Faculty of Law and Business at the Saarland University. His research interests include human capital management, high performance teams, international human resource management, changes in the work environment (Darwiportunism) and "Korporatismus als ökonomisches Gestaltungsprinzip für Universitäten" (KORFU). In the field of Human Resource Management he has been voted several times as one of the Top 40 experts in Germany.

Volker Stein is Professor at the University of Siegen, Germany, Chair of Business Administration, especially Human Resource Management and Organisational Behaviour. He is Founding Director of the "Südwestfälische Akademie für den Mittelstand – University Siegen Business School" and Visiting Professor at EM Strasbourg Business School. His current research focuses on HRM especially in mid-sized companies, human capital management, international empirical organisational research, market-based leadership in organisations, and university governance, in particular the research project "Korporatismus als ökonomisches Gestaltungsprinzip für Universitäten" (KORFU). Among others, Volker Stein is co-editor of "Bologna-Schwarzbuch" (Black Book Bologna, 2009) together with Christian Scholz.

Stefanie Müller is an assistant professor at the Chair for Organisational Behaviour, Human Resource Management and Information Systems at the Universität des Saarlandes. She received her doctoral degree for the research on ethics in human capital management. She is managing director of the Institute of Management Competence (imk) at the Universität des Saarlandes. Her research covers HRM in small and medium-sized enterprises, human capital measurement, employee surveys, and research on convergence versus divergence in HRM. Currently, she is member of the German research group for the ISO certification on Human Resource Management.

Tobias M. Scholz studied Business Administration at the TU Kaiserslautern, Goethe University Frankfurt and UCLA Anderson. After his diploma, in 2010 he started his Ph.D. at the Chair for Human Resource Management and Organisational Behaviour at the University of Siegen in Germany. He is primarily interested in the field of big data and the influence data can and will have on Human Resources and organisations – a field where a critical discussion is essential to reveal potential and risks. Other interests are concerning the increase in complexity and dynamics in modern Human Resources and organisations. He co-publishes the bi-annual eSports Yearbook, which is a collected edition about stories and research in the competitive gaming scene. He also published in the Thunderbird International Business Review and the Journal of Virtual Worlds Research.

CONFERENCE COMMUNIQUÉ
"THE DEAN IN THE UNIVERSITY OF THE FUTURE"
Saarbrücken / Germany, June 28, 2013

http://www. orga.uni-sb.de/dean/Dean_communique2013.pdf

The Conference "The Dean in the University of the Future"
is part of the research project KORFU (kor-fu.de),
which is funded by the German Federal Ministry of Education and Research and coordinated by DLR German Aerospace Center.
It is a joint project of the Universität des Saarlandes (Saarbrücken, Germany)
and the University of Siegen, Germany.

From June 26 to 28, 2013, the international academic conference "The Dean in the University of the Future – Learning From and Progressing with Each Other" took place at the Universität des Saarlandes in Saarbrücken, Germany.

As part of the project kor-fu.de, it brought together 45 participants, being deans, members of university management, and researchers in higher education from 21 countries and five continents (see Annex).

These participants endorse the following "Conference Communiqué".

In particular, the following researchers ("signatories") have signed the "Conference Communiqué":

Dr. Benjamin Akinyemi, Mount Kenya University, Rwanda

Ákos Barna, Saarland University, Germany

Dr. Rosemond Boohene, University of Cape Coast, Ghana

Mónica Bonifaz, Pontificia Universidad Católica del Perú, Perú

Thomas Brekke, Vestfold University College, Norway

Dr. Priscilla Brown Lopez, University of Belize, Belize

Prof. Dr. Christian Joseph R. Cumagun, University of the Philippines Los Baños, Philippines

Marina Elias, Universitat Autònoma de Barcelona, Spain

Prof. Dr. Dennis Farrington, South East European University, Republic of Macedonia

Prof. Dr. Rudolf Fisch, University of Administrative Sciences Speyer, Germany

Dirk Hans, scienceRELATIONS, Germany

Dr. Matthias Klumpp, University of Duisburg-Essen, Germany

Daniela Jänicke, International Science Management and Consultancy, Hamburg, Germany

Prof. Dr. António M. Magalhães, University of Porto, Portugal

Dr. Eriko Miyake, Doshisha Women's College of Liberal Arts, Japan

Prof. Dr. Michael Olbrich, Saarland University, Germany

Prof. Dr. Martin Paul, Maastricht University, The Netherlands

Prof. Dr. Christian Scholz, Universität des Saarlandes, Germany

Prof. Dr. Volker Stein, University of Siegen, Germany

Dr. Sauda Swaleh, Kenyatta University, Kenya

Prof. Dr. Célestin Tagou, Protestant University of Central Africa, Cameroon

Dr. Amélia Veiga, Centre for Research in Higher Education Policies, Portugal

Dr. Edgar Vogel, University of Talca, Chile

Prof. Dr. Kiyoshi Yamamoto, University of Tokyo, Japan

Prof. Dr. Ahmad F. M. Zain, University Malaysia Pahang, Malaysia

This "Conference Communiqué" will be presented to:

The Ministries of (Higher) Education and Research in the following countries: Albania, Andorra, Armenia, Australia, Austria, Azerbaijan, Belarus, Belgium, Belize, Bosnia and Herzegovina, Bulgaria, Cameroon, Canada, Chile, Costa Rica, Croatia, Cyprus, Czech Republic, Denmark, Estonia, Finland, France, Georgia, Germany, Ghana, Greece, Hungary, Iceland, Ireland, Italy, Japan, Kazakhstan, Kenya, Kosovo, Latvia, Liechtenstein, Lithuania, Luxembourg, Republic of Macedonia, Malaysia, Malta, Moldova, Monaco, Montenegro, the Netherlands, Norway, Peru, Philippines, Poland, Portugal, Romania, Russia, Rwanda, San Marino, Serbia, Slovakia, Slovenia, Spain, Sweden, Switzerland, Turkey, Ukraine, United Kingdom, Vietnam.

The Rectors' Conferences in the following countries: Austria, Belgium, Chile, Croatia, Cyprus, Czech Republic, Denmark, Estonia, Finland, France, Germany, Hungary, Ireland, Italy, Latvia, Lithuania, the Netherlands, Norway, Poland, Portugal, Romania, Slovakia, Spain, Sweden, Switzerland, Turkey, United Kingdom.

Other Institutions related to Higher Education such as: ARENA Center for European Studies, Center for Research in Higher Education Policies (CIPES), European Association for Quality Assurance in Higher Education (ENQA), European Association of Institutions in Higher Education (EURASHE), European Centre for Strategic Development of Universities (ESMU), European University Association (EUA), International Association of Universities (IAU), Network of Protestant Universities in Africa (NPUA), The Commission of Higher Education (CHED).

Preface

Wherever located in the world, universities play an important role in the production of knowledge and advancement of people and nations. Modern universities do not follow one general model but are highly different. They have a growing number of internal and external stakeholders and a broad understanding of diversity will be important in the university of the future.

The conference considers that empowering the dean is a critical part of ensuring that universities maintain and extend their innovative strength, autonomy, social influence, and competitive power in moving societies forward.

The Signatories, Having Discussed

- "Strategy of Deans and Faculties in Higher Education",
- "Management of Faculties and Dean's Competence Profile in Higher Education",
- "Faculty's Autonomy in Higher Education",
- "External Relations of Faculties in Higher Education", and
- "Performance Controlling of Faculties in Higher Education",

Suggest The Following:

(1) Deans can be elected or appointed according to criteria consistent with university autonomy.

(2) Deans are academic managers with appropriate academic qualification, experience, and skills.

(3) Recognising diversity of management approaches in universities, the dean has to design a management approach that incorporates performance management, open communication channels, articulation of faculty mission and values, HR management, and respects academic freedom of faculty members.

(4) Operating in a complex external environment, deans should assume the following important roles:
   - team leader under conditions of complexity,
   - translator of institutional strategy and responses,
   - manager of academic resources and strategy at the faculty level,
   - link between external and internal stakeholders,
   - educator empowering faculty, staff, and students,
   - advocate for the university system, and
   - key figure in upholding university standards and protecting academic freedom.

(5) The dean's role is pivotal in the university carrying out its societal role.

(6) Deans should lead the process of strategy formulation and implementation at faculty level.

(7) The strategic and operational decisions of a dean need to be evidence-based, academically justifiable, and sustainable.

(8) In order to increase transparency and to improve the decision making process, deans should have access to accurate information and data of the university.

(9) Deans as well as potential deans should have access to training courses in modern faculty management.

(10) Deans should inform all faculty members and students about university governance and the role of faculties within it.

(11) Deans make a vital contribution to university governance, and opportunities for them to collaborate in and provide collective input for university decision-making should be encouraged.

(12) Decision-making in faculties should be open, accountable and collegial.

(13) Ideally, faculties should independently manage and negotiate their financial resources, within established university parameters.

(14) Faculty strategies must be responsive to the development of new research and teaching entities within the university.

(15) Decisions on the extent of cooperation with external stakeholders should be consistent with the overall strategy of the faculty.

List Of Conference Participants

Akinyemi, Benjamin (Rwanda; Kigali Institute of Management, Rector)

Barna, Ákos (Germany; Universität des Saarlandes, Deputy Head of Strategic Controlling)

Bonifaz, Mónica (Perú; Pontificia Universidad Católica del Perú, Dean of the Faculty of Management)

Boohene, Rosemond (Ghana; University of Cape Coast, Department of Management Studies, School of Business)

Brekke, Thomas (Norway; Vestfold University College, Faculty of Business and Social Sciences)

Brown Lopez, Priscilla (Belize; University of Belize, Faculty of Education and Arts, Interim Dean)

Carr, Graham (Canada; Concordia University, Montréal, Department of History, Professor and Vice-President Research and Graduate Studies)

Cooper, Malcolm (Japan; Ritsumeikan Asia Pacific University, College of Asia Pacific Studies, former President)

Cumagun, Christian Joseph R. (Philippines; University of the Philippines Los Baños, College of Agriculture, Associate Dean)

Danowski, Iris (Germany; German Rectors' Conference HRK, Head of Section "Cooperation with Western and Southern Europe and Latin America)

de Wit, Inken (Germany; Universität des Saarlandes, Chair for Organisational Behaviour, Human Resource Management, and Information Management) (Session Organiser)

Elias, Marina (Spain; Universitat Autónoma de Barcelona, Sociology Department)

Escarré, Roberto (Spain; University of Alicante, International Relations)

Farrington, Dennis (Republic of Macedonia; South East European University, President of the Board)

Feldhaus, Anna (Germany, University of Siegen, Chair for Human Resource Management and Organisational Behaviour) (Session Organiser)

Fisch, Rudolf (Germany; University of Administrative Sciences Speyer, Chair for Empirical Social Research, former Dean, former Rector, former President)

Fumasoli, Tatiana (Norway; University of Oslo, Faculty of Social Sciences, ARENA Centre for European Studies)

Goedegebuure, Leo (Australia; University of Melbourne, LH Martin Institute for Higher Education Leadership and Management, Deputy Director)

Hans, Dirk (Germany; Executive Associate at scienceRELATIONS GbR, Head of (external) Communication, LCSB/SnT, University of Luxembourg, Lecturer, University of Oldenburg)

Huisman, Jeroen (United Kingdom; University of Bath, School of Management, Director of the International Centre for Higher Education Management ICHEM)

Jänicke, Daniela (Germany; International Science Management and Consultancy, Hamburg)

Klumpp, Matthias (Germany; University of Duisburg-Essen, Institute of Production and Industrial Information Management)

Kornacker, Julia (Germany; Technical University Dortmund, Chair of Management Accounting and Control)

Magalhães, Antonio (Portugal; University of Porto, Faculty of Psychology and Education Science, Center for Research in Higher Education Policies CIPES)

Müller, Stefanie (Germany; Universität des Saarlandes, Chair for Organisational Behaviour, Human Resource Management, and Information Management) (Session Organiser)

Miyake, Eriko (Japan; Doshisha Women's College of Liberal Arts)

Nguyen, Chi Ngon (Vietnam; Cantho University, College of Engineering Technology, Vice Dean)

Olbrich, Michael (Germany; Universität des Saarlandes, Faculty of Law and Management, Vice Dean of the Faculty for Law and Management)

Paul, Martin (The Netherlands; Maastricht University, President)

Rudolph, Dirk (Germany; Frankfurt School of Finance & Management, Programme Director Conception & Programme Development)

Scholz, Christian (Germany; Universität des Saarlandes, Chair for Organisational Behaviour, Human Resource Management, and Information Management, former Dean of the of the Faculty for Law and Management) (Conference Organiser)

Scholz, Tobias (Germany, University of Siegen, Chair for Human Resource Management and Organisational Behaviour) (Session Organiser)

Seidler, Hanns H. (Germany; Centre of Science Management ZWM, Managing Director)

Swaleh, Sauda (Kenya; Kenyatta University, Deputy Director of Student Affairs)

Stein, Volker (Germany; University of Siegen, Chair for Human Resource Management and Organisational Behaviour) (Conference Organiser)

Strauß, Natalie (Germany; Universität des Saarlandes, Chair for Organisational Behaviour, Human Resource Management, and Information Management) (Session Organiser)

Tagou, Célestin (Cameroon; Protestant University of Central Africa, Dean of the Faculty of Social Sciences and International Relations)

Trejos, Javier (Costa Rica; University of Costa Rica, Faculty of Science, Dean)

Veiga, Amelia (Portugal, Agency for Assessment and Accreditation of Higher Education A3ES, Center for Research in Higher Education Policies CIPES)

Vogel, Edgar (Chile; University of Talca, Faculty of Psychology, Dean)

Wagenfeld, Felix (Germany; German Academic Exchange Service DAAD, Deputy Head of Section Joint Higher Education Management Programme DIES)

Wells, Julie (Australia; RMIT University, University Secretary and Vice-President, Governance and Planning)

Winter, Stefan (Germany; Ruhr-University Bochum, Chair for Human Resource Management, Vice-Dean)

Yamamoto, Kiyoshi (Japan; University of Tokyo, Graduate School of Education)

Zain, Ahmad F. M. (Malaysia; University Malaysia Pahang, Faculty of Manufacturing Engineering)

CONFERENCE CONSEQUENCES:
IT'S JUST THE BEGINNING

Christian Scholz[1], Volker Stein[2]

[1]*Chair for Organisational Behaviour, Human Resource Management and Information Systems,*
Universität des Saarlandes, Campus A5 4, 66123 Saarbrücken, Germany
[2]*Chair for Human Resource Management and Organisational Behaviour, University of Siegen,*
Hoelderlinstrasse 3, 57076 Siegen, Germany
[1]*scholz@orga.uni-sb.de,* [2]*volker.stein@uni-siegen.de*

The international academic conference "The Dean in the University of the Future" is declared closed and the consequences are to be drawn: Where is the future relevance of the dean research? Which methodological approaches are promising? Which core results are already available and what do they tell us? And which future path is already visible for the research of deans, faculties and collegial university governance?

1. FURTHER RELEVANCE OF THE DEAN RESEARCH

"University governance" is coined to describe rules and regulations for the steering of university systems. This conference deals with that university governance issue and the role a dean plays in it. It is part of the KORFU research programme that is funded by the German Federal Ministry of Education and Research (BMBF) and administered by the German Aerospace Center (DLR). "KORFU" is the acronym for the German title "Korporatismus als ökonomisches Gestaltungsprinzip für Universitäten", to be translated as "collegialism as an economic governance principle for universities".

The proposed translation "collegialism" (the term "corporatisation" seems to be closer to the German "Korporatismus" but is a "false friend" with a completely different meaning) refers to the mostly voluntary participation of groups in political processes. A collegial university is one that is organised bottom-up in the sense of a civil society.

Faculties and their deans will play a decisive role in university governance.

Against this background, faculties perceive that they are responsible for performing university research and teaching, so that they have the legitimacy to claim responsibility also for the decisions on research and teaching. Therefore, there is a search for organisational solutions where the interplay of autonomous faculties will turn out to be the motor of progress. This progress does not only focus on faculty interests but in the end – at the aggregated level – on the competitiveness of the whole university. This leads to the question how to conceptualise decentralised, democratic management and governance models for modern universities.

Discussing challenges of universities (in particular, public funded universities) on a worldwide scope, university researchers from all over the world quickly address two issues: First, in which way do university strategies influence the work that is done in and by universities? And second, will a university be able to take decisions in favour of its own sustainable interests?

Because any strategy has to be implemented, the focus shifts from the overall "deciding" university perspective to the "implementing" perspective of subunits. Therefore, rethinking modern universities means discussing the balance of external determination and self-determination in order to make strategies work.

In universities, strategies are implemented in team structures that are usually organised according to research areas. These faculties are led by a dean and consist of researchers and lecturers, some administrative staff, and, of course, of students. As an organisation at the meso-level, faculties and their deans have to find a position where they can reach their objectives: the survival and future viability of their faculty within the university, and the optimisation of the general conditions for qualitative and innovative work.

Faculties all over the world have their unique environments. Besides of their specific local conditions, they evolve over time as an organisational form and can, therefore, be positioned in a stage model of university governance evolution (see pages 204-205 of this proceedings). It became obvious during the conference that new challenges for research and teaching require a matching position in the stage model. A typical mismatch in times of interdisciplinarity, multidimensional cooperation and flexibilisation is a centralistic university steering by university presidents and rectors. The logic of corporatisation being dominant, they try to move universities – their structure, their processes, their logic of thinking and deciding – in the direction of centrally planned companies in this stage. Although this steering type is completely outdated for companies, it is in many countries the legislators', the lobbyists' and the university top management's blueprint for university organisation. They intend to plan, steer and control faculties centrally by bodies at a higher level. A typical reason for such a "Presidential Feudalism" is the political discontent with universities which – from their point of view – work inefficiently and have to be tightly controlled. As a consequence, faculties and their deans are often perceived by university top

management exclusively as operative units. In their stereotypic view, faculties are ivory towers, inaccessible for interdisciplinarity, and moreover, unwilling to aim for efficiency and competitive market orientation.

Interestingly, centralistic steering in the sense of "Presidential Feudalism" is stretched to its limits. Regardless whether university development, budgeting, or new courses of studies are concerned, universities are such complex that a top-down steering will no longer be effective. A fatal consequence of centralistic steering problems and wrong decisions it can be observed, i.e. that failing university presidents do not react with delegating tasks, but with even enforcing centralism. In some national university systems (such as in Germany), the university president's plenitude of power meanwhile ranges from strategic policy decisions (capacity planning, appointsments to vacant chairs, discipline structure) to operational interventions in research and teaching (e.g., approval for the application for research grants). As a result, university bureaucracy is escalating, leading to countless control units such as controlling, public relation department, course planning, lecture hall allocation, international office, bureau for the transfer of knowledge, building administration or qualitiy management in hand of the university president or rector. That involves a great deal of expense.

Looking at the target group for a dean research, we se as one group the higher education policy makers which are responsible for university laws as framework condition for university governance. The second target group are decision makers within universites who can use their scope of decision in favour of centralistic or in favour of collegial university governance.

Further relevance of the dean research arises from the urgency of university decisions under financial restrictions. For a higher education policy which is forced to save money, it is the easiest way to steer top-down and to instrumentalise the university presidents to do the same. Centralism leads to arbitrary decisions without participation of those affected. Another case is the performance-based payment of university presidents. At this place, it should not be brought into question that university presidents are paid for performance, but, what the underlying performance criteria are. Situations can arise where the performance criteria, negotiated by the ministry and the university president, contradict the interests and strategic orientation of faculties but are imposed on them. Given a faculty that follows a consistent quality strategy by restricting student admission by capping and minimum grades, it will be dysfunctional when the university president is paid for approaching maximum capacity and, therefore, enforces unlimited student admission.

In centralistic university governance, faculties with their deans, researchers, teaching staff and students are not seriously involved in decision making. Instead, their information rights, participation rights, and self-defence rights are denied. There is the danger that by this kind of proceeding, the motivation, identity, and innovation resources of the performing parts of the university are undermined. Backlashes on the fundamental performance capacity of universities and the international competitiveness of single locations for science can be anticipated.

2. METHODOLOGICAL APPROACHES

A lot of writing and reseach deals with questions of organising universities in general and higher education systems in particular. Many of these contributions come from decision makers and stakeholders, all with their own agenda and definitely not working in an unbiased way. For instance, looking at Germany, any research and publication from the German Rectors' Conference (Hochschulrektorenkonferenz HRK), the lobby-group for university rectors and presidents, comes up with a laudation on centralistic systems. Therefore, we really need more of truly academic research beyond "research as a tool of lobbyists".

However, there is some appropriate methodology we found and used during the conference. It ranges from empirical research and case studies to pattern recognition and international empirical comparisons. These methods are directed to the analysis of sociological roles of deans, to the analysis of stakeholder interests and behaviour, and to the strategic and operational task of deans in their work of managing faculties.

In terms of organisational theory, research focuses on fundamental constructs such as decentralisation and subsidiarity, participation, identity building, and university governance with different steering logics (market versus hierarchy). These constructs are not only surveyed at the university level but also within faculties. A further target is the autonomous cooperation between faculties without the intervention of a university president.

In the beginning we had the belief that computerised simulation models would really help us a lot. It has, however, become obvious that these methods have only a limited degree of usefulness for the analysis of university governance. Algorithms and their logic are limited in modelling the actors' opportunistic striving for power.

What we also saw was the weakness of pure descriptive approaches. Just listing which kinds of university governance are used in which frequency might be interesting to politicians who usually try to follow the crowd. But without knowing the suational variables and, in particular, the goals of the stakeholders and their specific power, these descriptions do not make any sense. This means that there is the need for strictly empirical research.

3. CORE RESULTS OF RESEARCH ON THE DEANS

As the conference – the presentations and the discussion – showed, there are many results available in the field of university governance and, in particular, related to the dean's role in universities.

In respect to their *strategic role*, deans have to translate the external demands and requirements, mostly from higher education policy and university top management, into internal activities of their faculty. Therefore, their role is partly reactive. However, there is a more proactive role in strategy: Since deans have to shape their faculty's future viability, they can formulate a faculty strategy, addressing intra-faculty attitudes, cross-faculty cooperation, inter-faculty positioning, and supra-faculty competition.

In respect to their *management role*, deans have to steer their faculty towards performance. This includes the creation of productive work conditions for innovative research and teaching. The behavioural aspects and the financial aspects are the two sides of the same coin. Both the faculty academic and supportive staff on the one hand and the management systems of planning, implementing and performance controlling on the other hand have to be optimised according to recent management knowledge.

In respect to their *autonomy protection role*, deans have to act in a micropolitically as well as in a macropolitically intelligent way. Within the university, they have to negotiate their faculty's interests with the university top management, accepting that this relationship is potentially controversial. Going beyond their university, they may become lobbyists for the autonomy of faculties, knowing that decentralisation and collegialism can increase effectiveness and efficiency in highly complex systems as universities are.

Our conference "The Dean in the University of the Future" as an international academic conference also led to a Conference Communiqué. This remarkable document has been developed using the Model United Nation approach and calls for 15 requirements. They are printed in these Conference Proceedings on page 220 and describe collegial university governance within a decentralised faculty steering. These requirements cover such central aspects as motivation, engagement, retention, identity, and high performance, each being compatible with many fields of overall university governance. They reflect the shared deep sorrows and concerns for the future of universities.

The significance of the Conference Communiqué postulations stems from the variety of the discutants: Not only deans, but also university presidents, vice chancellors, and researchers in higher education contributed to the Conference Communiqué so that a broad formation of opinion took place. This process was organised as a plenum workshop, using the UN resolution principles. Starting with a formulated draft resolution that was based on the discussions from the first conference day, on the second conference day, amendments were used to modify operative clauses in the draft resolution. Those changes that were voted upon by the plenum were incorporated into the Conference Communiqué. By that, all "delegates" – in our conference from 41 countries – built a cross-national consensus on the question how to shape university governance in times of interdisciplinary performance demands in order to strengthen universities and national systems of higher education in international educational competition. In particular, it could be reached that the Conference Communiqué was more than a pure lamentation about disappointed hopes and more than a wish list with unrealistic postulations. In fact, it reflects the international interest in problems in university governance, while similar questions might be answered differently in different countries. It bears mentioning that the regionally and functionally highly diverse participants could, in spite of their different university systems, agree upon a combined position.

More results of research on the deans can be derived fom the KORFU project. In short, there are some other lines of discussion that may enhance further discussion:

- Based on empirical findings, the original stage model of university governance evolution was completed by the stage "Dean Steering". There are not only situations in which the university top management acts counter-productively against the interests of faculties. Even deans can opportunistically utilise their functional power in favour of own benefits or the benefits of their own institutes. An example is the staffing of the faculty for which a dean takes the responsibility. It can be steered in different directions – tenure tracks, full professorships etc. – with the result of arithmetic shifts between different branches of a faculty. Formally spoken, the original five-stage model became a six-stage model (with a symmetric 3x2 permutation of initial stage and degeneration stage). From the content side, a further organisational form that exists also in companies could be integrated.

- Our stage model of university governance evolution was made accessible for situational application: In which situations can which stages be applied and which effectiveness expectations are linked to that? In contrast to the presumptions, some stages of university governance contradict the objective of the long-term survival of faculties.

- The stages were internationally explored. From Australia, Japan, the Netherlands, the USA, Canada, and South and Central America, there are results available to characterise the national systems of university governance.

- The stage model of university governance was applied to the strategic behaviour of deans, to the cooperation of universities with companies, and made concrete for the institutionalisation of inter-faculty institutions.

- The stage model serves as basis for a dean training programme, transferring research findings for example to Latin America as part of the programme "Dialogue on Innovative Higher Education Strategies" (DIES) of the German Academic Exchange Service (DAAD).

- A comprehensive research agenda was sketched which is directed towards norms, codex and indices for university governance.

Two of the KORFU results are extremely interesting:

The first is the international comparison of university governance systems. The consequences of an excessive university centralisation can be observed. The example of Australia illustrates what happens if a coun-

try perceives higher education as export good and is heading for a massification of its universities. Faculties suffer from an exaggerated performance controlling which primarily focuses on international visibility in university rankings. At the same time, research output and the identity as a university fall by the wayside in those universities which resemble neo-tayloristic educational factories. Also, the example of the USA: there, faculty autonomy is the formula for success of the elite universities. They predominantly operate with very strong and relatively autonomous faculties. Excellence comes from decentralised specialisation. Finally, the Netherlands: in effect, their universities are based on a principle of consensus between "top" and "bottom" which leads to faculties that dispose of an independent financial basis and of voice within the university. The international comparison supports the idea that top universities benefit from a broad faculty autonomy, but centralism reduces research strength.

The second refers to the meta perspective. In many countries can be observed that research in higher education tends to back system conformism. Obviously, a critical perspective towards centralisation in university governance is in little demand. Predominantly, recent research takes the centralistic university governance system as given and tries to optimise its details, for example strategic university management, key performance indicators, performance-based resource allocation or university funding. However, this might be dangerous, because the reaction pattern "more centralisation" decreases overall effectiveness and efficiency. Moreover, this puts the long-term survival of faculties at risk. Faculties can – as the look into reality shows – be excellent in regard to their performance indicators, strategies, communication, and student attractiveness: as long as they are in the stage of "Presidential Feudalism", this does not prevent their liquidation. The only escape as seen from the faculty perspective might be collegialism.

4. THE PATH AHEAD

Higher education policy is responsible for the competitiveness of the country's respective society and economy. A broad academic education is for a country as important as excellent research outcomes are. Both are part of an academic tradition that has to be advanced. Higher education policy has to understand that this advancement is the core task of universities and, in particular, of the faculties as provider of excellence. Furthermore, higher education policy is responsible for university laws and can, therefore, influence the behaviour of university top management and faculty deans. If higher education policy acknowledges the importance of faculties, it can look for mechanisms that are directed towards long-term viability of faculties. In a "stress test for faculties" it can be assessed how faculties react if their existence is endangered from outside. How resistant and resilient are faculties and up to which degree will a collegial self-steering of faculties be able to guarantee performance and excellence?

As far as the *university top management* is concerned, it needs decision support instruments that give them advice which university governance system they can implement in order to reach a given set of objectives. While the situational variables are information transparency or the degree of maturity of faculties, the decision outcome is the university governance system with the degree of collegial participation and faculty autonomy. One idea is a stepwise, hierachic decision structure model. In general, university top management should examine all decisions where it forces faculties to act against their own faculty strategy, and start to negotiate the divergent positions.

Deans and faculties have a high self-responsibility for their future path. It is not enough to claim autonomy. In order to strengthen faculty autonomy, some basic guidelines are necessary:

- Deans should be acadmic managers with appropriate academic qualification, experience, and skills.

- Deans should lead the process of strategy formulation and implementation at faculty level.
- Decision-making in faculties should be open, collegial and accountable.
- Faculties should independently manage and negotiate their financial resources within extablished university parameters and should have access to accurate information and data of the university.
- Deans should inform all faculty members and students about university governance.

It becomes more and more important to define the strategic direction of the faculty in a collegial way (intra-faculty), to work together with other faculties without "silo thinking" (cross-faculty), to foster the similarities among faculties (inter-faculty) and to integrate themselves in the overall university system and competition (supra-faculty). For example, up to which degree can faculties build interdisciplinary inter-faculty research institutes without the initiative, approval or permission or of the university president? All of such decisions have later to be transformed into excellent research and teaching in order to serve the whole university.

Finally, *every single actor* involved in university governance will be responsible for the future viability of faculties and universities. In the stage of "Presidential Feudalism", there is a big danger that – in the sense of "run for your lives!" – single academics strive for bilateral collusion in order to optimise their individual interests. By obedient submission under the university president, they subvert "University Collegialism" to the disadvantage of the faculty. Therefore, it can be expected that the shift to less centralistic, more collegial university governance means to overcome a lot of problems.

All actors involved in university governance are called upon to reflect whether they meet all requirements of modern universities such as openness, transparency, collegialism, and accountability. If not, they must change. Or they will be changed. Because: It's just the beginning.

Christian Scholz holds the Chair of Business Administration, especially Organisational Behaviour, Human Resource Management and Information Management. He is founding Director of the MBA School as part of the Europa-Institute at the Universität des Saarlandes. From 2010 until 2012 he was the Dean of the Faculty of Law and Business at the Saarland University. His research interests include human capital management, high performance teams, international human resource management, changes in the work environment (Darwiportunism) and "Korporatismus als ökonomisches Gestaltungsprinzip für Universitäten" (KORFU). In the field of Human Resource Management he has been voted several times as one of the Top 40 experts in Germany.

Volker Stein is Professor at the University of Siegen, Germany, Chair of Business Administration, especially Human Resource Management and Organisational Behaviour. He is Founding Director of the "Südwestfälische Akademie für den Mittelstand – University Siegen Business School" and Visiting Professor at EM Strasbourg Business School. His current research focuses on HRM especially in mid-sized companies, human capital management, international empirical organisational research, market-based leadership in organisations, and university governance, in particular the research project "Korporatismus als ökonomisches Gestaltungsprinzip für Universitäten" (KORFU). Among others, Volker Stein is co-editor of "Bologna-Schwarzbuch" (Black Book Bologna, 2009) together with Christian Scholz.